Structured Systems Analysis and Design Methodology

Structured Systems Analysis and Design Methodology

GEOFF CUTTS, BSc, MSc, FBCS

Department of Computer Studies
Sheffield City Polytechnic

BLACKWELL SCIENTIFIC PUBLICATIONS

OXFORD   LONDON   EDINBURGH

BOSTON   MELBOURNE

Blackwell Scientific Publications
Editorial offices:
Osney Mead, Oxford OX2 0EL
8 John Street, London WC1N 2ES
23 Ainslie Place, Edinburgh EH3 6AJ
3 Cambridge Center, Suite 208
    Cambridge, Massachusetts 02142, USA
107 Barry Street, Carlton
    Victoria 3053, Australia

First published by Paradigm Publishing Ltd
    1987
Reprinted 1988
Reprinted by Blackwell Scientific
    Publications 1989

Set by Mathematical Composition Setters
    Ltd, Salisbury
Printed in Great Britain by Hollen Street
    Press Ltd, Slough, Berks

DISTRIBUTORS

Marston Book Services Ltd
PO Box 87
Oxford OX2 0DT
(*Orders:* Tel: 0865 791155
        Fax: 0865 791927
        Telex: 837515)

USA
    Publishers' Business Services
    PO Box 447
    Brookline Village
    Massachusetts 02147
    (*Orders:* Tel: (617) 524-7678)

Canada
    Oxford University Press
    70 Wynford Drive
    Don Mills
    Ontario M3C 1J9
    (*Orders:* Tel: (416) 441-2941)

Australia
    Blackwell Scientific Publications
    (Australia) Pty Ltd
    107 Barry Street
    Carlton, Victoria 3053
    (*Orders:* Tel: (03) 347-0300)

British Library
Cataloguing in Publication Data

Cutts, Geoff
    Structured systems analysis and design
    methodology.
    1. System analysis
    I. Title
    003   QA76.6

ISBN 0 632 02818 1

Contents

Acknowledgements

This book is a result of many years' experience with systems analysis and design. My experience with International Computers Limited and as Systems Development Manager for G.M.S. Computing Ltd. provides the industrial input to the book. My recent research, consultancy and study of systems analysis and design provide the academic input to the book.

The support of Learmonth and Burchett Management Systems made the book possible. The synopsis for the book was developed in conjunction with LBMS who also provided assistance by reviewing the book, by allowing me to attend some of their courses and by allowing their package Auto-Mate to be used for the development of the case study.

I have found that writing a book of this size is a large task. I must acknowledge the love and support of my family, Janet, Gareth and Nicky, and the tremendous efforts of Louise Morrey who tirelessly word processed my manuscript to produce the book. A sincere thank you to my wife and my father who both gave many hours to the task of proofreading.

Foreword

I am very pleased to be able to write a foreword to this book. Learmonth and Burchett Management Systems (LBMS) were involved in the development of the synopsis for the book as well as providing Auto-Mate software to assist the development of the case study.

Geoff Cutts has used his industrial and academic experience to produce a text which is informative, instructional and very readable. LBMS are happy to recommend the book as an excellent introduction and description of Structured Systems Analysis and Design Methodologies.

In 1980, LBMS were invited to work with the Central Computer and Telecommunications Agency (CCTA) to carry out a joint project to develop a standard analysis and design method for central government. This resulted in SSADM, which is now a mandatory standard for government projects. This method is marketed by LBMS as LBMS Structured Development Method (LSDM). There are minor differences, mainly notational, between LSDM and SSADM. The method described in this book is derived from LSDM. It illustrates the principles underlying LSDM but does contain some differences in the structure of the method and in the precise nature of some of the techniques. The differences existing in February 1987 are highlighted in Appendix B; however, LSDM is subject to a continual programme of revision and improvement.

Notwithstanding the above points, it is worth emphasising that the book remains a very valuable introduction to the subject.

Rainer Burchett
Director, LBMS

Preface

The purpose of this book is to explain a structured systems analysis and design methodology in a highly pragmatic fashion. I have tried to use my personal experiences as an analyst, designer and manager of many business development projects together with my academic studies to produce a book which would be helpful to potential computer users, existing computer users, systems managers, systems analysts, systems designers and students of analysis and design.

The book is in three parts. Part 1 introduces the Structured Systems Analysis and Design Methodology (SSADM). It describes the need for a different approach by the computing industry, the stages, tasks and techniques of SSADM and the benefits of adopting such an approach.

Part 2 describes the six stages within SSADM, with a chapter devoted to each. It is hoped that Part 2 could be used for education and for reference by the practising analyst and designer, as well as the student of analysis and design.

Part 3 provides a case study of the use of SSADM. It has been developed using Learmonth and Burchett Management systems software. Their package Auto-Mate was used throughout the development.

All classes of reader should appreciate the need for a different approach to systems analysis and design. Part 1 addresses this issue and should be studied by all readers.

Part 2 describes in detail the stages and tasks which comprise the methodology. Systems analysts, systems designers and students of systems analysis and design should study this part in detail.

User and management involvement in computer development projects is a vital ingredient for success. Users and management should understand the stages, tasks and techniques to be able to contribute fully. Part 2 should be read by users and management to gain this understanding.

No methodology can be mastered without practice. Part 3 provides a detailed case study which may be used to practice the methodology.

The methodology described is derived from LSDM: Learmonth and Burchett Structured Development Methodology. It is a structured approach to systems analysis and design; it is not the SSADM referred to earlier as the standard for government projects. However since the methodology described in this book is derived from LSDM, and the government's SSADM differs only in minor ways from LSDM, it is hoped that the structured analysis and design methodology described here will be of interest to government organisations. There are differences between the methodology described in this book and LSDM: those which I have introduced based on my experience, those which I have introduced to simplify and shorten the book, and the inevitable differences introduced because of the fact that LSDM is continually being enhanced.

Part 1

1

The environment of analysis and design

1.1 Introduction

The development of large computer systems is one of the most complex activities undertaken by organisations. The number of staff involved and the resources consumed often make computer development projects one of the most costly of all projects undertaken.

Projects which exceed their projected development costs and their projected development timescales are very often the norm. In addition, many of these systems do not provide the facilities the user required.

Improvements in the productivity of staff involved with systems development and the production of better-quality systems are vital if systems engineering is to be accepted as a true engineering discipline.

Techniques for programming, such as the many versions of structured programming, are now well established in many organisations. Improvements in productivity and quality cannot be achieved by the introduction of structured programming if the design specification from which the system is programmed and implemented is incomplete, ambiguous and contradictory.

Many of the problems stem from the use of natural language as the only language for design specifications. Many problems result from the lack of a methodology for analysis and design leading to the production of the design specification.

This book describes a methodology for systems analysis and design leading to a design specification which is specific, complete, unambiguous, non-contradictory, clear and concise.

It is in this section of the development cycle where improved productivity and quality can be achieved. This book therefore describes a methodology for systems analysis and design.

The use of techniques such as data flow diagrams and entity modelling for systems engineering is well established. Many organisations use their own methods. What is not so common is the structuring of the techniques into a practical methodology for system engineering. Structured systems analysis and design provides a methodology, incorporating the best available techniques, for the analysis and design of systems. The structured systems analysis and design methodology (SSADM) is not a collection of techniques, but is a well-developed step-by-step approach, which commences with an investigation of the current system and concludes with a detailed system design specification.

SSADM does not concentrate on any one technique. Some methodologies concentrate on functional analysis using data flow diagrams; some concentrate on data analysis using data models. SSADM regards functions and data with equal importance and uses a variety of techniques, some within more than one stage, to support the objectives of the stage. The techniques chosen for each task are the latest techniques which support the achievement of the task's objectives. SSADM is a structuring of well-known techniques into a comprehensive methodology which solves many of the problems associated with systems engineering.

1.2   The problems associated with systems engineering

The major problems associated with systems engineering can be deduced from the symptoms evident in many development projects. These symptoms are:

- development costs over budget
- development timescales over planned timescales
- the production of systems which do not meet the user's requirements, and which are difficult to modify and maintain

The massive increase in the size and complexity of systems being developed without any comparable change in the methods for analysis and design is perhaps the major reason for the problems being experienced by many organisations.

The system implemented must meet the user's requirements. The requirements must also be met within the costs and timescales agreed for the system development process. The cost and time of meeting the requirements increases in proportion to the time taken to reach the point where a specific, complete, unambiguous and clear statement of them is agreed with the user. Figure 1.1 shows this increase in cost.

It is vital to remove the errors from the design at an early stage. It is also important to accept that users' requirements will change as their environment changes. Maintenance and modification to all systems will be necessary. The methodology, therefore, must facilitate improvements in productivity and in the quality of development projects, maintenance projects and modification projects.

Point of agreement	Increase in cost
At the specification of requirements phase	None
At the end of the design phase	The cost to rework the analysis and design
At the end of programming	The cost to rework the analysis, design and programming
During user testing	The cost to rework the analysis, design, programming and testing
During live running by maintenance and modification	The very considerable costs required to rework the analysis and design and to modify the existing programs

Figure 1.1

Pressure from existing users for modifications and maintenance

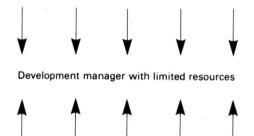

Development manager with limited resources

Pressure from potential users for new systems

Figure 1.2

Figure 1.2 shows the current position for many development managers.

The problem of proving the correctness of analysis and design is made difficult by the lack of a notation common to all stages of development. Changes from one notation to another as the development task progresses from stage to stage introduce errors of interpretation. If the statement of requirements is written in a vague fashion using natural language only, it is impossible to ensure the design meets the statement of requirements. Figure 1.3 shows typical proportions of the results of developing a system.

A specification of requirements written in natural language is shown below. It is vague, contradictory and incomplete.

Specification of Requirements
1. The new system must provide a fully on-line service for all sales accounting functions.
2. Statements should be printed at regular intervals showing all invoices and payments.

3. Each delivery should result in an invoice.
4. Invoices should be printed weekly showing all deliveries made to a customer during the week.
5. Credit notes should be treated as negative invoices.
   Vague
   > define regular interval - requirement number two
   > are invoices and payments printed forever? - requirement number two

   Contradictory
   > each delivery = invoice - requirement number three
   > invoice = all deliveries for one week - requirement number four
   > are credit notes printed? - requirements two and five

   Incomplete
   > how are new customers inserted into the system?
   > how are invoices priced?

A methodology for development of the specification of requirements and the design specification is required to overcome these problems.

A methodology is simply a way of structuring one's thinking about an area of study. It ensures that the appropriate sub-areas are considered at the appropriate time together with the proper reasoning about them. Further, a methodology should provide a framework which leads towards the

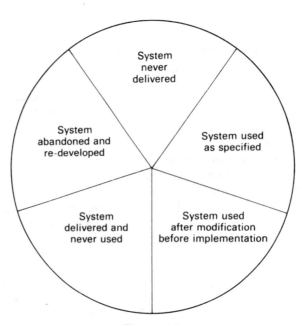

Figure 1.3

achievement of specific objectives. The achievement of the objectives is not guaranteed; it depends upon a number of criteria.

Questions such as 'Under what conditions is it sensible to seek to achieve the objectives?' and 'Do these conditions apply to the area of concern?' need to be asked and positively answered. Finally, one should ask if the skills and resources are available to implement the methodology. These questions and others are considered now.

1.3   The problems associated with systems analysis

The major problems associated with systems analysis arise in the understanding of the user's environment and the subsequent specification of the user's requirements. Both of these problem areas arise from problems in communication between the user and the systems analyst. The problem area is often considerably exasperated by the continuous change of the user's environment and the user's requirements for the new system.

The systems analyst can find it very hard to learn sufficient about the business to observe the system from the user's viewpoint. Similarly, the user community does not know enough about computer systems to be able to specify the requirements accurately, unambiguously and precisely. The analyst has no right to expect a lucid explanation of the systems requirements. The user has no right to expect a system which meets the requirements without such an explanation and subsequent documentation.

The analysis task is therefore a partnership between user and analyst which the analyst is usually asked to manage.

A large part of the investigation and analysis phases within any project is spent acquiring detailed information about the current system. During these phases the analyst can quickly get overwhelmed with detail; both the detail of the business and the technical detail of the new system. Unless there is one scheme or structure to organise these details, the analyst can become overloaded with facts and paper. The detail is needed and must be available when required, but the analyst must have techniques and tools to control it.

The document setting out the detail of the new system effectively forms a contract between the user and the project team. If the document is impossible for the user to understand, because of its sheer size and technical content, then no contract exists and the user possesses a free hand to change the requirements. Changing requirements during the design and implementation phases is one of the major reasons for project delay and overspend.

1.4   The problems associated with systems design

Problems associated with the user's understanding of the specification documents were discussed in the previous section. One solution might be to write a business specification using the user's terminology which would be totally understandable to the user. However, if a specification document were written in such a way it may not be very useful to the designers and programmers who will be involved during the later phases of the project.

Often a considerable amount of re-analysis takes place defining data and functions in design terms. This work essentially duplicates the work of the analyst.

The second major problem for the designer is the separation of system design, data and processes from technical design. Exactly how can the design be implemented on the given hardware and software. The designer needs to be able to design a logical database and logical processes before the technical detail is added to the documentation.

What is required, therefore, is a systems analysis and design methodology which, as far as possible, overcomes these problems.

1.5   The need for a structured methodology

The need for a structured methodology is evident from the many sets of survey results which report the ever-increasing problems with current methods of developing computer systems. The major problem is related to project costs and timescales. Only a small proportion of projects are completed within their budget and on time. There are many reasons given for this situation, ranging from poor estimating to continued change in the user's requirements. In addition to the problems of cost and timescale, systems are still developed that do not meet the user's requirements, are difficult and costly to modify and maintain, and are poorly documented.

The need for a structured methodology is not solely based upon the problems associated with current approaches. There exists a requirement in all areas of computing to improve the productivity of development staff and the quality of the final product. Productivity and quality may be partially linked to user and management involvement; they should, however, not depend entirely on the involvement of users and management. A requirement exists in parallel with the productivity and quality requirement, to provide a basis for progress measurement and resource planning.

Published statistics by many organisations show that very few systems, as initially implemented, meet the user's requirements. The cost of rectification increases from zero, if the user's requirements are specified exactly during the analysis phase of a project, to very large sums, if the system is implemented and then modified to meet the requirements. The reduction of this rectification cost is another reason to follow a structured methodology.

1.6   Characteristics of a 'good' systems analysis and design methodology

This initial chapter has established a need for a structured methodology which will contribute towards improved development productivity and system quality. It is now necessary to establish a set of characteristics of a 'good' systems analysis and design methodology against which SSADM might be measured.

Two important characteristics of any systems analysis and design methodology are the degree to which they assist user–analyst–designer–implementor communication and the ease of understanding both of the methodology itself and of the documentation produced by it. The systems being considered for the 1990s and beyond are large and complex. Therefore to aid understanding some form of top–down modelling is required. The modelling techniques must provide high-level views which can be exploded piece by piece to provide more and more detailed local views. The view of a system must encompass three basic concepts: a view of the data within a system, a view of the flow of information around the constituent parts of the system, and a view representing the effect of information flow or functions on the data due to the passage of time.

The development of these three views of the system can be undertaken in a structured manner if the methodology provides for decomposition of the system. In this way a manageable number of system elements can be considered at one time.

The concept of considering a small number of elements at any time ensures that they are carefully selected for analysis. Elements may comprise functions and data structures. This process effectively defines the boundary of the project; all selected elements being initially inside the boundary.

Understanding also depends upon clarity of expression. A good methodology should wherever possible provide graphical representations. Such representations are capable of conveying large quantities of information in a simple and concise form. This makes the models represented graphically easy for users to understand and relatively easy to change. The ability to gradually transform a set of diagrams from a representation of the current system through a representation of the requirements towards a detailed design specification is a vital characteristic. This ensures the methodology leads from analysis of the current system into requirements specification and on into detailed design specification.

1.7 The specification

Two formally documented specifications are necessary: the specification of requirements and the detailed design specification. In each case a good methodology should lead to concise, unambiguous specifications which are not excessively wordy, physical or redundant. Many specifications are unclear, inconsistent and incorrect. The product of a structured methodology should be graphic and concise and overall it should accurately reflect the user's requirements. The specifications must be also totally understandable by their recipients.

1.8   The systems development cycle

There are many different representations of the systems development cycle. The following phases are used in this book:

(1) Terms of reference including business objectives
(2) Feasibility study
(3) Investigation
(4) Analysis
(5) Design
(6) Implementation
(7) Operation, maintenance and modification

All projects must pass through these phases, with a different emphasis being placed on each according to the type of project.

Very often the first phase has been completed before the project commences, with the terms of reference and business objectives forming the project brief. The first phase in these cases is a feasibility study. No feasibility study should commence without clearly stated terms of reference and overall business objectives.

1.8.1   Feasibility study

A feasibility study is required to determine if the objectives are realistic, that is, they are able to be done and put into effect. The feasibility study must address technical, economic and social areas of concern.

At the end of a feasibility study, a stop–go decision must be made for the project. The study must therefore present a detailed specification of the objectives together with an analysis of the impact on the organisation of any project aimed at meeting them.

Techniques such as cost benefit analysis, discounted cash flow and return on investment are used to establish economic feasibility. Technical feasibility needs to be established by estimation of processing and data requirements while social feasibility can only be determined by discussions with the proposed user.

The feasibility study is a project within a project incorporating investigation, analysis, design and possibly a pilot implementation/operation. A good methodology should provide for high-level investigation, analysis and design leading to the feasibility study report followed by more detailed investigation, analysis and design leading to the final system design specification. This is termed the two-pass systems development cycle and is shown in Figure 1.4.

The feasibility study should refine the business objectives within the terms of reference to provide objective measures against which success or failure of the project may be judged. It should further consider alternative system

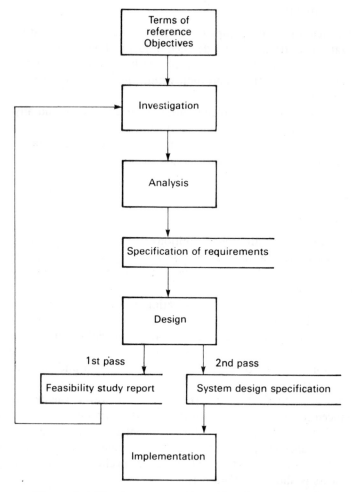

Figure 1.4 The two-pass systems development cycle

designs, rejecting unacceptable ones according to economic, technical and social feasibility criteria, finally choosing a number of designs for development. The feasibility study should report when a forecast can be made of the effect on the objective measures previously defined.

At this stage the feasibility study report should lay the foundations for subsequent planning and control of the project by documenting the investigation, analysis and design work done so far. This documentation should allow any subsequent project team to benefit from the work of the feasibility study team.

1.8.2   Investigation

The investigation phase comprises a detailed study of the existing system. Investigation continues until a detailed model of how the current system is implemented can be drawn and agreed with the user. The model should include both the functions and data within the system and the volume of processing and data.

Finally, the identified problems with the current system and any requirements for the new system should be documented.

Investigation techniques include the study of existing data, i.e. documents and reports, observation, the use of questionnaires and, of course, interviewing.

1.8.3   Analysis

There are very many different definitions of systems analysis with no real common agreement about the precise meaning of the term. One of the reasons may be the diversity of systems themselves, making a common approach impossible.

One useful definition is 'the organisation of information gathered during the investigation phase into a meaningful form'. This generally means the building of a model which represents what the current system accomplishes, not how it is accomplished. The model is logical not physical, and should include both the functions carried out by the system and the data stored within the system.

The model first reflects the current system. However, the definition may be enhanced to include the improvement and optimisation of the model to solve the identified problems with the current system. Further, the model should be enhanced to provide the stated requirements making the final product of analysis a required logical model or specification of requirements. This process is shown in Figure 1.5.

1.8.4   Design

The specification of requirements forms the input to the design phase. The objective of this phase is to specify the system in a way suitable for implementation on the chosen hardware with the chosen software. The design phase may therefore include the choice of hardware and software.

The design phase may be divided into logical design and physical design. The logical design sub-phase will transform the specification of requirements into detailed specifications of both data and processing requirements; what, in detail, is required of the new system. The physical design sub-phase will transform the logical specifications into physical specifications, database and program specifications, by including within the specifications

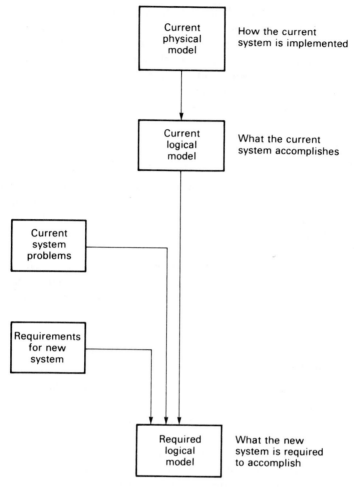

Figure 1.5 Analysis

consideration of the constraints imposed by the chosen hardware and software.

During the physical design sub-phase, details such as input and output formats will be designed along with file formats, screen formats etc.

The design phase will conclude with the production of a detailed system design specification.

1.8.5   Implementation

Implementation is the phase where the system design is translated into an operational system. It includes programming, program testing, hardware and software acquisition and installation, system testing, system set up, user education and training, user testing, and changeover to the new system.

Programming and program testing are sometimes identified as a separate phase. The use of SSADM will reduce the reliance on program and system testing to identify analysis and design errors. For this reason, programming and program testing are included as a necessary part of the implementation phase without any special importance.

1.8.6   Operation

The operational life of any system should include its review at agreed intervals. Business objectives will have changed during the life of the system and the degree with which they are met by the operational system should be established. Operational problems and requests should also be considered so that a planned modification and maintenance programme for the system can be established.

All systems require unplanned emergency maintenance. This area of work for analysts, designers and programmers is consistently increasing. The use of SSADM aims to reduce this effort by ensuring high-quality, well-documented system implementations.

1.9   The Structured System Analysis and Design Methodology (SSADM)

SSADM is a structured methodology appropriate for the analysis and design of systems which exist in a well-structured environment. It is less appropriate for ill-structured environments; these must be analysed and transformed into well-structured environments.

The differentiation of well-structured from ill-structured environments can be undertaken by assessing a number of key parameters, some of which are listed below. Well-structured environments are definable and sustainable whereas ill-structured environments are generally unsustainable.

Parameter	Well-structured	Ill-structured
Objectives	Realistic, clear, consistent	Unrealistic, vague, inconsistent
Problem areas	Known, relevant	Vague, not recognised
Requirements	Consistent, useful	Intuitive
Communication	Effective, reliable	Uncertain, unreliable
Attitudes	Flexible, co-operative	Obstructive

Most environments will exhibit some well-structured and some ill-structured characteristics. It is essential to only consider the use of SSADM in an environment which is predominantly well-structured.

SSADM is divided into six stages (see Figure 1.6). In this way a stage

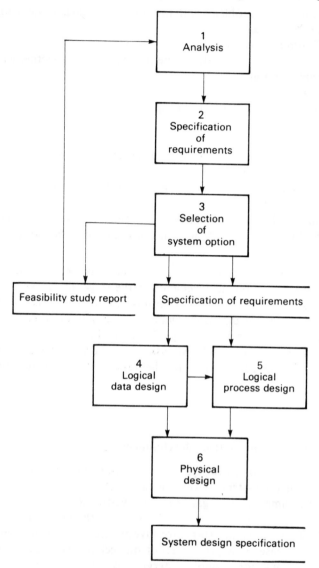

Figure 1.6 SSADM—six stages

represents the activities of a well-defined section of the development cycle.
Each stage has its own carefully defined set of objectives.

The objectives of each stage are:

1 *Analysis*
   To construct a logical model of the current system.

To document the problems with the current system and the requirements for the new system.

2 *Specification of requirements*
To construct a logical model of the required system together with detailed documentation.

3 *Selection of system option*
To identify and document the operational requirements for the new system.

4 *Logical data design*
To complete a detailed logical data design specification.

5 *Logical process design*
To complete a set of detailed logical process designs.

6 *Physical design*
To translate the logical data design into the file or database specification and the logical process designs into program specifications.

Each stage comprises several tasks. The tasks provide a structured approach leading to the achievements of the stage objectives.

Techniques such as data flow diagrams, are used by tasks to provide a mechanism for their completion. Data flow diagrams are used for the completion of specific tasks within stages 1, 2, 3 and 6. Techniques in SSADM are used as appropriate. SSADM tasks use a variety of techniques, each chosen for its appropriateness to the task; SSADM is not technique-dependent.

1.9.1 SSADM in the systems development cycle

SSADM is a methodology for systems analysis and design. Figure 1.7 shows its coverage of the systems development cycle.

SSADM commences by organising the investigation notes and concludes by producing a detailed design specification for the implementors.

SSADM does not include stages for investigation or implementation. The investigation phase of a project relies on techniques common to many business situations, for example, interviewing. Skills in the application of investigation techniques should be possessed by all systems analysts; SSADM may commence following any detailed investigation.

Implementation commences with programming and program testing. Structured programming existed well before structured analysis and design, and many organisations have adopted it as an installation standard. SSADM, therefore, completes a total structured approach. Stage 6 of SSADM is tailored to a user's environment to ensure that the structured design interfaces with existing programming methods.

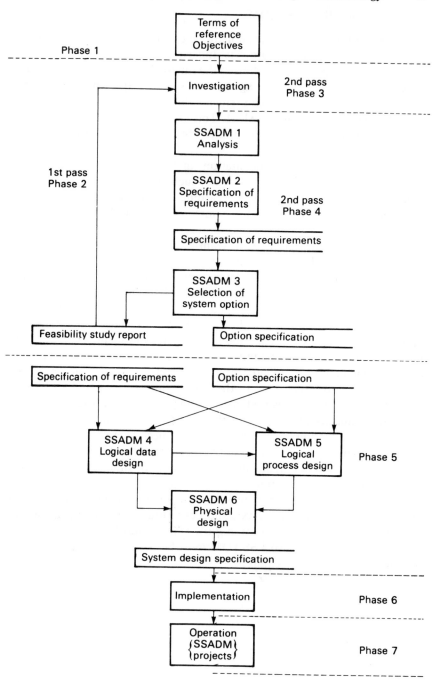

Figure 1.7 SSADM in the systems development cycle

1.9.2 The benefits of SSADM

Many users of SSADM have demonstrated that it does not increase the cost or timescale of development projects. Indeed, the experience has shown that there exists great potential to shorten the timescale and decrease the cost of development projects by meeting the user's exact requirements first time.

The meeting of the user's requirements, first time, is perhaps the greatest benefit to be accrued from SSADM. This can be attributed very largely to the methodology's involvement of the user throughout the development process.

The format of the documentation makes the system specification understandable by the user. Techniques, such as data flow diagrams, allow users to make their own decisions regarding information requirements and implementation options without becoming involved in the design technical detail.

SSADM forces the development team to consider the detail early in the project to ensure that the specification of requirements and the design specification are correct. Many more analysis and design decisions are forced into the earlier stages. This contrasts with many methods of working whereby the true costs of analysis and design are hidden. They are hidden because many decisions taken during the analysis and design stages are based on insufficient knowledge and are corrected during programming and implementation. The costs and timescales associated with the programming and implementation are inflated by this correction factor which has been shown to be up to 100 per cent of the implementation costs and timescales.

The final benefit is realised after implementation: SSADM includes detailed documentation as part of the methodology. This ensures that all documentation is completed as part of the project whereas documentation following analysis and design is rarely completed fully. The documentation provides a means of reducing the costs and timescales of system maintenance and modification.

SSADM, therefore, brings benefit to many phases of the system development process from initial analysis and design through to implementation, and maintenance and modification during live running.

The major benefit of using SSADM must be restated: it enables users to obtain the systems they require.

2

SSADM techniques

2.1 Introduction

SSADM is not based on any one technique but is a framework comprising six stages.

Each stage is designed to achieve a specific objective or set of objectives. The achievement of these objectives is engineered by using a set of tasks within each stage. Each task is based upon the most appropriate technique for the task. A stage may therefore use several techniques to achieve its objective and, conversely, a technique may be used during more than one stage.

Chapter 3 describes in detail the stages and tasks within SSADM, while this chapter introduces the techniques. SSADM uses many techniques. A set of techniques and related documentation that users can easily understand form the basis of SSADM.

The prime techniques are:

(1) Data flow diagrams which show the boundary of the system and its relationship to the external world. They also show the functions, data stores, input and output for the system.
(2) Entity models, which show the data structures and data relationships for the system. Groups of data structures or entities will eventually form the data stores on the final data flow diagram.
(3) Entity life histories, which show how each entity is affected by system functions and provide a dynamic view of a system. They model the effect of functions, modelled on the data flow diagram, on the entities, modelled on the entity model.
(4) Normalisation, which transforms complex data structures into simple lists, is used to build entity models bottom-up from the input and output data structures.
(5) Process outlines, which specify the operations necessary to process a

transaction in the system. These lead towards the production of program specifications.

(6) Physical design control, which provides sets of rules for transforming
logical specifications into physical specifications. A different set of rules
is required for each hardware and software product.

An improvement in the quality of developed systems is one of the claimed
benefits of SSADM; it uses a number of techniques to assist in this. Cross-
referencing is a technique used in several stages, to ensure the completeness
and accuracy of the models at that stage. Data store entity cross-references
are built during stage 1 and entity function cross-references are built during
stage 2.

User reviews, in the form of walkthroughs for quality control purposes
as well as for monitoring project progress, are a formal part of the
methodology.

The final technique is related to documentation. SSADM includes an
integrated set of documents which support the methodology. Documentation is very much a part of SSADM, not a task which is undertaken when
the project is completed.

2.2   Data flow diagrams

Data flow diagrams provide a view of the system understandable to the
user; a user's view. The user, in any system, produces output, very often
in the form of new or amended documents, based upon the flow of data into
the function the user performs. The user, therefore, observes data flow and
is able to describe in detail this view of the system. Data flow diagrams are
used in four forms: current physical, current logical, required logical and
required physical during stages 1, 2 and 3.

The user's view of the system is modelled by data flow diagrams. They
are system models against which analysts can test their understanding by
first constructing the model and secondly by performing a structured
walkthrough of the model with the user. Data flow diagrams are a simple
graphical representation of data flow, data storage and functions which
users readily accept. Many users quickly learn sufficient about them to be
able to contribute directly to their construction.

The various forms of data flow diagrams represent models of the system
during its various stages of refinement.

- Current physical - how the existing system operates
- Current logical - what the current system accomplishes
- Required logical - what the new system is required to accomplish
- Required physical - how the required system will be implemented

DATA FLOW DIAGRAM

SYSTEM: CHAPTER 2	DATE:
AUTHOR: G. CUTTS	PAGE: 1 of 2

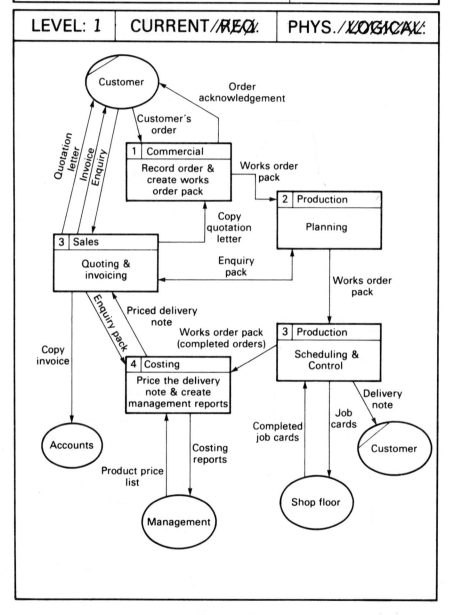

Figure 2.1

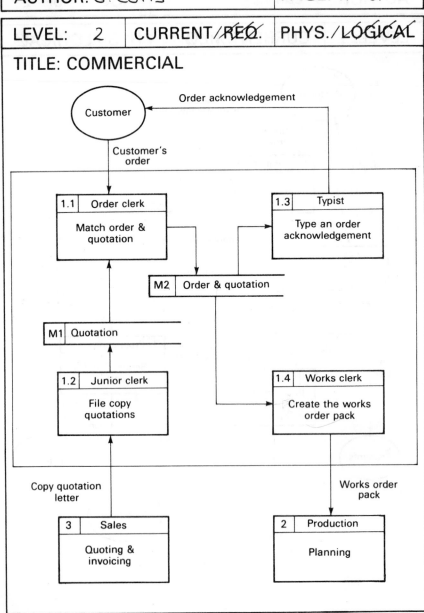

DATA FLOW DIAGRAM

SYSTEM: CHAPTER 2	DATE:
AUTHOR: G. CUTTS	PAGE: 2 of 2

LEVEL: 2	CURRENT/~~REQ.~~	PHYS./~~LOGICAL~~

TITLE: COMMERCIAL

Customer

Order acknowledgement

Customer's order

1.1	Order clerk
	Match order & quotation

1.3	Typist
	Type an order acknowledgement

M2	Order & quotation

M1	Quotation

1.2	Junior clerk
	File copy quotations

1.4	Works clerk
	Create the works order pack

Copy quotation letter

Works order pack

3	Sales
	Quoting & invoicing

2	Production
	Planning

Figure 2.2

Figure 2.1 shows a current physical data flow diagram, and Figure 2.2 shows an explosion of function 1 from Figure 2.1.

Data flow diagrams provide an excellent graphical descriptive tool that is easy for users to understand. They provide a clear view of the system functions and the system boundary and are therefore one of the techniques used to assist analyst–user communication.

The representation of exceptions and errors on data flow diagrams makes them over-complicated, losing the advantage of clarity. In addition, data flow diagrams can become very complex with many levels being required to express very detailed functions. This complexity can lead to omission and errors on the diagrams. Additionally, a methodology based solely on data flow diagrams would not include the structure of data. Data flow diagrams should, therefore, be just one of a set of complementary techniques.

2.3   Entity models

Entity models provide a system view of the data structures and data relationships within the system. All systems possess an underlying generic entity model which remains fairly static in time. The entity model reflects the logic of the system data, not the physical implementation.

There are many examples where different departments of the same organisation perform identical functions in very different ways. Their respective current physical data flow diagrams would reflect the differences. Their entity models would be very similar, since the data and data relationships required to perform the function are the same.

Entity models are logical not physical; they represent logical groups of data, called entities, and the relationships between the entities. Customer and order are examples of entities; places (i.e. a customer places an order) is an example of a relationship between the entity customer and the entity order. Figure 2.3 shows an entity model.

Entity models are used in stages 1, 2 and 4. They progress from early attempts to understand the underlying data structures and relationships (during stage 1), through to the construction of the final entity model (during stage 4).

Entity models provide an excellent graphical representation of the generic data structures and relationships. They provide a clear view of the logical structure of data within the boundary of interest and allow the analyst to model the data without considering its physical form. Entity modelling provides a system view independent of current processing; it is a system-wide view not a functionally decomposed view.

The technique of entity modelling complements data flow diagrams providing the missing system view of the data structures and relationships.

ENTITY MODEL

SYSTEM: CHAPTER 2 · EXAMPLE	DATE:
AUTHOR: G. CUTTS	PAGE: 1 of 1

VERSION: 1

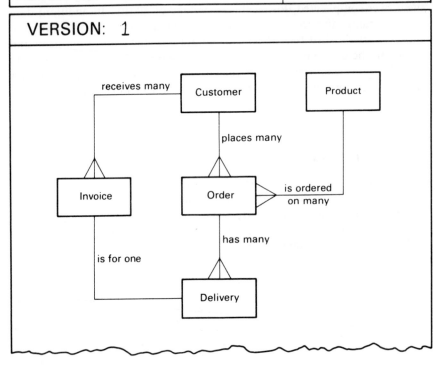

Entity	Relationship	Entity
Customer	receives many	Invoice
Customer	places many	Order
Product	is ordered on many	Order
Invoice	is for one	Delivery
Order	has many	Delivery

Figure 2.3

2.4 Cross-reference

The technique of cross-referencing one set of objects to another is used during stages 1 and 2 to provide tests of completeness and accuracy.

The open-ended rectangles on data flow diagrams represent data stores.

DATA STORE/ENTITY X REF.

PHYSICAL/~~LOGICAL~~

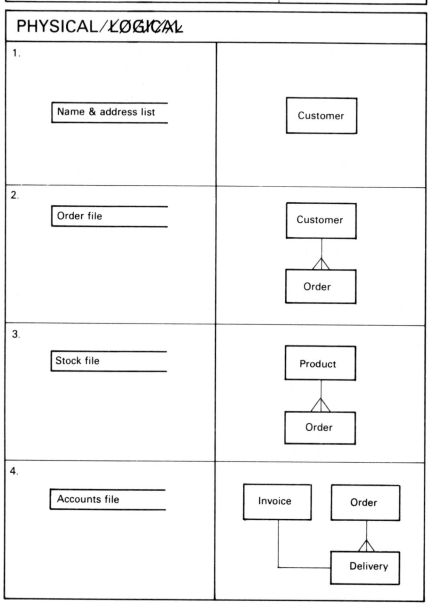

Figure 2.4

Each data store comprises part of an entity, a complete entity, a number of entities or several parts and complete entities. It is possible to cross-reference the data stores from a set of data flow diagrams with the entity model.

Figure 2.4 shows a cross-reference between a set of current physical data stores and the entity model for the same system.

If a current physical data store cannot be referenced to one or more entities, then either the entity model is incomplete or the physical data is not required within the system. If an entity from the entity model is not cross-referenced, then the entity may not be required in the current system.

Errors may have occurred during the construction of either model. The construction of a cross-reference highlighting problem areas serves as an early proof mechanism on the completeness and accuracy of the data flow diagrams and the entity model.

The cross-reference also provides an early insight into the areas of duplicated information within the current physical system. Duplication of data is often necessary to avoid lengthy access times but nearly always leads to inconsistencies. Figure 2.4 shows that data on orders is held on three physical files: the order file, the stock file and the accounts file.

2.5   Entity function matrix

The construction of an entity function matrix is a technique which leads to the construction of entity life histories and logical process outlines. The technique is used to construct a matrix in which the entities form the rows and the functions form the columns. The rows are formed by listing all the entities from the entity model and the columns are formed by listing all the functions on the data flow diagram. Figure 2.5 shows an entity function matrix without any entries.

Matrix entries comprise single or combinations of the letters I, R, M, D. I indicates that an entity occurrence is inserted by the function; R indicates that an entity occurrence is read by the function; M indicates that an entity occurrence is modified by the function; and D indicates that the entity occurrence is deleted by the function. The entries into the matrix can be made by reference to the data flow diagrams and the data store entity cross-reference. Figure 2.6 shows an example of a completed entity function matrix.

The matrix acts as a further proving technique. It is easy to identify that the customer entity needs functions to modify and delete the entity; the product entity needs a maintenance function; the invoice entity is inserted but never accessed; and the delivery entity is simply inserted, then deleted. These potential anomalies require further investigation with satisfactory reason being found for them, or with action being taken to eliminate them before continuation of the project.

ENTITY/FUNCTION MATRIX

SYSTEM: CHAPTER 2 EXAMPLE	DATE:
AUTHOR: G. CUTTS	PAGE: I of I

Function name / Entity name	1.1 Order entry	1.2 Produce order acknowledgement	1.3 Record delivery	1.4 Produce invoice	2.1 Create new customer account						
Customer											
Order											
Product											
Delivery											
Invoice											

Figure 2.5

Reading across a row of the matrix gives the entity life history. The entity order is inserted by function 1.1, order entry; modified by functions 1.2, produce order acknowledgement, and 1.3, record delivery; and eventually deleted by function 1.4, produce invoice. Reading down a column gives the processing that a function has to carry out. Function 1.3, record delivery, modifies the order and product entities and inserts the delivery entity.

The entity function matrix, therefore, provides a technique for plotting the effect of functions on entities. It also provides a way forward into entity life histories and process outlines.

Cross-references such as those of the data store entity and the entity function provide a technique for proving the models, therefore improving the quality of the final system.

ENTITY/FUNCTION MATRIX

SYSTEM: CHAPTER 2 EXAMPLE	DATE:
AUTHOR: G. CUTTS	PAGE: 1 of 1

Function name / Entity name	1.1 Order entry	1.2 Produce order acknowledgement	1.3 Record delivery	1.4 Produce invoice	2.1 Create new customer accounts						
Customer	R	R			I						
Order	I	M	M	D							
Product			M								
Delivery			I	D							
Invoice				I							

Figure 2.6

2.6   Entity life history

Each row of the entity function matrix shows how an entity is affected by functions. It does not show the sequence of functions nor does it show when it is valid to carry out a function. The matrix also only shows the normal functions which affect the entity. The entity life history technique provides a graphical representation which shows the sequence of functions and when it is acceptable to carry out a function. Entity life histories also show abnormal functions. Figure 2.7 shows a simple entity life history with no abnormal functions.

The squares represent functions, the circles show the current status of the

ENTITY LIFE HISTORY

SYSTEM: CHAPTER 2 EXAMPLE

DATE:

AUTHOR: G. CUTTS

PAGE: / of /

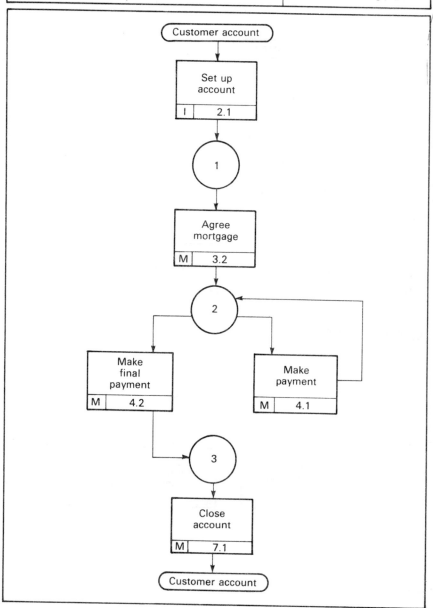

Figure 2.7

ENTITY LIFE HISTORY

SYSTEM: CHAPTER 2 EXAMPLE   DATE:

AUTHOR: G. CUTTS   PAGE: 1 of 1

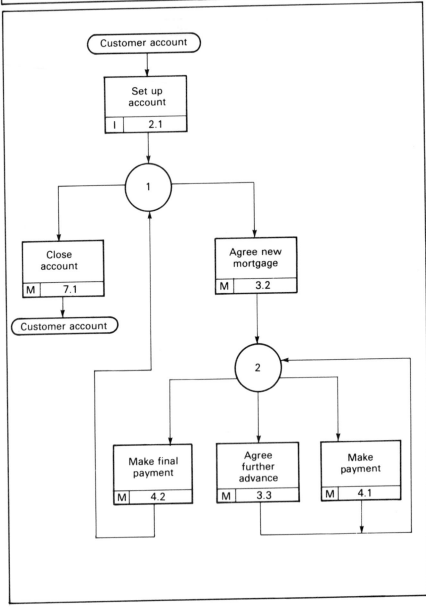

Figure 2.8

entity occurrence. The function, make payment, 4.1, modifies the entity customer account. It is only valid to make payments when the entity occurrence has a status of two. The status of the entity occurrence should be reset to two, in this instance, on completion of successful processing. The function, make final payment, 4.2, is only valid if the status is two; the 'set to' status, in this case, is three. The only valid function, when the status is three, is close account. Each function possesses, for each entity it affects, a valid previous status and a set to status.

Entity life histories allow the analyst to concentrate on a particular entity. In this case, perhaps the entity life history should be amended to allow subsequent mortgage agreements. Figure 2.8 shows an amended entity life history for the entity, customer account.

2.7 Normalisation

Normalisation is the technique used within stage 4 to produce data structures in third normal form, from input and output specifications. Input and output data structures are progressively transformed from UNF (unnormalised form) through 1NF and 2NF (first and second normal forms) to 3NF (third normal form).

Normalisation is a technique for transforming complex data structures into simple tables. The tables form the building blocks for data design; the methodology uses the tables to create entities and an entity model.

Figure 2.9 shows a complex data structure representing orders for books. Much of the data relating to books is duplicated in the data structure, which is unnormalised. Note also that with this data structure, customer details and book details cannot be stored unless an order exists. Normalisation would result in three simple tables, shown in Figure 2.10; these tables are in third normal form. First and second normal forms represent steps towards the target, third normal form.

Normalisation results in the discovery of entities and entity descriptions, bottom up, from detailed input and output descriptions.

2.8 Process outlines

A process outline collects together all the operations that are necessary for a process to execute. The entities affected by the processing can be established from the entity function matrix. The previous status of the entity occurrence, for which the function is valid, can be established from the entity life histories. The entity life history will also provide the 'set to' status on the successful completion of the function.

A skeleton process outline comprising the entity name, the effect on the

Customer Number	Name	ISBN	Title	Author	Price	Qty. Ordered
A471	J. Allen	0-13-47917-3	Data Processing	A. Downs	15.00	10
		0-12-27947-1	Program Design	J. Smith	12.00	5
		0-17-11001-2	IKBS	F. Williams	22.00	1
J419	J. Jones	0-12-27947-1	Program Design	J. Smith	12.00	7
K579	A. Keith	0-17-11001-2	IKBS	F. Williams	22.00	2
		0-21-100001-3	Novel Architecture	N. Wills	15.00	3

Figure 2.9

Customer Table

No.	Name
A471	J. Allen
J419	J. Jones
K579	A. Keith

Book Table

ISBN	Title	Author	Price
0-13-47917-3	Data Processing	A. Downs	15.00
0-12-27947-1	Program Design	J. Smith	12.00
0-17-11001-2	IKBS	F. Williams	22.00
0-21-100001-3	Novel Architecture	N. Wills	15.00

Order Table

Customer No.	ISBN	Qty. Ordered
A471	0-13-47917-3	10
A471	0-12-27947-1	5
A471	0-17-11001-2	1
J419	0-12-27947-1	7
K579	0-17-11001-2	2
K579	0-21-100001-3	3

Figure 2.10

entity occurrence, the valid previous status and the set to status can easily be constructed (see Figure 2.11).

The skeleton process outline can now be enhanced to include a description of the processing for each operation required to complete the process. Each process outline will include one or more function boxes from the data flow diagrams.

A completed process outline is shown in Figure 2.12.

2.9   Physical design control

Physical design control is not a single technique, but a number of rules for converting the logical data design and logical process outlines into physical

Create invoice

Entity	Effect	Valid previous	Set to
Order line	M	3	3
Delivery	M	2	3
Invoice	I	—	1

Figure 2.11 Skeleton process outline for create invoice

LOGICAL PROCESS OUTLINE

SYSTEM: CHAPTER 2 EXAMPLE	DATE:
AUTHOR: G. CUTTS	PAGE: 1 of 1

EVENT NAME: Create Invoice	VOLUME:

BRIEF DESCRIPTION: Invoices are created from the input of actual quatity despatched taken from a copy of the delivery note.

Op. No.	Entity Name	Status Eff.	Ind. prev	set	Description / Narrative	Ref.	I/O Ref.	Err. Ref.
1					Read input delivery details. Validate the input fields as described in VIO. If errors are detected follow the procedure described in E2 and the details in format O2.	VIO	O2	E2
2	Order line	M	3	3	Find the relevant order line. If not found reject the transaction, see O3, E3. If found but status error, see EI. Add 1 to the number of invoices field.		O3	E3 EI
3	Delivery	M	2	3	Find the relevant delivery. If not found reject the transaction, see O3, E3. If found but status error, see EI. Modify the quantity to the quantity input.		O3	E3 EI
4	Invoice	I	—	1	Insert invoice			

Figure 2.12

specifications. The result of physical design control is a database or file specification and a series of program specifications.

The conversion rules will vary according to the target hardware and software.

Database or file specifications are enhanced or modified entity models. The entity model is enhanced to show access points and access methods, then modified to satisfy the constraints of the database or file management software available.

Physical program specifications are enhanced process outlines. Several process outlines may be merged to create one program specification. Enhancements to the process outline include the details of how each entity is accessed via the database implementation.

2.10 Walkthrough

A walkthrough is a meeting of all interested people to discuss the content of the project. It is not a progress review.

2.11 Stages technique cross-reference

SSADM comprises six stages; the techniques used within each stage are listed below:

Stage 1 Analysis	Data flow diagrams
	Entity models
	Cross-reference
	Walkthroughs and documentation
2 Specification of requirements	Data flow diagrams
	Entity models
	Cross-reference
	Entity life histories
	Walkthroughs and documentation
3 Selection of system options	Data flow diagrams
	Walkthroughs and documentation
4 Logical data design	Normalisation
	Entity models
	Walkthroughs and documentation
5 Logical process design	Process outlines
	Walkthroughs and documentation
6 Physical design	Physical design control
	Walkthroughs and documentation

2.12 Summary

The objective of SSADM is to provide a framework for systems analysis and design. The framework comprises several techniques, and a system of documentation.

The techniques have been chosen for their applicability to the stage and task within the stage as well as being usable and teachable.

The major techniques are data flow diagrams, for representing information flows; entity models, for representing data structures and data relationships; entity life histories, for representing the effect of time; normalisation, for building third normal form data structures; process outlines, for specifying detailed process logic; and physical design control, for establishing optimum physical database, file and program specifications.

The techniques are now fitted into the detailed framework of stages and tasks in chapter 3.

3

SSADM stages and tasks

3.1 Introduction

The terms of reference are the starting point for SSADM. They state the business objectives for the proposed development and the resources available for it. In many cases, a feasibility study report will have been completed which will form a second input into SSADM.

The outputs from SSADM are a set of program specifications, a database or files specification, an implementation plan, a user manual and an operations manual. SSADM systems analysis can also be used to produce feasibility study reports.

Figure 3.1 shows SSADM inputs and outputs.

The stages of SSADM have been constructed so that each has a clear objective with limited scope. Each stage has a defined set of outputs which provide a clear, clean interface between the stages.

Figure 3.2 shows the six stages of SSADM, SSADM inputs and outputs, and the output produced by each stage.

The division of SSADM into six stages provides a high-level project management tool. Since each stage is self-contained and has a precise objective and a set of outputs, management monitoring of completion is relatively easy. A walkthrough should be undertaken at the end of each stage to monitor both progress and quality. The six stages of SSADM could be used to create six project milestones.

The inputs and outputs from each stage are listed below:

Stage 1 Analysis
      Input   Terms of reference
                             Feasibility study report (optional)
      Output   Current logical data flow diagrams
                             Current entity model
                             Problems and requirements list

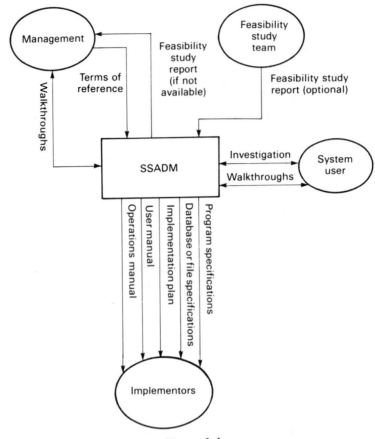

Figure 3.1

Stage 2 Specification of requirements
Input	Current logical data flow diagrams
	Current entity model
	Problems and requirements list
Output	Required logical data flow diagrams
	Required entity model
	Entity descriptions
	Input and output descriptions
	Function descriptions
	Entity function matrix
	Entity life histories

Stage 3 Selection of system option
Input	Required logical data flow diagrams
Output	Required physical data flow diagrams

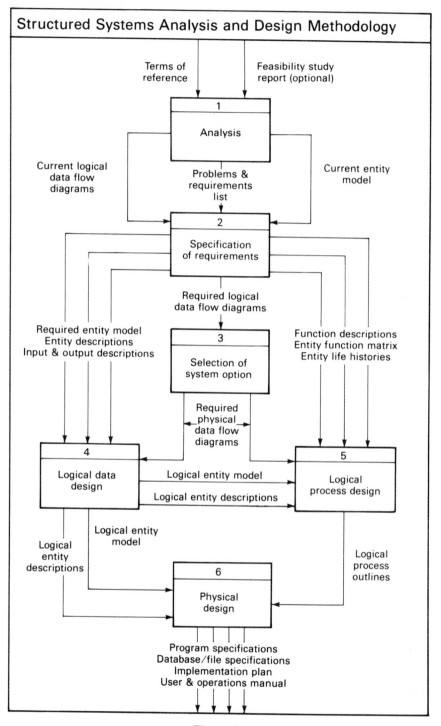

Structured Systems Analysis and Design Methodology

Terms of reference

Feasibility study report (optional)

1 Analysis

Current logical data flow diagrams

Problems & requirements list

Current entity model

2 Specification of requirements

Required logical data flow diagrams

Required entity model
Entity descriptions
Input & output descriptions

Function descriptions
Entity function matrix
Entity life histories

3 Selection of system option

Required physical data flow diagrams

4 Logical data design

Logical entity model

Logical entity descriptions

5 Logical process design

Logical entity descriptions

Logical entity model

Logical process outlines

6 Physical design

Program specifications
Database/file specifications
Implementation plan
User & operations manual

Figure 3.2

Stage 4 Logical data design

Input	Required physical data flow diagrams
	Required entity model
	Entity descriptions
	Input and output descriptions
Output	Logical entity model
	Logical entity descriptions

Stage 5 Logical process design

Input	Required physical data flow diagrams
	Logical entity model
	Logical entity descriptions
	Function descriptions
	Entity function matrix
	Entity life histories
Output	Logical process outlines

Stage 6 Physical design

Input	Logical process outlines
	Logical entity model
	Logical entity descriptions
Output	Program specifications
	Database or file specifications
	An implementation plan
	A user manual
	An operations manual

3.2   System manual

The inputs shown for each stage form the major source of information to the stage. One of the major benefits of SSADM is the gradual completion of the system documentation, stage by stage. The system manual or system documentation is therefore not a specific deliverable from any of the stages, but from all of the stages. The system manual, comprising the output from all stages, is available throughout the life of the system and therefore forms a secondary input to each stage.

3.3   SSADM stages

3.3.1   Stage 1: Analysis

Stage 1 of SSADM uses the terms of reference and optionally the feasibility study report to produce a logical model of the current system. The logical model comprises a set of current logical data flow diagrams and a current entity model. Stage 1 commences with a planned investigation of the current system, the results of which are used to build the data flow diagrams and entity model. During the building of the models, and during the investigation, problems with the current system, and requirements for the new system, will be identified. A list of problems and requirements forms the third deliverable item from stage 1, along with the current logical data flow diagrams and the current entity model.

The objectives of stage 1 are to obtain a thorough understanding of the functions and data within the current system; to build logical models of what data flows, data stores, functions, data structures and data relationships exist; to identify problems with the current system; to record requirements for the new system and to agree the logical models, problems and requirements with the user.

3.3.2   Stage 2: Specification of requirements

Stage 2 of SSADM can be divided into three sections. Section one uses the current models as input and optimizes them before creating the required models. The required models reflect solutions to the problems documented, as well as building into the models the requirements for the new system. The required logical data flow diagrams are created from the current logical data flow diagrams and the required entity model is created from the current entity model.

Section two provides the detailed documentation for the models. Entity descriptions and input/output descriptions are documented as attribute lists. The input/output descriptions form part of the detailed documentation of the data flow diagrams along with the entity descriptions, which effectively document the data stores. To complete the documentation of the data flow diagrams, function descriptions are required. Each function which is not further decomposed should be documented.

Section three provides a detailed third view of the system. A view, in addition to the static views provided by data flow diagrams and entity models, which models the effect of functions on entities in time. This view is dynamic and provides early proving of the model building tasks.

The objective of stage 2 is to provide a clear, concise, unambiguous, complete set of documents which specify the required system in terms that the user can understand. A walkthrough at the end of stage 2 must reach agreement on what is required of the new system; it is a statement of the logical requirements for the new system.

3.3.3   Stage 3: Selection of system option

This stage is concerned with taking the logical specification of requirements and developing a physical statement of requirements. During stage 3, the required logical data flow diagrams are transformed into the required physical data flow diagrams. The logical diagrams model what is required of the system, and the physical diagrams model how the requirements are to be provided.

The objective of stage 3 is to select a particular physical implementation for further development. The selection, from a short list of implementation options, should be made by the user, assisted by the project team. Each option will have a different impact on the problems and requirements, and on the user; and will also have different costs and implementation times. It is these considerations, along with technical guidance from the project team, which will lead the user to a final selection.

This final section forms the specification of requirements.

3.3.4   SSADM systems analysis

The specification of the required system marks the conclusion of systems analysis, a major milestone in any project. Stages 1, 2 and 3 comprise analysis stages, their objective being to produce a detailed specification of requirements. For this reason, a major milestone walkthrough should be planned for the end of stage 3.

A different view of SSADM is shown in Figure 3.3, a view which shows the specification of requirements as a major interface in the methodology.

SSADM may be used in two modes up to stage 3, single-pass and two-pass analysis. With two-pass analysis, stages 1, 2 and 3 are used as a methodology to provide an overview of the system and to provide the information necessary for the production of the feasibility study report.

Stages 1, 2 and 3 appear in the methodology twice. The full two-pass methodology for SSADM systems analysis is shown in Figure 3.4.

3.3.5   Stage 4: Logical data design

Stage 4 uses the input and output descriptions to produce data structures in third normal form. An entity model and entity descriptions are created from the data structures. The entity models and entity descriptions from stage 2 are compared with those just produced, differences are resolved by reference to the requirements and the user, and a set of logical entity descriptions and a logical entity model are delivered to stages 5 and 6.

The objective of stage 4 is to ensure that the data structures and data relationships are fully described and understood. Stage 4 produces entity descriptions and the entity model bottom up, whereas, during stage 2, they were produced top down. The two approaches ensure that a high-quality logical entity model and logical entity descriptions are delivered to stages 5 and 6.

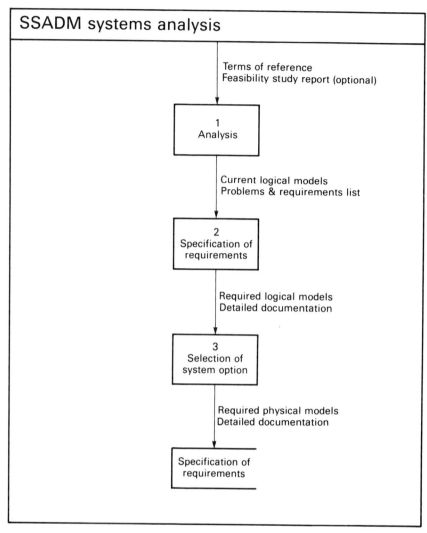

Figure 3.3

3.3.6 Stage 5: Logical process design

The first task in stage 5 is to catalogue the functions from the required physical data flow diagrams. The functions are catalogued according to their type of processing (on-line, batch), the timescale of processing (daily, weekly) and the access requirements (sales ledger, order file). Each process will comprise one or more data flow diagram functions.

For each logical process, a process outline is created which describes the operations necessary to execute the process. This logical process outline

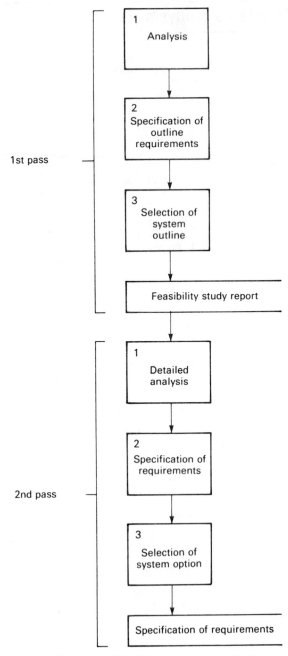

Figure 3.4 SSADM two-pass analysis

represents a logical program or module specification, the output from stage 5 passed to stage 6.

The objective of stage 5 is to group the functions into logical processes according to processing requirements, and to provide detailed descriptions of the logical processes.

3.3.7   Stage 6: Physical design

In physical design, the logical entity model and logical entity descriptions are transformed into a database or file specification by the application of rules specifically designed to reflect the target hardware and software. The database or file specifications are then used, along with a second set of rules, to transform the logical process outlines into program specifications.

Optimisation and tuning of the specifications is considered before production of the final database or file specifications and the final program specifications.

The system specification is now complete and stage 6 can conclude by producing an implementation plan covering programming, conversion etc., an operations manual and a user manual.

3.3.8   SSADM systems design

SSADM systems design includes stages 4, 5 and 6. Systems design is the transformation of the specification of requirements into a detailed logical specification and secondly into a detailed physical specification.

There are two major milestones during system design. These are at the end of stage 5, when a complete logical design is available for review, and at the end of stage 6, when the complete physical design is available for review. Note that the target hardware and software are not considered until stage 6; detailed knowledge of the hardware and software is not required to be able to complete the logical design. System designers, therefore, need not be technical experts to be able to undertake logical design. Indeed, systems design can proceed up to detailed logical design followed by several stage 6s, each targeted on a different hardware and software system.

Systems design within SSADM is clearly separable into logical design and physical design.

3.4   SSADM tasks

Each stage within SSADM possesses clearly defined objectives, a set of inputs and a set of outputs. The inputs are transformed into the outputs to meet the objectives of the stage by a set of tasks. Each task within each stage possesses a clearly defined objective, a sub-objective of the stage objectives. Similarly, each task possesses a set of inputs and a set of outputs.

The stages were numbered 1 to 6; the tasks are numbered within each stage. Task 5 in stage 1 is therefore numbered 1.5. The user of the methodology can clearly understand the stage and task being undertaken, the inputs, the outputs, the objective and the techniques to be used for the task. SSADM provides a structured approach to systems development.

This chapter will now document each task, its objective, its inputs and its outputs, a list of techniques to be used and a brief description of the task.

Chapters 4 to 9 will describe each stage in detail.

3.4.1 Stage 1: Analysis, tasks

There are six tasks, shown in Figure 3.5.

Stage 1, Task 1.1: Investigate the current system
Objective To document the functions and data within the current system.
Input Terms of reference; feasibility study report; interview notes; results of investigations of current files, procedures etc.; results of questionnaires etc.
Output A detailed set of investigation notes/documentation.
Technique Any investigation technique or techniques available, such as interviews, questionnaires, current documentation etc.
Description This task is common to all development methodologies. It uses the standard skills all systems analysts possess and seeks to gain a thorough understanding of the current system.

Stage 1, Task 1.2: Create the current physical data flow diagrams
Objective To model the physical functions, data flows, data stores and external entities associated with the current system. The model represents how the current system operates.
Input Investigation documentation; terms of reference.
Output A set of physical data flow diagrams.
Technique Data flow diagrams; walkthroughs.
Description This task provides a graphic representation of the current system which models the user's view of the system. The user's view comprises the document flow, the files and stores of data, the providers and recipients of documents and the functions carried out.

The current physical model will model all of the problems and anomalies of the current system since it should be a faithful representation of current practice.

Stage 1, Task 1.3: Create the current entity model
Objective To model the logical data structures (entities) and entity relationships required to support the current system.
Input Investigation documentation.
Output Current entity model.
Technique Entity modelling.
Description This task provides a graphical representation of the current system which models the system view of the system. The system view comprises the entities and relationships necessary to support the processing requirements of the system. The model represents the underlying generic data structures and is a logical model. It does not, therefore, reflect the current files and data stores directly.

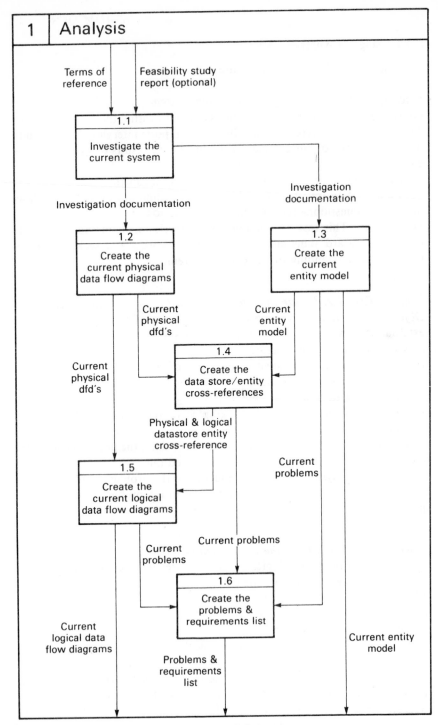

Figure 3.5

Stage 1, Task 1.4· Create the data store entity cross-reference
Objective To provide a physical data store to logical data store cross-reference which will enable the logicalisation of the data flow diagrams.
Input Current physical data flow diagrams; current entity model.
Output Physical data store entity cross-reference; logical data store entity cross-reference.
Technique Cross-reference.
Description This task first provides a cross-reference between the current physical data stores and the entities of the entity model. It provides a check on the completeness and accuracy of the data flow diagrams and the entity model. It also allows each data flow, to or from a physical data store on the current physical data flow diagram, to be annotated with one or more entity names.

The task secondly provides a cross-reference between current logical data stores and the entities. This is obtained by partitioning the entity model into logical groups.

Stage 1, Task 1.5: Create the current logical data flow diagrams
Objective To model the logical functions, data flows, data stores and external entities associated with the current system. This model represents what the current system accomplishes.
Input Current physical data flow diagrams; physical data store entity cross-reference; logical data store entity cross-reference.
Output Current logical data flow diagrams.
Technique Data flow diagrams.
Description This task uses a four-step procedure to transform the physical model into a logical model. The steps include logicalising the data flows, data stores and functions as well as removing physical time dependencies and physical only functions.

The logical model represents what is accomplished by the current system, not how the current system operates.

Stage 1, Task 1.6: Create the problems and requirements list
Objective To document the problems with the current system and the requirements for the new system.
Input Terms of reference; investigation documentation; perceived problems and requirements.
Output The problems and requirements list.
Technique Itemised formatted list.
Description The investigation task, particularly during the interview procedure, should reveal the problems with the current system. Requests for new system functions and data are received during the investigation. The problems and requirements are formally documented by this task. The construction of logical models of the current system also reveal problems and

requirements. The problems and requirements list therefore documents all the problems with the current system and requirements for the new system discovered during stage 1.

Stage 1 review
Objective   To agree with the user the accuracy and completeness of the current system model and the list of problems and requirements.
Input   The current logical data flow diagrams; the current entity model; the problems and requirements list.
Output   An agreement.
Technique   Walkthrough.
Description   This task ensures that the final models of the current system, together with the problems and requirements, are 'signed off' by the user. The walkthrough may result in an iteration of some or all of the tasks within stage 1. Stage 1 cannot be considered complete until a successful walkthrough with the user has taken place.

3.4.2 Stage 2: Specification of requirements, tasks

There are seven tasks, shown in Figure 3.6.

Stage 2, Task 2.1: Create the required logical data flow diagrams
Objective To model the logical functions, data stores, data flows and external entities associated with the required system.
Input The current logical data flow diagrams; the problems and requirement lists.
Output The required logical data flow diagrams.
Technique Data flow diagrams.
Description This task generates the required functional model from the current functional model. Solutions are found to the problems generally by providing an enhanced system. The data flow diagrams are therefore optimised and enhanced or recreated to solve the problems and to satisfy the new requirements.

Stage 2, Task 2.2: Create the required entity model
Objective To model the logical data structures (entities) and relationships associated with the required system.
Input The current entity model; the required logical data flow diagrams.
Output The required entity model.
Technique Entity modelling.
Description This task transforms the current entity model into the required entity model. The required logical data flow diagrams may well differ from the current logical data flow diagrams. New data stores and modifications to the existing data stores will be required to solve the problems with the current system and to satisfy the requirements for the new system.

The new data stores and the modifications to existing data stores effectively introduce new entities, new relationships, entity modifications and relationship modifications. These modifications are used to transform the current entity model into the required entity model.

Stage 2, Task 2.3: Document the entity descriptions
Objective To document the attributes for each entity.
Input Required entity model; investigation documentation.
Output A set of entity descriptions.
Technique Standard format document.
Description This task documents, for each entity, the attributes which comprise the entity description.

The entity descriptions are completed, at this stage, top down by allocation of attributes to entities.

At this stage, the entity descriptions are logical. They are simply lists of attributes with no indication of their physical format etc.

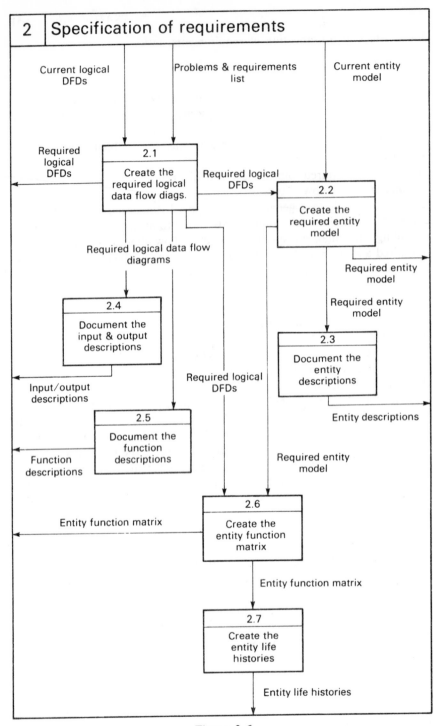

| 2 | Specification of requirements |

Current logical DFDs

Problems & requirements list

Current entity model

Required logical DFDs

2.1
Create the required logical data flow diags.

Required logical DFDs

2.2
Create the required entity model

Required logical data flow diagrams

Required entity model

Required entity model

2.4
Document the input & output descriptions

2.3
Document the entity descriptions

Input/output descriptions

Required logical DFDs

Entity descriptions

2.5
Document the function descriptions

Function descriptions

Required entity model

2.6
Create the entity function matrix

Entity function matrix

Entity function matrix

2.7
Create the entity life histories

Entity life histories

Figure 3.6

Stage 2, Task 2.4: Document the system input, system output and data flow descriptions

Objective To document the attributes for each input and output.

Input Required logical data flow diagrams.

Output A set of system input descriptions; a set of system output descriptions; a set of internal data flow descriptions.

Technique Standard format document.

Description This task uses the required logical data flow diagrams to identify those data flows which cross the system boundary. These data flows comprise the system input and output. All other data flows are either internal or entity data flows.

This task documents, for each input, each output and each internal data flow, the attributes which comprise the data flow.

At this stage, the descriptions are logical descriptions, not screen formats, report layouts etc.

Stage 2, Task 2.5: Document the function descriptions

Objective To describe the processing carried out by each primitive function.

Input Required logical data flow diagrams.

Output A set of function descriptions.

Technique Structured English; pseudo-code; decision tables; decision trees; any other descriptive technique available to the analyst and acceptable to the user.

Description This task uses one or more of the techniques to describe, and therefore document, the detailed processing carried out by each function. Only functions which are not further decomposed, that is, primitive functions, require to be described.

Each description should use a technique and style which is understandable by the user.

Stage 2, Task 2.6: Create the entity function matrix

Objective To chart the effect, in time, of the functions on the entities.

Input Required logical data flow diagrams; required entity model.

Output A set of function descriptions.

Technique Cross-reference.

Description This task creates a matrix or cross-reference of the functions against the entities. The functions, which form the columns of the matrix, represent primitive functions from the required logical data flow diagrams. The entities, which form the rows of the matrix, are simply listed from the required entity model.

The entries of the matrix may be one or more of the following.

I the function INSERTS an occurrence of the entity into the database
M the function MODIFIES an occurrence of the entity in the database
R the function READS an occurrence of the entity in the database
D the function DELETES an occurrence of the entity from the database
space the function has no effect on the entity.

Stage 2, Task 2.7: Create the entity life histories
Objective To document, for each entity, the sequence or sequences of functions which affect the entity.
Input The entity function matrix; the required logical data flow diagrams.
Output A set of entity life histories.
Technique Entity life history.
Description The entity life history, drawn for each entity, shows the sequence or sequences of functions which chart the normal processing of an entity occurrence from insertion into to deletion from the database. In addition, abnormal and error functions are charted. Finally, a status is attributed to each entity. The status defines which function or functions may access and process the entity occurrence.

Stage 2 review
Objective To agree with the user the accuracy and completeness of the specification of requirements.
Input The seven sets of documents which form the specification of requirements.
Output An agreement.
Technique Walkthrough.
Description This task ensures that the logical specification of requirements is fully understood and accepted by the user: this is vital to stage 3. A successful walkthrough of the documents which comprise the specification of requirements must be completed to conclude stage 2.

3.4.3   Stage 3: Selection of system options, tasks

There are three tasks, shown in Figure 3.7.

Stage 3, Task 3.1: Postulate system options
Objective   To document a number of possible physical implementations of the required system.
Input   The required logical data flow diagrams.
Output   For each option: a set of required physical data flow diagrams, supporting cost benefit and impact analyses, and supporting narrative.
Technique   Data flow diagrams; cost benefit and impact analyses; narrative.
Description   This task identifies a number of implementation or business options represented by physical data flow diagrams. Each option will

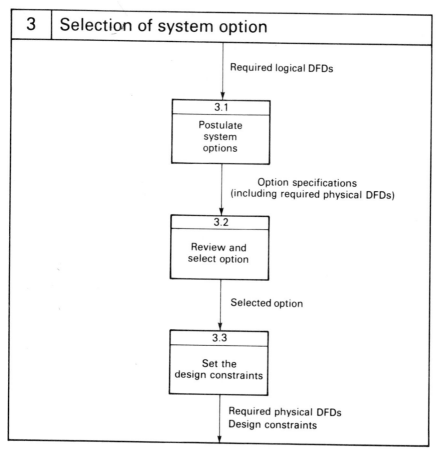

Figure 3.7

comprise a set of required physical data flow diagrams supported by a description of the costs, benefits and impact on the user of the option. For example, one option may specify more on-line processing than a second or even third option.

Each option effectively documents a different business solution.

Stage 3, Task 3.2: Review and select option
Objective To select one of the physical implementation options for continued development.
Input The required physical data flow diagrams; the cost benefit and impact analyses; supporting narrative.
Output A set of required physical data flow diagrams.
Technique Presentation; walkthrough.
Description Since each of the options presents a different business solution, the user, assisted by the project team, must select one of them for continued development. The project team should prepare a presentation of the system options and be prepared to walkthrough each one with the user.

This task represents the major milestone of stages 1, 2 and 3, systems analysis.

Stage 3, Task 3.3: Set the design constraints
Objective To set further constraints on the design not already documented.
Input The specification of requirements; the selected implementation option.
Output The complete specification of requirements.
Technique Narrative.
Description This task documents the constraints on the final design that are not apparent from the specification of requirements documentation already completed. The constraints include security, privacy and recovery requirements.

Design objectives may also be set or revised during this task. The design objectives include resource usage, for example direct access space and device utilisation, and performance objectives, for example response times and batch run times.

Stage 3 review
Objective To 'sign off' the specification of requirements.
Input The specification of requirements.
Output An agreement.
Technique Walkthrough.
Description The reviews of stages 1 and 2 were very much user reviews. Stage 3, particularly task 3.2, involves the user in a process which requires a full understanding of the specification of requirements.

The stage 3 review is more a project management review. It is a major project milestone where analysis finishes and design commences. A management walkthrough is therefore necessary to ensure the completeness of all systems documentation required for the design stages.

3.4.4   Stage 4: Logical data design, tasks

There are six tasks, shown in Figure 3.8.

Stage 4, Task 4.1: Select data structures
Objective   To select a set of data structures for task 4.2, normalisation. The set must include sufficient data structures to enable a complete and accurate entity model to be produced while minimising the effort required for the task of normalisation.
Input   The required physical data flow diagrams.
Output   A selected data structures list.
Technique   Walkthrough.
Description   All of the data structures, that is, input, output, data flow and data stores, are represented on the required physical data flow diagrams. A set of data structures is selected for output to task 4.2 by walkthrough, according to a number of selection guidelines. The walkthrough should be by members from the analysis team and the design team.

Stage 4, Task 4.2: Normalisation
Objective   To transform the selected data structures into simpler structures thus removing various anomalies associated with complex data structures.
Input   A set of selected data structures; the data structure descriptions.
Output   A set of simple data structures.
Technique   Normalisation.
Description   Normalisation is a mathematical technique which transforms complex data structures or unnormalised data structures into simple structures in third normal form. A series of prescriptive rules is applied to unnormalised data structures to produce, initially, first normal form, then second normal form and finally third normal form. The various anomalies associated with unnormalised data structures are gradually removed during the process of normalisation.

Stage 4, Task 4.3: Create the entity descriptions
Objective   To create a list of entities, and for each a list of attributes.
Input   The data structures in third normal form.
Output   A set of entity descriptions.
Technique   Set of rules.
Description   This task simply merges together all of the third normal form data structures which have identical keys. The combined lists of attributes form the entity description. The entity itself is uniquely identified by its key, which often provides a pointer to an appropriate entity name.

Stage 4, Task 4.4: Create the entity model
Objective   To create an entity model from the entity descriptions.

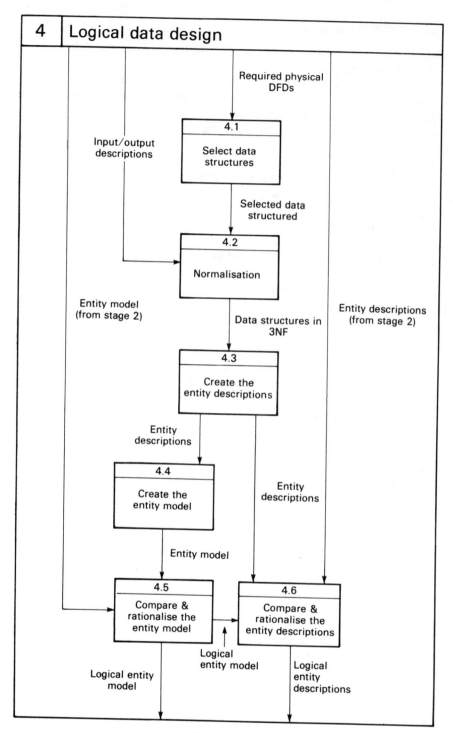

4	Logical data design

Required physical DFDs

4.1

Select data structures

Selected data structured

Input/output descriptions

4.2

Normalisation

Entity model (from stage 2)

Entity descriptions (from stage 2)

Data structures in 3NF

4.3

Create the entity descriptions

Entity descriptions

4.4

Create the entity model

Entity descriptions

Entity model

4.5

Compare & rationalise the entity model

4.6

Compare & rationalise the entity descriptions

Logical entity model

Logical entity model

Logical entity descriptions

Figure 3.8

Input   The entity descriptions obtained during stage 4, task 4.3.
Output   An entity model.
Technique   The application of a set of prescriptive rules.
Description   Each entity description forms an entity in the entity model. A set of rules based on the key or keys within the entity description is then used to build entity relationships and thus complete the entity model.

Stage 4, Task 4.5: Compare and rationalise the entity models
Objective   To produce the final entity model, the logical entity model, one of the major outputs from stage 4.
Input   The entity model from stage 2; the entity model from stage 4.
Output   The logical entity model.
Technique   Inspection.
Description   A series of steps is used in this task to bring together the two entity models. During stage 2, the entity model was created by top down analysis and during stage 4 it was created bottom up from raw data. This task compares the two, rationalises the difference, often by reference to the user's requirements, to produce the logical entity model.

Stage 4, Task 4.6: Compare and rationalise the entity descriptions
Objective   To produce the final set of entity descriptions, the logical entity descriptions, the second major output from stage 4.
Input   The entity descriptions from stage 2; the entity descriptions from stage 4; the logical entity model.
Output   A set of logical entity descriptions.
Technique   Inspection.
Description   The two sets of entity descriptions are compared, any differences are rationalised, and a logical entity description is produced for each entity on the logical entity model.

3.4.5 Stage 5: Logical process design, tasks

There are three tasks, shown in Figure 3.9.

Stage 5, Task 5.1: Review the stage 2 documentation
Objective To update the entity function matrix, the entity life histories, and the function descriptions as a result of the further development carried out during stages 3 and 4.
Input The entity function matrix; the entity life histories; the function descriptions.

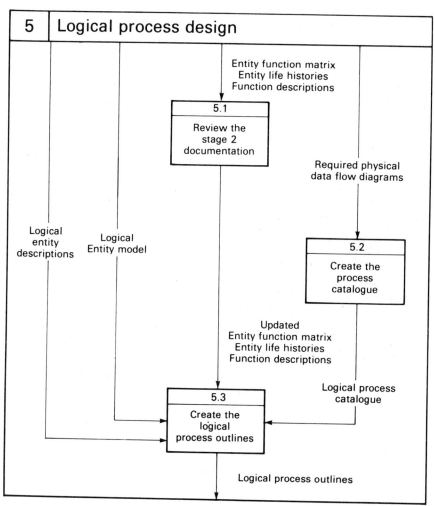

Figure 3.9

Output   An updated entity function matrix; an updated set of entity life histories; an updated set of function descriptions.

Technique   Inspection or walkthrough.

Description   New entities and relationships, and modifications to current ones, may well have resulted from the detailed data design tasks during stage 4. Other modifications to the stage 2 specification of requirements, for example, modifications to functions, may well have resulted from stage 3. The modifications need to be reflected in the entity function matrix, entity life histories and the function descriptions, before these documents can be used to develop the logical process outlines.

Stage 5, Task 5.2: Create the process catalogue

Objective   To group and catalogue the functions by type of processing, by processing frequency and by access requirements.

Input   The required physical data flow diagrams.

Output   The process catalogue.

Technique   Inspection and walkthrough.

Description   This task identifies individual processes in the required system by grouping one or more primitive functions into a single process. Each process will be catalogued under the headings: processing mode, on-line/batch; frequency of processing; access requirements; and will be for one mode, one frequency and one set of access requirements.

Stage 5, Task 5.3: Create the logical process outlines

Objective   To create for each identified process a detailed specification of the operations which satisfy the processing requirements.

Input   The updated entity function matrix; the updated entity life histories; the updated function descriptions; the logical entity model; the logical entity descriptions; the logical process catalogue.

Output   A set of logical process outlines.

Technique   Process outlines.

Description   This task expands the set of function descriptions, which comprise each process, into a detailed, operation-by-operation, description of the process.

The entities affected by the functions within the process are identified from the entity function matrix; the effect on each entity from the entity life history; and the processing required from the function descriptions.

Stages 4 and 5 review

Objective   To 'sign off' the logical design specification.

Input   The logical entity model; the logical entity descriptions; the logical process outlines.

Output   An agreement.

Technique   Walkthrough.

Description   This task ensures the logical process outlines can be satisfied by the data design. Each logical process outline should be 'dry run' against the data design to ensure the data design will fully support the processing required.

3.4.6 Stage 6: Physical design tasks

There are seven tasks, shown in Figure 3.10.

Stage 6, Task 6.1: Create the physical files/database specification
Objective To transform the logical data design into a physical data specification.
Input The logical entity model; the logical entity descriptions; the logical process outline.
   The technique used and the output produced depend upon the target hardware and software. For example, if the target software is a network database, then an appropriate technique might be Bachmann diagrams and the expected output a schema definition.

Stage 6, Task 6.2: Specify the access paths
Objective To document for each process outline the access mechanism for each entity referenced within the process outline.
Input The logical process outlines; the physical file or database specification.
Output A set of entity access paths.
   The technique is dependent upon the hardware and software support available for the physical files or database. The use of the data manipulation language verbs supported by the software is an appropriate method of specifying entity access paths.

Stage 6, Task 6.3: Create the program specifications
Objective To combine the logical process outlines with the access methods to create the program specifications.
Input The logical process outlines; the access paths.
Output A set of program specifications.
   The technique is dependent on the target hardware, software and installation standards. The output must be acceptable to the installation team. It may be a complete rewrite of the logical process outline and access paths, together with physical screen, report, menu and dialogue designs, or simply the addition of the designs to the process outlines and access path documents.

Stage 6, Task 6.4: Design tuning
Objective To ensure the file or database design and the program designs meet the design constraints set during stage 3.
Input The file or database specification; the program specifications.
Output A revised file or database specification; a revised set of program specifications.
Technique Walkthrough.

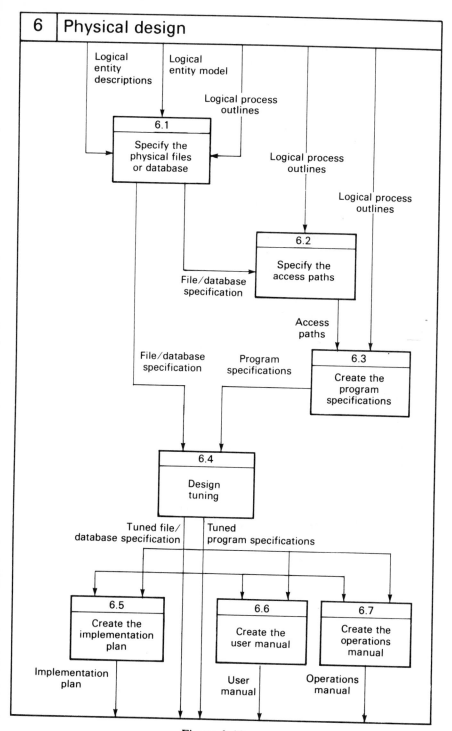

6	Physical design

Logical entity descriptions

Logical entity model

Logical process outlines

6.1
Specify the physical files or database

Logical process outlines

Logical process outlines

6.2
Specify the access paths

File/database specification

Access paths

File/database specification

Program specifications

6.3
Create the program specifications

6.4
Design tuning

Tuned file/ database specification

Tuned program specifications

6.5
Create the implementation plan

6.6
Create the user manual

6.7
Create the operations manual

Implementation plan

User manual

Operations manual

Figure 3.10

Description Design tuning involves the estimation of the system's resource usage and performance, the comparison of those estimates against the objectives and the subsequent review of the design and/or the objectives.

Stage 6, Task 6.5: Create the implementation plan

Objective To create a plan for the final part of the systems development cycle, the implementation.

Input The system specification.

Output An implementation plan.

The technique and therefore the specific outputs are installation dependent. For example, the development team, by discussion with the implementation team, could hand over to them a bar chart showing activities and timescales for the completion of the project.

Stage 6, Task 6.6: Create the user manual

Objective To complete the major part of the user manual.

Input All of the system documentation.

Output A part-completed user manual.

Technique Data flow diagrams; narrative.

Description This task uses the system documentation together with the experience of the development team and the user to complete the major part of the user manual. The manual will be completed and agreed with the user by the implementation team.

Stage 6, Task 6.7: Create the operations manual

Objective To complete the major part of the operations manual.

Input All of the system documentation.

Output A part-completed operations manual.

Technique Data flow diagrams; narrative.

Description This task uses the system documentation, together with the experience of the development team, the user, and the operations department, to part complete the operations manual. The manual will be completed and agreed with the user and the operations department by the implementation team.

3.5   SSADM project control

SSADM is not a project control system; it does, however, provide a structure by which projects may be planned and monitored.

Strategic plans may be created using the system development cycle and the stages within SSADM. Tactical plans may be created using the stage tasks. Since each stage and task has a specific objective or set of objectives, with given deliverable items from the stage or task, then monitoring completion is made easier. A stage or task is complete when the documented output has been produced and agreed. Similarly, each stage or task may commence only when required inputs are available.

SSADM comprises six stages and thirty-two tasks. The techniques used by SSADM are only necessary to provide an efficient mechanism for completing tasks. SSADM is therefore a development methodology, not a collection of techniques.

3.5.1 SSADM for small systems

It is feasible to use a cut-down version of SSADM for small systems. With small systems, the effort required to carry out all of the stages and tasks may not be justified. The cost of analysis and design may make the total system not feasible.

Figure 3.11 shows a cut-down methodology.

The tasks chosen from stage 1 are tasks 1.1, Investigation, and 1.6, Create the requirements list. The formal modelling of the current system is omitted. The input to tasks 2.1 and 2.2 of stage 2, the creation of the required logical models, is therefore restricted to the requirements list. These tasks now rely much more on the analyst's ability to model the requirements directly, which is feasible with a smaller number of functions and entities. A review of the requirements should now be undertaken with the user before more detailed work commences.

The number of system options with small systems is likely to be very low. Indeed, in many systems, for example those based on micro-computers, the number of system options may be one only. To economise on further detailed specification effort, tasks 3.1 and 3.2 from stage 3 are carried out at this point. The detailed documentation of inputs and outputs can then be undertaken for computer inputs and outputs only.

The early cross-referencing of data flow diagrams and entity models was omitted. Tasks 4.2 to 4.6 from stage 4 are merged into two tasks to provide a cross-reference and proving stage.

The input and output descriptions are converted to third normal form entity descriptions. The entity descriptions are compared with the required entity model to produce the logical entity model and the logical entity descriptions.

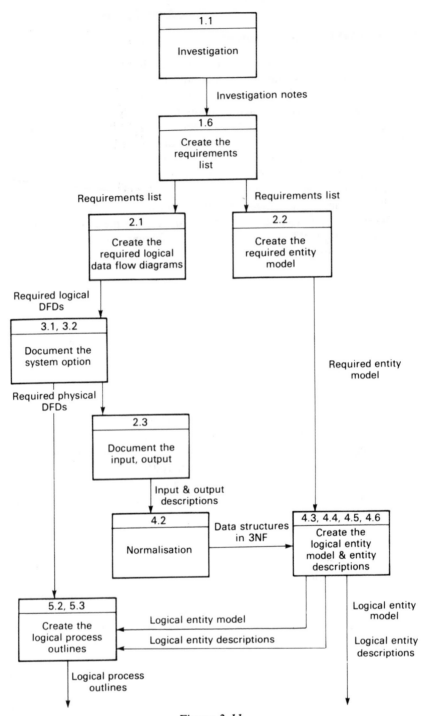

Figure 3.11

Finally tasks 5.2 and 5.3 from stage 5 are used to create the logical process outlines. Note that the logical process outlines are created without the input of function descriptions or entity life histories. Again this task is feasible for small systems.

The outputs from the logical stages of SSADM are identical to the full version. Stage 6 should now progress as in the full version.

Note that the cut-down version of SSADM works equally well for totally new systems and replacement of existing ones.

3.6 SSADM for new developments

The development of a new system for a totally new environment is very rare. Few new systems are developed for newly created organisations or departments. Most systems replace an existing or current system.

If no current system exists, then some of the tasks during stage 1 cannot be carried out. Stage 1 would be cut down to tasks 1.1 and 1.6 only, an investigation and documentation of the requirements.

The stage 2 tasks which create the required logical models must now take as their only input the requirements list. After this point, the stages and tasks can progress as in the full version of SSADM.

3.6.1 The systems development cycle phases, SSADM stages, sections, tasks and sub-tasks

The systems development cycle comprises seven phases. Phases four and five, analysis and design, are the subject of this book. SSADM comprises six stages, each stage comprises a number of tasks and sub-tasks. Stages 1 and 2 of SSADM contain many tasks. For ease of understanding, they are grouped into sections.

The hierarchy is:

Phases
  Stages
    Sections
      Tasks
        Sub-tasks

Figure 3.12 shows all of the phases, stages, sections, tasks and sub-tasks and forms a reference for the remainder of the book.

SSADM

Systems development cycle phase	Stage	Section	Task	Sub-task
1 Terms of reference & business objective	—			
2 Feasibility study	—			
3 Investigation	—			
4 Analysis	1 Analysis	1 Creation of the current physical model	1.1 Investigate the current system	—
			1.2 Create the current physical data flow diagrams	1.2.1 Document flow diagrams
				1.2.2 Data flow diagrams
				1.2.3 Validation of the diagrams
			1.3 Create the current entity model	—
		2 Creation of the current logical model	1.4 Create the data store entity cross references	—
			1.5 Create the current logical data flow diagrams	—
		3 Creation of the problems & requirements list	1.6 Create the problems & requirement list	—
	2 Specification of requirements	1 Creation of the required logical model	2.1 Create the required logical data flow diagrams	—
			2.2 Create the required entity model	—
		2 Detailed documentation of the required logical model	2.3 Document the entity descriptions	—
			2.4 Document the system input, system output & data flow descriptions	—
			2.5 Document the function descriptions	—
			2.6 Create the entity function matrix	—
			2.7 Create the entity life histories	—
		3 Validation of the model		—
	3 Selection of system option (for further development)	—	3.1 Postulate system options	—
			3.2 Select the required option	—
			3.3 Set the design constraints	—

5 Design	4 Logical data design	4.1 Select data structures	
		4.2 Normalisation	4.2.1 First normal form (1NF)
			4.2.2. Second normal form (2NF)
			4.2.3. Third normal form (3NF)
			4.2.4 Validation of the 3NF data structures
		4.3 Create the entity descriptions	—
		4.4 Create the entity model	—
		4.5 Create the logical entity model	—
		4.6 Create the logical entity descriptions	—
	5 Logical process design	5.1 Review the stage two documentation	—
		5.2 Create the process catalogue	—
		5.3 Create the logical process outlines	—
	6 Physical design	6.1 Specify the physical files or database	—
		6.2 Specify the access paths	—
		6.3 Specify the programs	—
		6.4 Design tuning	—
		6.5 Create the implementation plan	—
		6.6 Create the user manual	—
		6.7 Create the operations manual	—
6 Implementation			
7 Operation			

Figure 3.12

Part 2

Part 2

4

Analysis

4.1 Introduction

This chapter describes the first stage in SSADM, analysis, shown in Figure 4.1. The stage commences with an investigation of the current system and concludes by producing three documents: the current logical data flow diagrams, the user's view of the system; an entity model, a system view; and a combined list of problems with the existing system and requirements for the new system.

The tasks within stage 1 must be considered as an iterative set of tasks. It is not possible to fully investigate the current system to an extent where no questions will be raised during the creation of the data flow diagrams and the entity model. The creation of the diagrams organises the investigation notes into meaningful models. The execution of these tasks will reveal missing facts and alternative interpretations which can generally only be solved by further investigation.

Task 1.2, creation of the current physical data flow diagrams, and task 1.3, creation of the entity model, are the tasks which organise the investigation notes into meaningful models. Many analysts experienced with data flow diagrams and entity models use the modelling techniques as their format for investigation notes.

Tasks 1.4 and 1.5 convert the current physical data flow diagrams into the current logical data flow diagrams. The objective is to remove from the data flow diagrams any reference as to how the current system operates. The move is to the logic of the system, what is carried out, not how it is carried out. Task 1.4 creates a set of cross-reference diagrams between the physical and the logical to assist the conversion task.

The final task within stage 1, task 1.6, produces a combined list of problems with the current system and requirements for the new system. This list will be used in stage 2, along with the models of the existing system, to create a specification of requirements. This specification should solve the problems and include the stated requirements for the new system.

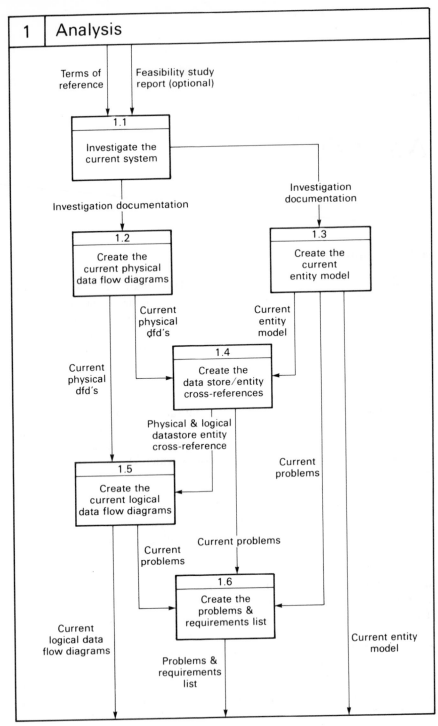

Figure 4.1

Stage 1 of SSADM may therefore be considered as three distinct sections:

Section 1: Creation of the current physical model
Section 2: Creation of the current logical model
Section 3: Creation of the problems and requirements list

4.2   Section 1: Creation of the current physical model

4.2.1   Task 1.1: Investigate the current system

The investigation of the current system should include functional analysis, data analysis, problem analysis and requirements for the new system. The objective is to provide sufficient data to be able to construct a set of data flow diagrams, an entity model, and a problems and requirements list.

Investigation techniques, such as questionnaires and interviewing, are skills all systems analysts should possess. These are the techniques required to undertake task 1.1; they are basic techniques required when using any systems analysis and design methodology. The objective of this text is to describe a specific analysis and design methodology assuming the analysts and designers possess the basic skills. Investigation techniques are not, therefore, described in detail.

Task 1.1 should provide detailed notes for task 1.2, create the current physical data flow diagrams, and task 1.3, create the current entity model.

No investigation can ever be 100 per cent complete. Ambiguity as well as missing facts will be revealed during the modelling of the system. Problems can only be sorted out by further discussion and further investigation. For this reason, tasks 1.1, 1.2 and 1.3 should be considered to be an iterative loop rather than a fixed sequence of tasks.

Functional analysis
Functional analysis leads to documentation of how the current system operates. The documentation comprises information on the documents within the system, the documents received into the system and produced by the system, the source and destination of documents, the storage of documents and the transformation which take place on documents.

The movement of documents represents data flow, the storage of documents is represented by data stores and transformation on documents by functions. Functional analysis therefore produces a set of data flows, sources of data flow, destinations of data flow, data stores and functions. Investigation, analysis and documentation is carried out top down, high-level functions being identified first with lower levels being introduced by successive function decomposition. Functional analysis provides a good understanding of the system and leads directly into task 1.2, creation of the current physical data flow diagrams.

Data analysis
The objective of data analysis is to identify the logical data within the system. Investigation of the data within the system should be carried out independently of functional analysis. Again the investigation, analysis and documentation should be carried out top down with relevant data groups being identified before the content of a data group is considered. Data analysis leads directly into task 1.3, creation of the entity model, where data analysis is discussed in detail.

Problem analysis and requirements
Interviewing is perhaps the most used and most effective way of identifying problems with the current system and requirements for the new one. Many of the problems and requirements will be identified during the investigations for functional analysis and data analysis. These should be carefully noted for documentation later, task 1.6. Additionally, a section of each interview should be reserved for discussion of problems and requirements. Again these discussions should be carefully noted for later formal documentation.

4.2.2   Task 1.2: Create the current physical data flow diagrams

This task is the first one in SSADM to use data flow diagrams. Before describing current physical data flow diagrams, data flow diagrams (DFDs) will be described.

Data flow diagrams
Figure 4.2 shows an example of a data flow diagram (DFD) for a hospital X-ray department, produced from the following investigation notes.

X-ray management investigation notes
Reception: Patients present to reception X-ray request forms which were obtained from their GP. Each X-ray request form is allocated an appointment which is written on to an appointment card and given to the patient. X-ray request forms are filed. A diary is maintained which contains details of all the appointments. When patients arrive for X-ray, they present their appointment card. A nurse checks the validity of the appointment, passes the appointment card to a clerk and takes care of the patient. The clerk generates an X-ray film/report request for the filing section. The X-ray request form is retrieved from the file and given to a radiographer. X-ray film/report requests are placed in a temporary file for collection by the filing section.
Radiographer: On receipt of the X-ray request form, the radiographer takes the appropriate photographs (called films) and places them in a temporary file for collection by the filing section. Each appointment results in a set of X-ray films.

DATA FLOW DIAGRAM

SYSTEM: X-RAY MANAGEMENT	DATE:
AUTHOR: G. CUTTS	PAGE: 1 of 3

LEVEL: 1	CURRENT/R̶E̶Q̶.	PHYS./L̶O̶G̶I̶C̶A̶L̶

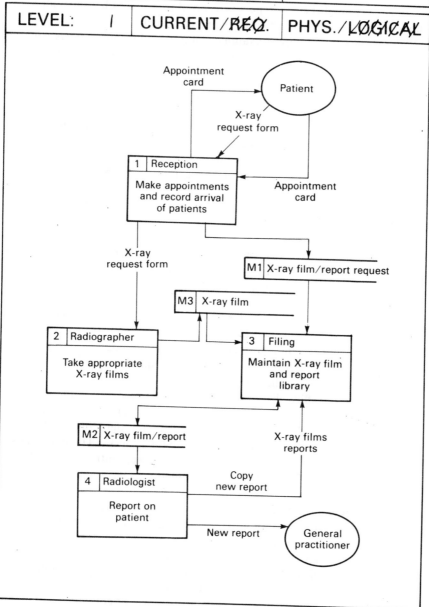

Figure 4.2

Filing clerk: The filing clerks collect the X-ray film/report requests. These request all X-ray films and reports previously generated for the patients. Patients can have many X-ray films and reports. The new X-ray films are attached and the complete set placed in a temporary file for the attention of the radiologist who makes out a report for the appointment.

When a copy of the new report is received from the radiologist, all X-ray films and reports are returned to their permanent file.

Radiologist: The radiologist examines all X-ray films and reports which a patient has and makes out a new report. The report is sent to the GP with a copy to the filing section.

The DFD shows the functions within the system, make appointments and records arrival of patients, take appropriate X-ray films, maintain X-ray film and report library, and report on patients. These functions are carried out currently by reception, radiographers, filing clerks and radiologists respectively. Further, since the total X-ray department function has been decomposed into four functions, then they have been simply numbered one through four.

Functions are the dominant feature of data flow diagrams and are represented by a rectangle.

The diagram also shows the sources and destinations for information. These are shown by ellipses, patient and GP. The patient makes an X-ray request, receives an appointment card and returns to the X-ray department with that appointment card. The GP receives a report on the patient. The boundary of the system to be further investigated is also implicitly shown by the diagram. Functions are inside the system and sources and destinations for information outside. The information passing between patient and GP is outside the system and does not cross the boundary; the system can therefore have no effect on this relationship. Data flow diagrams are used in this text to illustrate the stages and tasks of SSADM.

Arrows on data flow diagrams illustrate flows of data. In the example, the flows of data represent documents and X-ray films. For example, an X-ray request form flows from reception to the radiographers and a copy new report flows from the radiologists to the filing clerks. These data flows are internal flows as opposed to the data flows appointment card, X-ray request forms and new report which form the input and output of the system.

Finally, the data flow diagram shows open-ended rectangles to indicate stores of data. The description data store is carefully chosen since data is stored in many forms including files. For example, the data stores in the X-ray department could be an in-tray of requests for the filing clerk to retrieve previous X-rays and reports from a filing cabinet and a simple pile of previous X-rays and reports together with the new X-ray films for reference by the radiologist. Further data stores will be contained within the functions.

Data flow diagrams provide a user's view of the system showing:

- functions by rectangles
- the sources of data by ellipses
- the destinations of data by ellipses
- data flows by arrows
- data stores by open-ended rectangles

Templates and sophisticated software packages are available for the construction of data flow diagrams.

Levels of decomposition

The X-ray department shown in Figure 4.2 has been decomposed into four functions. There are no rules governing the number of functions that should be shown on a single DFD other than that of understandability. This means that any more than, say, ten functions on a single diagram may lead to confusion. The basic concept of the DFD is that it represents the user's view and must therefore be totally understandable by the user.

Further decomposition and thus a greater level of detail and understanding is obtained by zooming in and decomposing any or all of the function rectangles. Figure 4.3 shows a further decomposition of the 'make appointments and record arrival of patients' function. Note that the input and output exactly correspond with the data flows corresponding to function 1, Figure 4.2.

Note also that since the functions make appointment, check appointment and patient care, and retrieve X-ray request form and write out X-ray film/report request are all sub-functions of function 1; they are numbered 1.1, 1.2 and 1.3 respectively. It is also possible to conclude that the receptionists, nurses and clerks are all part of the staff of reception. Two new stores of data also emerge as being within reception, a diary and a file of X-ray request forms.

Figure 4.2 is labelled the level 1 DFD, which may be decomposed into up to four level 2 DFDs which may be further decomposed to levels 3 and 4. Rarely are more than four levels of decomposition necessary even for the largest most complex systems.

Decomposition should cease when the function can be described accurately, precisely and unambiguously. This may well mean that some functions have more levels of decomposition than others. Each function at its lowest level, its primitive level, should process only a single transaction type. For example, the transaction types for a sales accounting system might be: issue an invoice, issue a credit note and receive a payment. A primitive function should exist for each type of transaction.

Figure 4.4 shows the level 2 DFD for the level 1 function, maintain X-ray film and report library.

DATA FLOW DIAGRAM

SYSTEM: X-RAY MANAGEMENT	DATE:
AUTHOR: G. CUTTS	PAGE: 2 of 3

LEVEL: 2	CURRENT/~~REQ~~. PHYS./~~LOGICAL~~

TITLE: RECEPTION

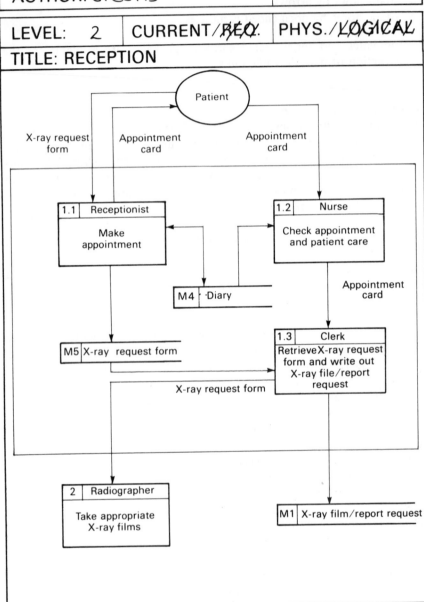

Figure 4.3

DATA FLOW DIAGRAM

SYSTEM: X-RAY MANAGEMENT

DATE:

AUTHOR: G. CUTTS

LEVEL: 2 | CURRENT/~~REQ.~~ PHYS./~~LOGICAL~~

TITLE: FILING

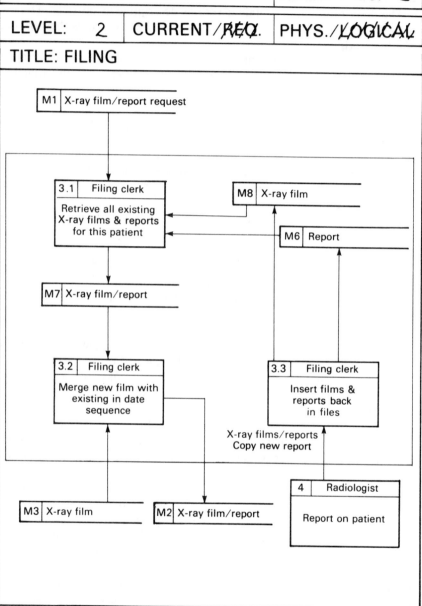

Figure 4.4

Diagram conventions

Functions are represented by rectangles containing a short but meaningful description. The function is given an identification number, a single number at level 1 with compound numbers at subsequent levels, and are annotated with the responsible authority for completing the function.

The description must contain a verb as descriptive as possible. The use of verbs such as 'update' and 'process' should be avoided as they are not highly descriptive.

The responsibility box will commence as the person or department responsible and may conclude as a program reference. If the function remains external to the computer system, the new person or department responsible may be inserted into the responsibility box.

The ellipse is used to show the source or destination of a data flow. Each ellipse should be carefully named. To avoid over-complication, the ellipse may be repeated on a DFD. To show that there exists more than one ellipse representing an external source or destination, a line is introduced into the top left-hand corner of the ellipse. This line is then present in every occurrence of the ellipse.

Data flows are shown by arrows suitably annotated. The arrow may be double-headed to show, for example, the reading and subsequent modification of a data store. Occasionally the movement of goods represents a data flow. It is, however, more frequent that goods movement does not represent a flow of data and therefore they should not be shown on a DFD. In Figure 4.5, returned goods represent a data flow made up of product number and quantity of goods returned. This data is processed within the system. The movement of goods is represented by a broad arrow.

The final diagram structure is the open-ended rectangle to represent a data store. The name data store is carefully selected to represent not only files but also wall charts, lists, private reference books etc., any store of data within the system. Data stores are named, e.g. invoices, given an identification number and a type. Types are typically M for manual data store and C for computer file. Finally, the double bar at the closed end of the rectangle indicates that this data store is repeated elsewhere on the DFD.

Data flows into or out of data stores need not be named as part of this task.

Figure 4.5 shows a function 'type invoice form' which is a decomposed function from function 2. It is the responsibility of a typist. Figure 4.5 further shows a customer source or destination and an occurrence of the accounts department as a source or destination. Data flows shown are credit note and a two-way flow regarding appointments. Also the flow of returned goods represents the data flow product number and quantity. Finally, Figure 4.5 shows an occurrence of the manual data store, invoices, identification number seven. It is only one of the occurrences on the diagram since the open-ended rectangle possesses a double line at its closed end.

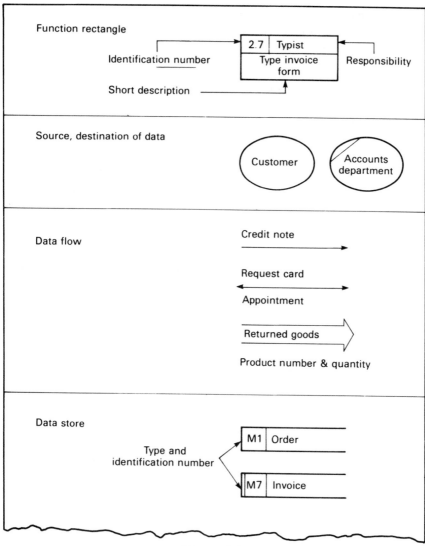

Figure 4.5

Developing the current physical data flow diagram

The first use of DFDs occurs in stage 1, task 1.2, create the current physical data flow diagrams. The diagrams are current in that they reflect the system as it exists, the current system, and they are physical in that they reflect how the system operates. The current physical DFDs model functions which, at level 1, might be the departments or sections; sources, providers of data to the system; and destinations, users of data from the system. Document flows and data stores, representing current files, lists, wall charts, reference books etc., are also modelled on the current physical DFDs.

Three sub-tasks comprise task 1.2:

1.2.1   Development of a document flow diagram.
1.2.2   Conversion of the document flow diagram to the current physical level 1 data flow diagrams and decomposition to subsequent levels.
1.2.3   Validation of the diagrams.

Sub-task 1.2.1: Document flow diagrams
This sub-task identifies the source and destination of data and its flow between them. The only diagram structures required are the ellipse and the arrow.

Data flows represented by arrows are real document or goods flows. Sources and destinations of data may be external to the organisation, e.g. supplier, customer; departments within the organisation, e.g. accounts department, senior management or existing computer systems such as sales ledger.

The interview notes should be read and a list of sources and destinations created with a second list of documents. The document flow diagram can now be drawn. Figure 4.6 shows a simple document flow for the sources, destinations and document flows listed below.

Sources and destinations	Customer
	Despatch
	Warehouse
	Sales
	Accounts
	Supplier
	Computer sales ledger
Documents	Delivery note and copy
	Despatch instruction set
	Order
	Internal order form
	Order acknowledgement
	Weekly credit limit list
	Re-order card
	Goods received note
	Purchase order form
	Purchase ledger transactions
	Invoices, payments and credit notes list
	Invoice and credit note
	Financial statement
	Sales statement

DOCUMENT FLOW

SYSTEM: *EXAMPLE*	DATE:
AUTHOR: *G CUTTS*	PAGE: 1 of 1

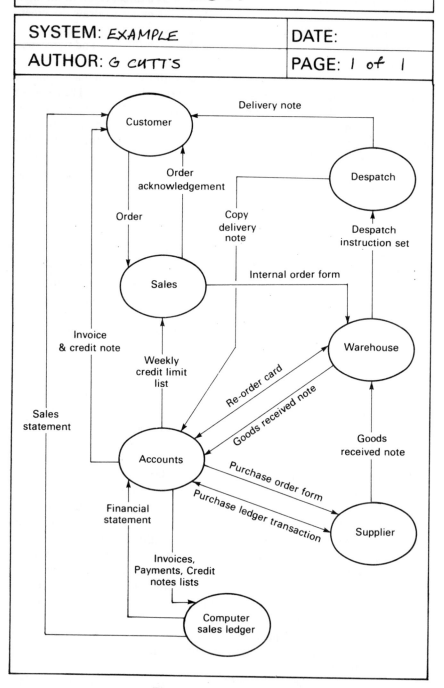

Figure 4.6 Document flow

The diagram can be built in real-time, that is as a direct result of an interview. Many experienced systems analysts find it easier to draw document flow diagrams rather than take interview notes.

The document flow diagram should be shown to the user and agreement on its accuracy obtained.

The final step in sub-task 1.2.1 is to agree with the user management the boundary of the system. Figure 4.7 shows a system boundary. The required system to be further investigated and analysed comprises functions for sales, despatch and the warehouse with sources or destination of data, customer, accounts and supplier. The data flows from accounts to supplier and accounts to computer sales ledger are completely outside the system; they do not cross the system boundary nor are they within the boundary. The new system, therefore, can have zero effect on these data flows. Several boundaries may be discussed before agreement is reached.

Sub-task 1.2.2: Data flow diagrams

The level 1 current physical data flow diagram (Figure 4.8) is now easily constructed by redrawing the document flow shown in Figure 4.7, replacing sales, despatch and warehouse by function rectangles and by omitting all sources, destinations and data flows not affecting the system.

Level 2 current physical data flow diagrams can then be drawn for each of the level 1 functions. A simple example is shown in Figures 4.9 and 4.10: the decomposition of 3, stock control; and 3.3, monitor stock levels.

Decomposition

Before decomposition of the level 1 current physical data flow diagram is commenced, the diagram must be agreed with the user. A structured walkthrough is the best approach. The user can become totally involved with DFDs and often give a high level of commitment to the accuracy of the diagrams.

Two potential problems arise at the point of decomposition. They are the identification of sub-functions and the incorporation of data stores.

The investigation notes identified the level 1 functions as data sources or destinations. These level 1 functions may represent departments within an organisation such as accounts. The sections within the department may form the level 2 functions. These sections may be identifiable from the existing investigation notes or it may be necessary to return to task 1.1, investigation to obtain more information about the sections within the department. The first investigation would have regarded the department's inputs and outputs of major importance to the production of the document flow diagram. Since the department is inside the boundary, a further investigation may be necessary to determine the internal data flows, data stores and level 2 functions.

The boundary of the level 2 DFD is easily obtained; it is the function

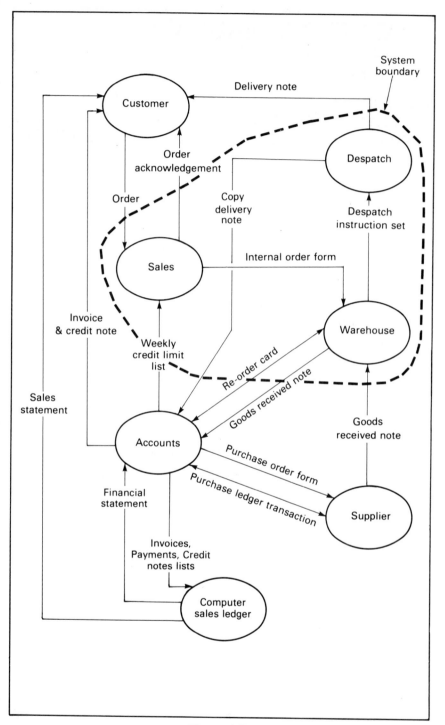

Figure 4.7

DATA FLOW DIAGRAM

SYSTEM: *CHAPTER 4 EXAMPLE*	DATE:
AUTHOR: G. CUTTS	PAGE: 1 of 4

LEVEL: 1	CURRENT/~~REQ.~~	PHYS./~~LOGICAL~~

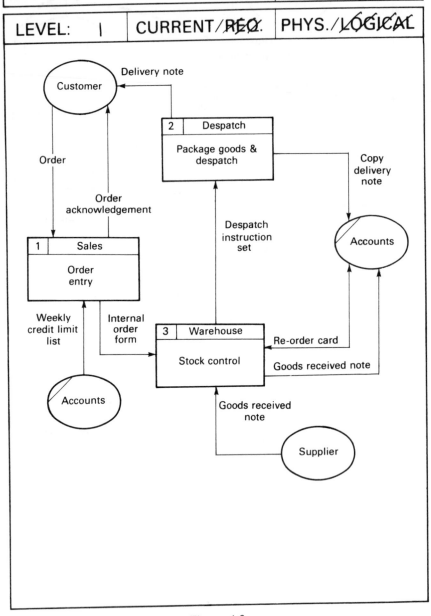

Figure 4.8

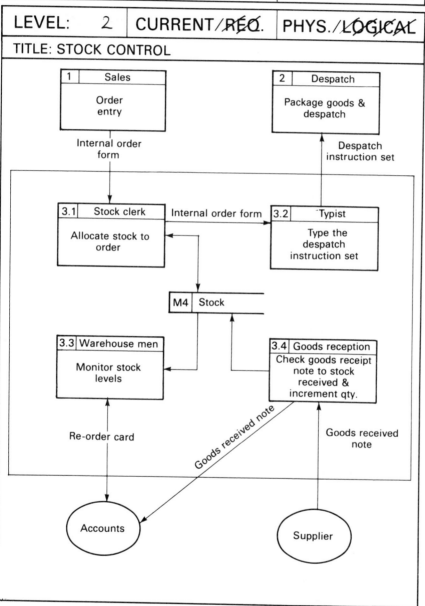

DATA FLOW DIAGRAM

SYSTEM: CHAPTER 4 EXAMPLE	DATE:
AUTHOR: G. CUTTS	PAGE: 2 of 4

LEVEL: 2	CURRENT/~~REQ.~~	PHYS./~~LOGICAL~~

TITLE: STOCK CONTROL

1	Sales
	Order entry

Internal order form

2	Despatch
	Package goods & despatch

Despatch instruction set

3.1	Stock clerk
	Allocate stock to order

Internal order form

3.2	Typist
	Type the despatch instruction set

M4	Stock

3.3	Warehouse men
	Monitor stock levels

3.4	Goods reception
	Check goods receipt note to stock received & increment qty.

Re-order card

Goods received note

Goods received note

Accounts

Supplier

Figure 4.9 Stock control

DATA FLOW DIAGRAM

SYSTEM: CHAPTER 4 EXAMPLE	DATE:
AUTHOR: G. CUTTS	PAGE: 3 of 4

LEVEL: 3	CURRENT/REQ.	PHYS./LOGICAL

TITLE: MONITOR STOCK LEVELS

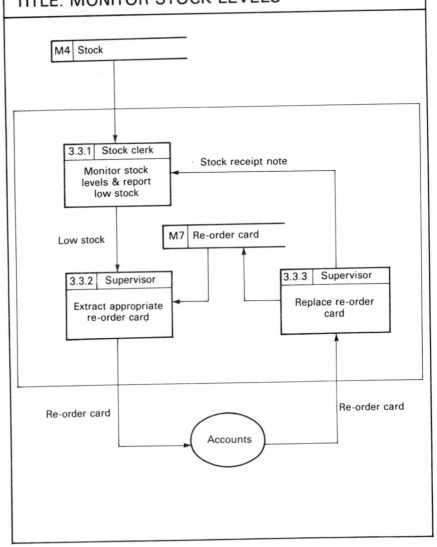

Figure 4.10 Monitor stock levels

rectangle on the level 1 diagram. Similarly, the input, output, sources and destinations are defined by the level 1 diagram, see Figure 4.8. Figure 4.11 shows the boundary of function 3, stock control.

Each input or output must connect to a function. The easier starting point for construction of the level 2 diagram is by identification of the functions which receive the inputs. The functions can be added to the diagram, Figure 4.11, to give Figure 4.12.

The functions which generate output should now be examined. Ask the question 'Does the process have access to all the data necessary to generate the output?' The answer most likely will be 'No'. The inputs to the generation process must be investigated. They will either originate from data stores or from further internal functions. In some instances, an internal function will connect inputs to outputs. The answer to the question 'Does the process have access to all the data necessary to generate the output?' may in these cases be 'Yes'. Manual functions such as 'Write out the internal order form' may connect the input 'Customer order' to the output 'internal order form'.

Data stores and functions can now be added until the diagram is complete. It is worth re-emphasising at this stage that the DFDs represent the current physical system. Data stores represent wall charts and private books of data as well as current files; functions have their responsibility annotated and data flows are very often document flows.

The problem of when to introduce a data store on to the diagram always needs careful handling. Below are three instances of current systems which might yield the diagrams shown in Figure 4.13.

(1) Documents are date stamped and checked before being left in the out tray for collection by order processing.
(2) Documents are date stamped and checked before being placed in the central store room for order processing to collect.
(3) Documents are date stamped and checked before being sent directly to order processing where they are stored prior to processing.

Each diagram is correct. The data store is always present and is introduced on to the diagrams at an appropriate point. Data stores which are completely internal to a function need not be shown at that level, which is the case in situations (1) and (3).

In situation (1), documents are stored within function 1.1 and a batch of documents flows to the sales department; whereas in situation (3), documents flow individually to be stored within function 1.2.

Data flows to or from data stores need not be named at this stage.

Sub-task 1.2.3: Validation of the diagrams
The first step in the validation of the diagrams is to check for inconsistencies.

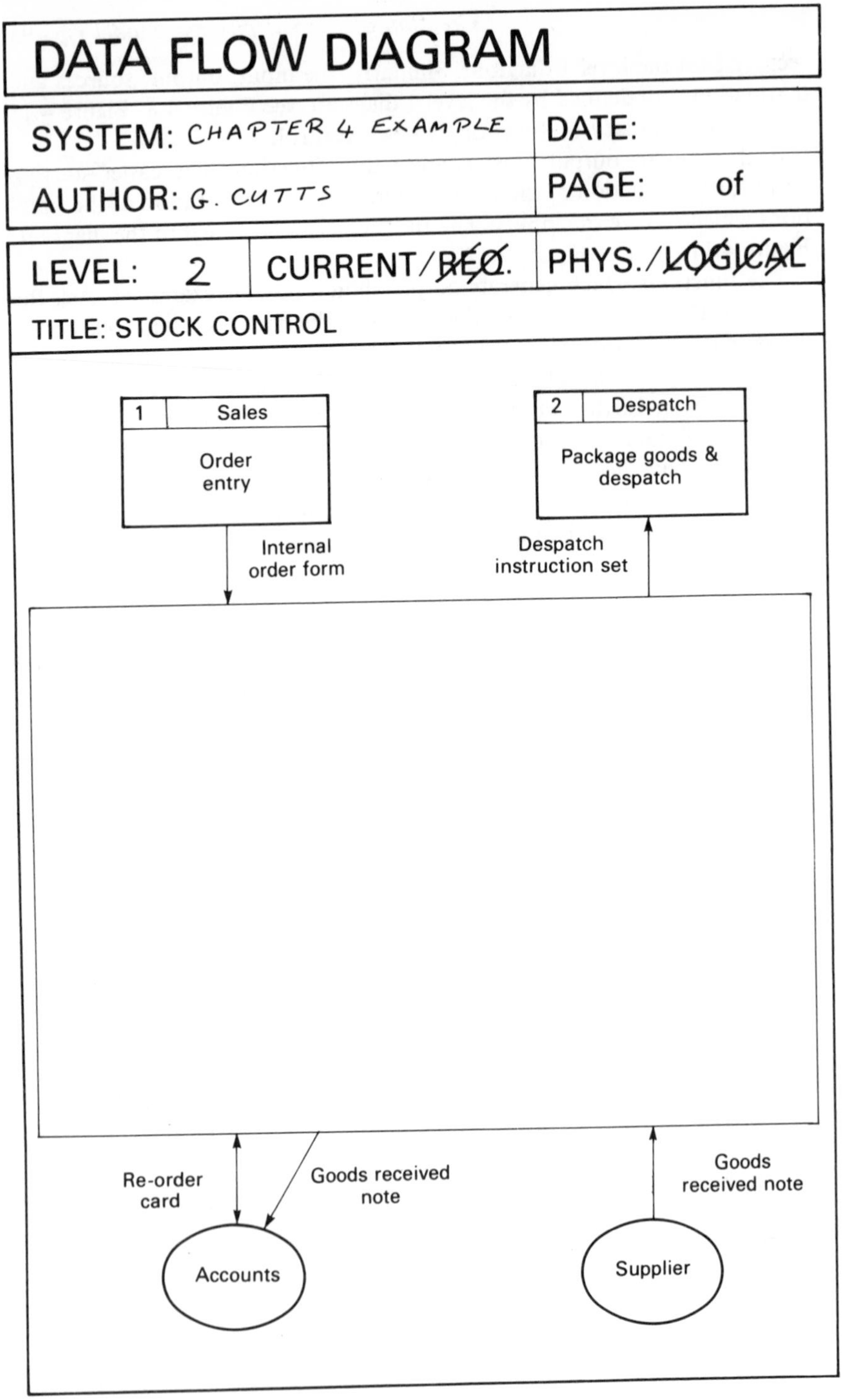

DATA FLOW DIAGRAM

SYSTEM: CHAPTER 4 EXAMPLE	DATE:
AUTHOR: G. CUTTS	PAGE: of

LEVEL: 2	CURRENT/~~REQ.~~	PHYS./~~LOGICAL~~

TITLE: STOCK CONTROL

1	Sales
	Order entry

2	Despatch
	Package goods & despatch

Internal order form

Despatch instruction set

Re-order card

Goods received note

Goods received note

Accounts

Supplier

Figure 4.11 Stock control—level 2

DATA FLOW DIAGRAM

SYSTEM: *CHAPTER 4 EXAMPLE*	DATE:
AUTHOR: *G . CUTTS*	PAGE: of

LEVEL: 2	CURRENT/~~REQ~~.	PHYS./~~LOGICAL~~

TITLE: STOCK CONTROL

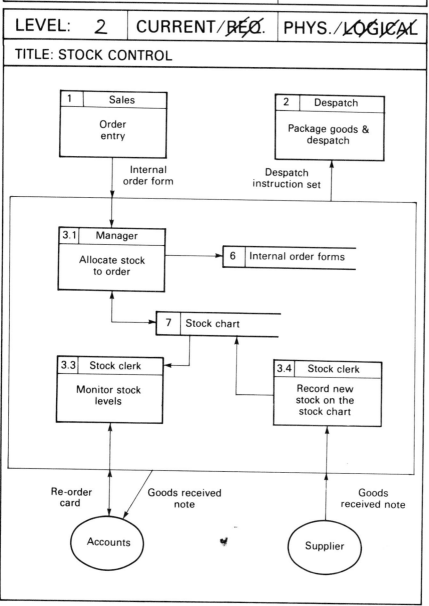

Figure 4.12 Stock control—level 2

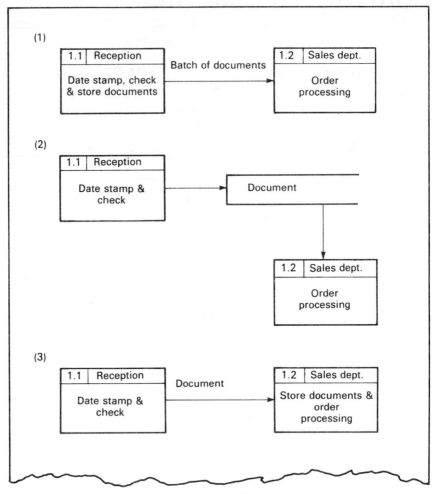

(1)

1.1	Reception
Date stamp, check & store documents	

Batch of documents →

1.2	Sales dept.
Order processing	

(2)

1.1	Reception
Date stamp & check	

→ | Document |

1.2	Sales dept.
Order processing	

(3)

1.1	Reception
Date stamp & check	

Document →

1.2	Sales dept.
Store documents & order processing	

Figure 4.13

Functions should not be total sources of data or destinations for data. Those which are total sources generate data without reference to other data, those which are total destinations perform no useful purpose. Generally, if such a situation exists, then further investigation is necessary to establish the exact processing performed.

Similarly, data stores should not be total providers of data nor total destinations for data. Data is stored by one function to be used by another. There are, however, exceptions. The data store 'archived pay advices' is necessary for legal purposes. Pay advices are required to be stored for a set period just in case a query may arise in later years. This query function may not be shown on the DFD since it is of extremely low volume and includes a wide variety of query processing. The data store 'archived pay advices' may therefore be a legitimate total destination.

There are also situations where a file, particularly a computer file, is maintained by one system and used solely as a reference file by another. The latter system would show the file as a total source. All situations where data stores are total sources or destinations should be investigated, reasons established for the situation or additional data flows created if necessary.

Finally, the validation process should examine data flows. All data flows should have a source, an external entity, a function or a data store, and a destination, again an external entity, a function or a data store. Inevitably, some data flows will not have a destination. These again require further investigation to determine their destination or, if none can be identified, their need to be generated in the first place. Similarly, some data flows will have no source: again this is a situation for further investigation and clarification.

The context diagram

Figures 4.7 and 4.8 effectively show the boundary of the system. If there is any problem in clearly understanding the boundary, a level zero current physical data flow diagram may be drawn. This diagram puts the complete system into context and is sometimes termed the context diagram. Figure 4.14 shows a level zero current physical data flow diagram for a system comprising the functions of sales, warehousing and despatch.

The system is represented as a single function making absolutely clear that everything outside the function is external to the system. The input and output data flows and their sources or destinations are equally clear. The context or level zero data flow diagram is therefore a useful representation of the system boundary, together with the system input and output.

The task of constructing the current physical data flow diagrams has so far followed a series of sub-tasks in sequence. There are, however, many instances during the task when iteration to task 1.1, investigation, is necessary. This may be to sort out a problem discovered during validation. Other reasons for re-opening the investigation arise from problems in agreeing the boundary and in identifying the functions and data stores during the decomposition.

Problems with boundary identification

The boundary shown in Figure 4.7 neatly encloses all of the functions undertaken by sales, the warehouse and despatch. If only part of the functions for the warehouse were required to be inside the boundary, then a diagram similar to Figure 4.15 would result.

The warehouse function needs to be decomposed to identify those sub-functions which fall inside the boundary and those which fall outside. The inside sub-functions and the outside sub-functions can be grouped to form

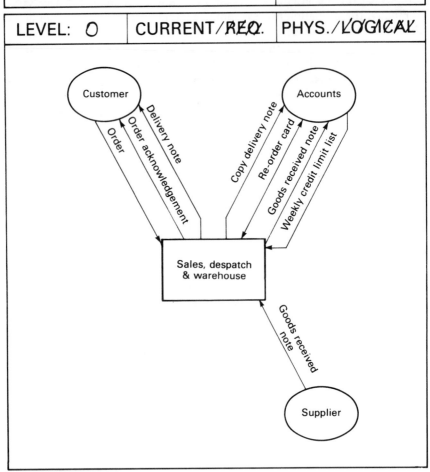

DATA FLOW DIAGRAM

SYSTEM: *CHAPTER 4 EXAMPLE*	DATE:
AUTHOR: *G. CUTTS*	PAGE: *I* of *I*

| LEVEL: *O* | CURRENT/~~REQ~~. | PHYS./~~LOGICAL~~ |

Figure 4.14

two functions representing the warehouse. In this case, Figure 4.16, the inside function, is concerned with goods out and the external function with goods in. The system boundary can now be drawn, and the construction of the current physical data flow diagrams can proceed.

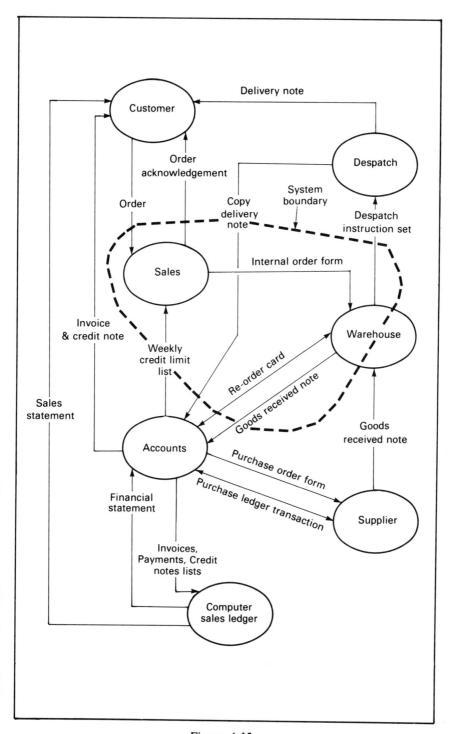

Figure 4.15

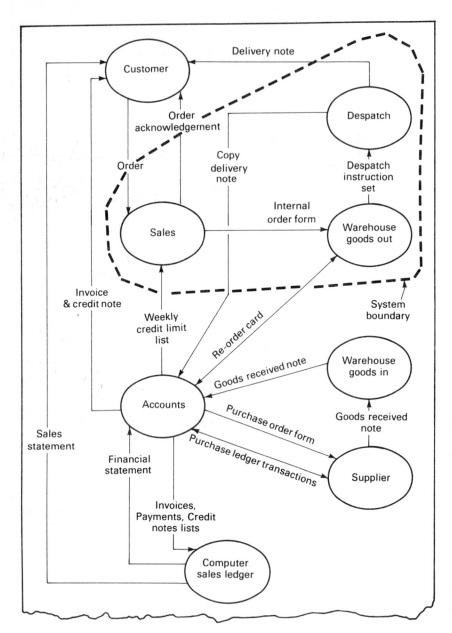

Figure 4.16

4.2.3 Task 1.3: Create the current entity model

This task is again a first in that it introduces entity models which will be used in stages 1, 2 and 4. Entity models result from data analysis, whereas the DFDs resulted from functional analysis. Data analysis provides a way of structuring data, removing inconsistencies and testing the use of data before detailed design.

Data analysis must be undertaken independently of functions or processing to enable data to be shared. The analyst must take a wide view of the data, a top down approach, producing a view of the data, and the relationships between data, inside the system. It is an internal view within the boundary of the system of the data and of data relationships, and represents the generic underlying structure of the data. This view, a system view, contrasts with the use of DFDs which produced a user's view.

Definitions

Each entity represents a data group of interest to the system. A sales and accounting system may have data grouped together relating to customers, orders and invoices. The entities would therefore be customer, order and invoice.

Each entity represents a data group. A group of data items, called attributes, are held in the system for each entity. Examples of attribute lists for each of the entities customer, order and invoice are given below:

Customer:
- Customer number
- Customer name
- Customer address
- Credit limit
- Delivery address
- Date of last order

Order:
- Customer number
- Product number
- Product description
- Quantity ordered

Invoice:
- Invoice number
- Invoice date
- Customer number
- Customer name
- Customer address
- Product number
- Product description
- Quantity delivered
- Price each
- Total value

Entities can be identified by extracting the nouns or noun phrases from the investigation notes. These nouns or noun phrases provide a list of candidate entities.

The X-ray management investigation notes might yield the following set of nouns as candidates for entities:

Patient	X-ray request
Diary	Appointment
Report	X-ray film/report request
X-ray film	

It is better at this stage to identify too many possible entities than too few. The entity model will be revised later during stage 4.

A matrix, Figure 4.17, can then be constructed. In fact, only half is required since the matrix will be used to indicate relationships between entities.

	Patient	Diary	X-ray request	Appointment	X-ray/report request	X-ray film	Report
Patient							
Diary							
X-ray request	Presents						
Appointment		Contains	Is allocated				
X-ray film/ report request				Generates			
X-ray film	Has			Results in			
Report	Has			Results in			

Figure 4.17

A second analysis of the investigation notes, this time for verbs, provides candidate relationships between the entities.

For example, 'patients present to reception X-ray request forms':

Entity	Patient
Relationship	Present
Entity	X-ray request

'patients can have many X-ray films and reports':

Entity	Patient	Patient
Relationship	Have	Have
Entity	X-ray film	Report

The relationships can be marked on to the matrix, Figure 4.17.

An alternative methodology or, indeed, a good method of double checking is to compare the entities in pairs. For each pair, ask the question, 'Does a relationship exist between this pair of entities?'

Relationship degree

The following entities and relationship have degree 1 : 1 (read 1 to 1):

Entity	Husband
Relationship	Has
Entity	Wife

A husband can only have one wife and a wife can only have one husband (well, to be legal in the UK). The relationship is 1 : 1.

Most relationships have degree 1 : M (read 1 to many):

Entity	Patient
Relationship	Has undergone
Entity	Operation

A patient can have many operations but an operation can have only one patient (transplants are regarded as two operations). The relationship is 1 : M.

Some relationships are M : N (read many to many) where M is not necessarily equal to N:

Entity	Ship
Relationship	Docks
Entity	Port

A ship docks at many ports and a port has many ships. The relationship is M : N where the number of ports per ship is usually different from the number of ships per port.

Diagram conventions (Figure 4.18)

Entities are represented by rectangles annotated with the entity name, which

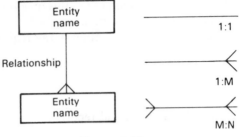

Figure 4.18

should be meaningful. The attribute which provides the key to the entity may provide a meaningful name.

Lines are used to represent relationships with the crow's foot representing the many part of the relationship. The one entity of the relationship is called the owner and the many entity is called the member. Owner entities therefore have many member entities. The crow's foot is sometimes replaced by an arrow head.

Figure 4.19 shows several entities and relationships. The entities are customer, order, order line and product. The three relationships are shown below:

Entity	Relationship	Degree	Entity
Customer	Places	1:M	Order
Order	Has	1:M	Order line
Product	Ordered on	1:M	Order line

A customer places many orders, each order has many order lines, each order line being for one product. An order therefore can be for one or more products. A product has many order lines from different orders; each order line is from one order and each order is from one customer.

Note that customer is the owner of the customer–order relationship and order is the member; order is the owner of the order–order line relationship and order line is the member; product is the owner of the product–order line relationship and order line is the member. The order entity is both a member and an owner and the order line entity is a member of two relationships.

An entity model represents the complete set of entities and relationships for a system. The version of the entity model created at this stage represents the current understanding at this early stage within the project.

Figure 4.20 shows the entity model for the X-ray system drawn directly from Figure 4.17.

Many : many relationships
The entity models drawn so far have only used 1:1 and 1:M relationships.

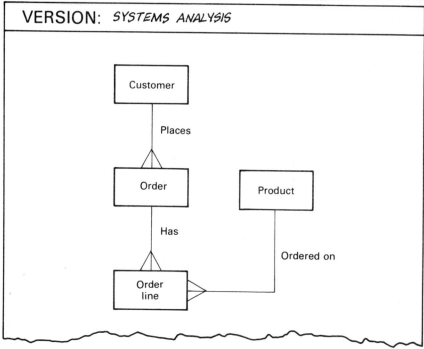

ENTITY MODEL

SYSTEM: ORDER PROCESSING	DATE:
AUTHOR: G. CUTTS	PAGE: 1 of 1

VERSION: SYSTEMS ANALYSIS

Figure 4.19

Many to many relationships are difficult to implement so they are generally eliminated on the entity model. Figure 4.21 shows a M : N relationship. A patient may consult many doctors and a doctor will certainly deal with many patients. A list of the attributes for patient and doctor shows some common attributes.

Patient: Patient number
Name
Address
Health history
List of appointments
   date
   time
   location

Doctor: Doctor identification
Name
Qualifications
Specialisms
List of appointments
   date
   time
   location

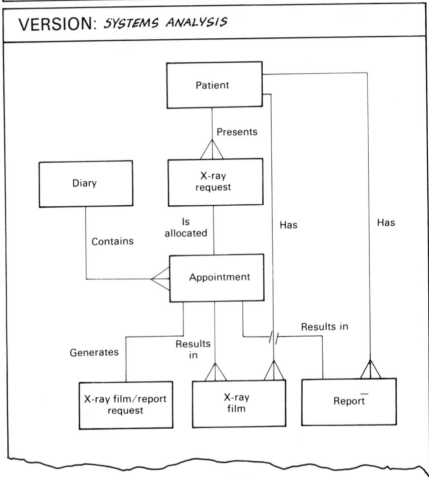

ENTITY MODEL

SYSTEM: X-RAY MANAGEMENT	DATE:
AUTHOR: G. CUTTS	PAGE: 1 of 1

VERSION: SYSTEMS ANALYSIS

Figure 4.20

The patient has a list of appointments, with several doctors; the doctor has a list of appointments, with several patients. A single appointment is common to one patient and one doctor. The relationship patient to appointment is 1:M, and the relationship doctor to appointment is 1:M; appointment is common to both entities. The M:N relationship (Figure 4.21) can

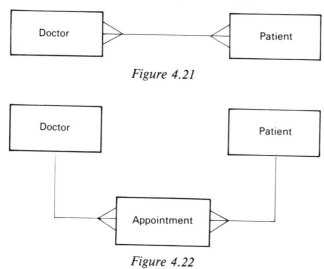

Figure 4.21

Figure 4.22

be replaced by two relationships and the creation of a third entity, appointment, representing the common data from the two original entities. The entity model which results is shown in Figure 4.22.

Note that order line in Figure 4.19 provides a link between order and product. An order is for many products and a product is for many orders.

One : one relationships
One to one relationships create some problems which need to be resolved. The first is which entity to make the owner and which the member. One way around the problem is to merge the entities into one. Consider two entities, enquiry and quotation. If one enquiry always results in one quotation, the relationship is 1:1 and one entity will suffice, enquiry and quotation, i.e. the entities may be merged.

A second solution is to examine the time dependencies. For example, consider an order line entity which will have one invoice line entity. However, the order line entity will exist in the system from order entry through stock allocation processing and delivery before the invoice line entity is inserted. In this case, the order line should be the owner.

In many instances, neither of the above will apply. In this case, the choice of owner is arbitrary.

Convoluted relationships
The entity model (Figure 4.23) shows a new type of relationship. The entity doctor appears on both ends of the relationship: doctor works with doctor. The relationship, works with, requires further investigation. It may mean doctor, works with, on an operation, doctor. The common data is the

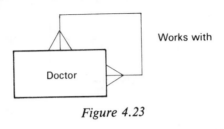

Figure 4.23

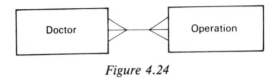

Figure 4.24

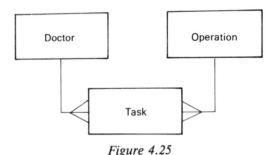

Figure 4.25

operation; the entity operation can therefore be inserted to link doctor to doctor (Figure 4.24). This results in a M:N relationship. The common data between doctor and operation is required for a link. A possible link is the tasks performed, such as surgeon, assistant, anaesthetist (Figure 4.25).

Optional relationships
The entity model (Figure 4.26) shows three entities: company, capital project and department. The relationships between company and project and company and department are clear. A company is organised into departments and undertakes capital projects. However, some projects are solely for a particular department; in this case there is a link between department and project. Projects are always undertaken for the company and optionally for a department.

The optional link is shown by the standard relationship arrow annotated with the letter O for optional. These optional relationships will be treated differently in stage 6, physical design.

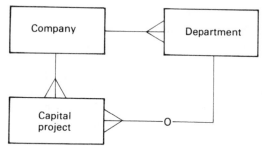

Figure 4.26

Multiple relationships
All of the entity models constructed so far have shown a maximum of one
relationship between an owner and a member. Figure 4.27 shows an entity
model where two relationships connect order and order line.

Relationship (a) represents orders with outstanding order lines, relationship (b) represents orders with despatched order lines. This is quite common
and basically divides the order lines into two groups, order lines waiting
despatch and order lines that have been despatched.

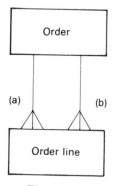

Figure 4.27

4.3   Section 2: Creation of the current logical model

4.3.1   Task 1.4: Create the data store entity cross-references

The physical data store entity cross-reference
The inputs to task 1.4 are the data stores from the current physical data flow
diagrams and the entity model. Every data store on the current physical
data flow diagrams must be represented by one or more entities on the entity
model. If a cross-reference cannot be found, then either a data store has

been inserted or, more likely, the entity model is not complete. This type of cross-referencing and high-level proving during the early stages of the project is a feature of the methodology which leads to good-quality systems being produced.

Figure 4.28 shows two data stores on a DFD and an entity model. Customers place orders, where each order contains many order lines, a single order line for each product ordered. For each despatch against an order line, normally only one but possibly more than one, an advice note is sent with the goods. A copy advice note is used by a typist, function 1.7, to create an invoice for each despatch. Function 1.7 references a name and address list to check the invoice address. Copy invoices are sent to accounts where a clerk inserts invoice data on to the sales ledger, function 2.3. An

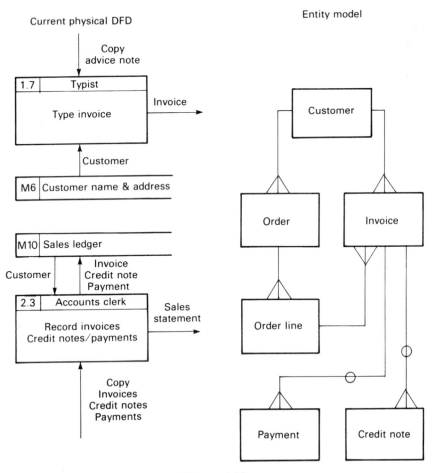

Figure 4.28

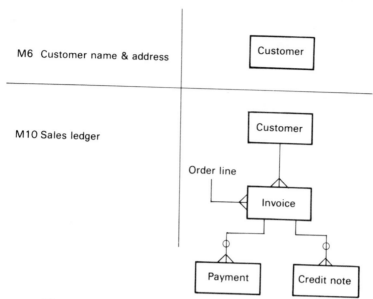

Figure 4.29 Physical data store/entity cross-reference

order line has an invoice for each despatch and, therefore, may have many invoices. Payments against invoices or the part credit of invoices are also processed by the accounts clerk. Figure 4.29 shows the cross-reference. Note that the full customer entity appears in both existing data stores. This shows a duplication of this data in the current physical system.

Figure 4.30 shows the cross-reference for the X-ray system. Note that patient data is repeated in manual data stores 1, 2, 4 and 6; and that patient data together with X-ray films and patient reports can be physically located in one of three manual files 2, 7 and 8.

Many of the current physical data stores contain data on more than one entity. This leads to storage anomalies which will be discussed in Chapter 7. Finally, note that data store M3 only includes a reference to the patient entity, name and date of birth perhaps, whereas data store M6 contains the full patient data. This is because of the problems of including any more than a minimum amount of text on an X-ray film.

The current physical data stores may contain several entities. Functions which access data stores may not require access to all of the entities, and it is therefore good practice at this time to return to the current physical data flow diagrams and to annotate each of the data flows to or from data stores with the names of the entities accessed. These names will be useful during task 1.5, the creation of the current logical data flow diagrams.

Figure 4.31 shows a section of a current physical data flow diagram with data flows to and from the data store sales ledger annotated. Figure 4.32

DATA STORE/ENTITY X REF.

SYSTEM: X-RAY MANAGEMENT

DATE:

AUTHOR: G. CUTTS

PAGE: 1 of 1

PHYSICAL/~~LOGICAL~~

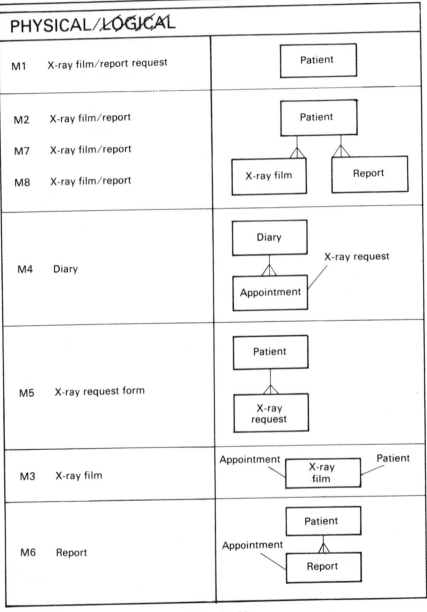

M1	X-ray film/report request
M2	X-ray film/report
M7	X-ray film/report
M8	X-ray film/report
M4	Diary
M5	X-ray request form
M3	X-ray film
M6	Report

Figure 4.30

Data store entity cross-reference

M7   Sales ledger

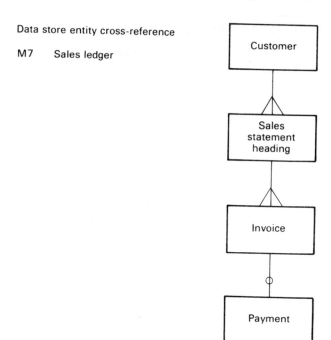

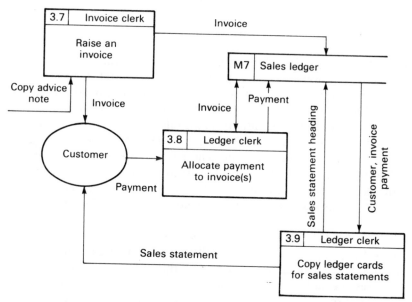

Figure 4.31

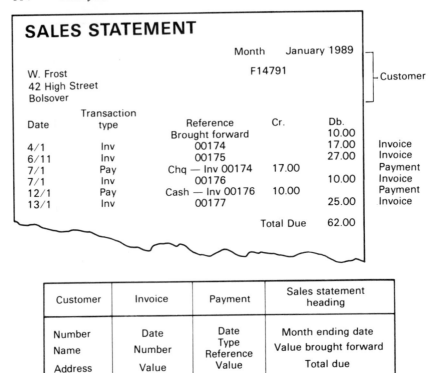

SALES STATEMENT

Month   January 1989

W. Frost   F14791
42 High Street   Customer
Bolsover

Date	Transaction type	Reference	Cr.	Db.	
		Brought forward		10.00	
4/1	Inv	00174		17.00	Invoice
6/11	Inv	00175		27.00	Invoice
7/1	Pay	Chq — Inv 00174	17.00		Payment
7/1	Inv	00176		10.00	Invoice
12/1	Pay	Cash — Inv 00176	10.00		Payment
13/1	Inv	00177		25.00	Invoice
			Total Due	62.00	

Customer	Invoice	Payment	Sales statement heading
Number	Date	Date	Month ending date
Name	Number	Type	Value brought forward
Address	Value	Reference	
		Value	Total due

Figure 4.32

shows an example of a sales statement showing the data from each of the four entities customer, invoice, payment, and sales statement heading.

To complete the cross-reference, it is necessary to investigate the attributes within each physical data store and to group them according to the entity names. Examine the entry from the sales ledger shown in Figure 4.32: it contains customer data, invoice data, payment data, and data which can only be allocated to the sales statement itself. This exercise provides a first look at the entity descriptions, i.e. the attributes which make up the entity. Entity descriptions will be formally completed during stage 2 but a start can be made at this stage in recording candidate attributes for each entity.

The logical data store entity cross-reference

The next step is to decompose the entity model into logical data stores. The topology of the diagram often helps with this process. A logical data store comprises the entities which form logical groups. A logical group often represents a series of entities referenced by a single process. A complementary method to arrive at logical groups is to examine the time relationships within the entities.

Consider the entity model, Figure 4.20, for the X-ray management system.

Patient records, their X-ray films and their reports are all stored until the patient death is recorded, whereas data on specific X-ray requests and appointments is transient data, only stored until the appointment including

DATA STORE/ENTITY X REF

SYSTEM: X-RAY MANAGEMENT	DATE:
AUTHOR: G. CUTTS	PAGE: 1 of 1

P̶H̶Y̶S̶I̶C̶A̶L̶/LOGICAL

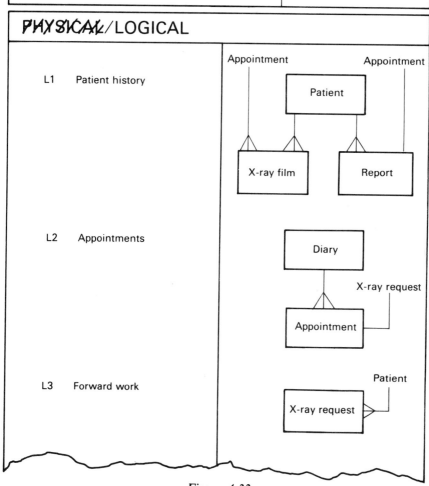

Figure 4.33

ENTITY MODEL

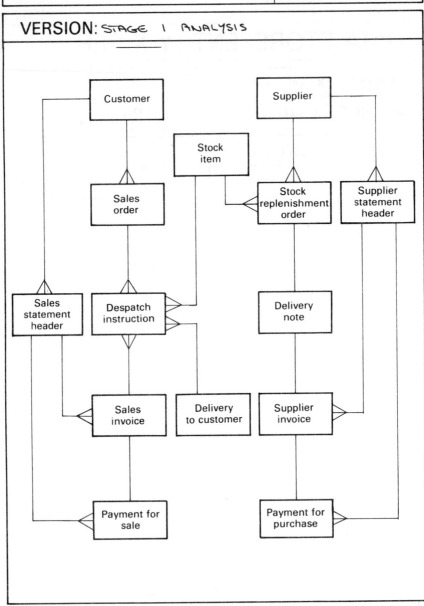

Figure 4.34

ENTITY MODEL

SYSTEM: ABC

DATE:

AUTHOR: G. CUTTS

PAGE: 1 of 1

VERSION: STAGE 1 ANALYSIS

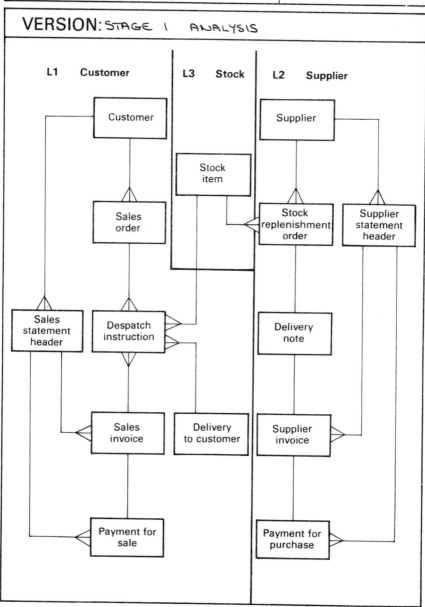

Figure 4.35

ENTITY MODEL

SYSTEM: ABC

AUTHOR: G. CUTTS

DATE:

PAGE: 1 of 1

VERSION: STAGE 1 ANALYSIS

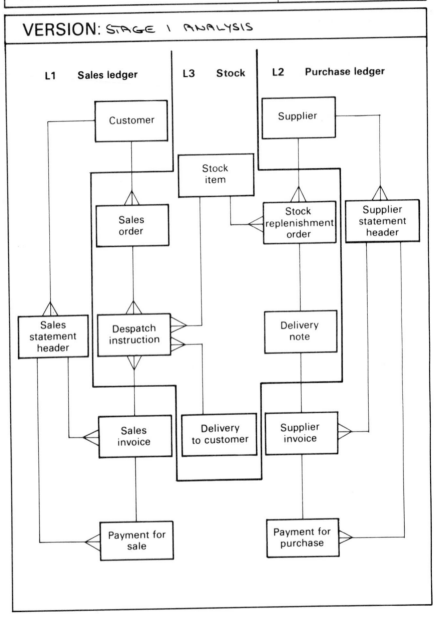

Figure 4.36

a new report is complete. Logically, three data stores exist: logical data store 1 comprising patient, X-ray film and report entities; logical data store 2 comprising the diary and appointment entities; and logical data store 3 the X-ray request entities.

A cross-reference can now be simply constructed between logical data stores and entities. Figure 4.33 shows such a cross-reference for the X-ray management system.

The choice of the logical data store names should reflect the basic content of the data store. Logical data store 1 contains a patient history of X-ray films and reports, logical data store 2 represents all appointments, and logical data store 3 represents all the outstanding requests for X-ray, the forward load.

The decomposition of the entity model into logical data stores requires a good knowledge of the entity model. It is, however, a process which requires the application of common sense rather than absolute rigour. Any decomposition which can be argued to be a logical decomposition is correct. Figure 4.34 shows an entity model with two possible decompositions, both are correct.

The first decomposition (Figure 4.35) places an emphasis on accounting with orders being close to customers along with the invoice record and stock replenishment orders similarly being close to suppliers.

The second decomposition (Figure 4.36) places the emphasis on stock with current stock, orders, and future stock, which is represented by stock replenishment orders being close. Note in both cases the links via relationships are preserved.

Task 1.4 is now complete: two cross-references have been produced. The physical data store entity cross-reference provided a degree of high-level proving of the DFDs and the entity model and the means by which entity names could be entered on to the current physical DFDs. The logical data store entity cross-reference provides one of the inputs to task 1.5.

4.3.2 Task 1.5: Create the current logical data flow diagrams

Data flow diagrams were used in task 1.2 to provide the user's view of the current system. The diagrams showed how the current system works. They were drawn to assist the analyst understand the functions, data stores and data flows within the current system.

The construction of current physical DFDs also provided an insight into the problems within the system since the current physical diagrams should model the anomalies of the current system. Anomalies such as redundant data stores and redundant processing should have been easily identified.

Since the goal of system analysis is to provide a logical requirements specification derived from solutions to the problems, the new requirements and the logical model of the current system, the construction of logical DFDs to complement the entity model is a necessary next step.

The current logical DFDs will provide a model of what the current system accomplishes, not how it is accomplished. It provides a model of the underlying functions and data, independent of the current implementation. The task of logicalising the DFDs often leads to further identification and clarification of potential problem areas.

Four steps are required to convert the current physical DFDs into the current logical DFDs. The lowest level diagrams should be converted first.

Step 1 removes physical implementation constraint from the data flows along with their physical state; step 2 removes time dependencies associated with the current implementation; step 3 removes functions which only serve the current implementation and examines the remaining functions to remove physical associations; and step 4 incorporates the logical data stores on to the DFDs already modified by steps 1 to 3.

Logicalisation of the data flows

The first and perhaps easiest procedure is to remove all physical references on the data flows. For example, if a request document is known as the pink request form, then the words 'pink' and 'form' may be deleted. The pink form represents the current implementation of a request, logically what is required is a request. The data flow label 'pink request form' is changed to 'request'. This also removes the physical format, that is a form.

This change will ensure that when the new system is implemented all possible new physical forms for a request will be considered. A request could be made using a request form, via a screen and keyboard, or perhaps by a voice input terminal. The design of the new system should not be influenced by the current physical implementation, that is 'the pink form'. Similarly, the state of a document or set of documents should be removed. States such as 'entered on to magnetic tape' represent current physical manifestations of the data flow.

Listed below are some transformations of data stores from their physical descriptions to logical descriptions. The descriptions are transformed to reflect what the data content is, not how it is presented.

Physical	*Logical*
Pink top copy	Order
Works docket	Order
Re-order card	Request for stock replenishment
Price ticket	Price
X-ray request	X-ray request
Annotated delivery note	Quantity of parts under delivered

Step 1, therefore, is to examine each data flow, suitably renaming those which indicate a physical form or state within the name. New names should be chosen to accurately describe the data on the documents. Data flows to and from data stores should already be named with their logical entity names and therefore need no further modification.

Note that now the physical format of the 'pink top copy' and the 'works docket' have been removed, the data contained on the documents is revealed to be identical, the order. If both of these documents are input to a single function, one of them must be redundant. The final activity within step 1 is to remove redundant data flows.

Removal of physical time dependencies

Delay is often built into physical implementations to enable efficient processing. If orders are received by telephone at a steady rate throughout the day, it might be inefficient to take each order to the warehouse as it is received. A solution might be to record orders until twenty have been received, then to take them to the warehouse. A temporary file of orders is therefore constructed by the current physical implementation. Figure 4.37 shows the appropriate section of the current physical DFD.

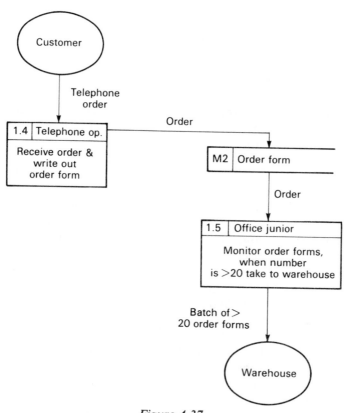

Figure 4.37

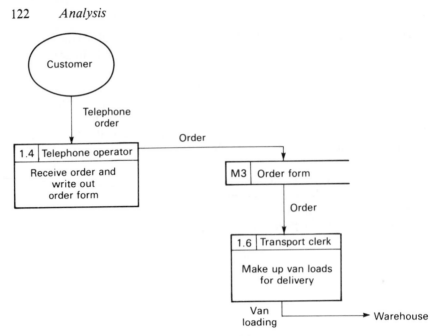

Figure 4.38

Data store M2, order form, is only required to save the office junior from constantly having to take forms to the warehouse. Logically what is required is the receipt of an order via the telephone and the data being made available to the warehouse staff. Data store M2 builds in a time dependency for purely physical considerations. It should therefore be deleted from the current logical DFD.

Care should be taken to ensure that data stores which do introduce time delays for valid reasons are not deleted. Figure 4.38 shows such a situation.

In this case, the function 'make up van loads' cannot be implemented without all the orders for a given route or day's delivery, depending upon the van-loading algorithm. This data store introduces a time dependency but it should not be deleted as it is logically necessary.

Logicalisation of the functions

The process of removing physical references from the data flows provides a first method of identification of purely physical functions. Many physical functions serve only to transform documents with identical data content. These functions will become obvious, see Figure 4.39.

With the 'pink top copy' and the 'works docket' renamed with their data content 'order', function 1.7, 'create works order documentation', is logically redundant and should therefore be deleted.

Figure 4.37 showed a function 'monitor order forms, when number >20,

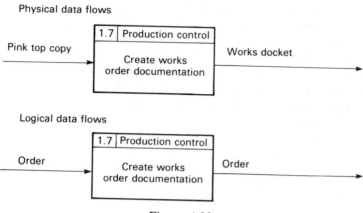

Figure 4.39

take to warehouse'. This function does not carry out any logical processing; it is purely physical. Again this function should be deleted and not carried forward to the logical DFD.

The change of state of a data flow by a function often reveals further purely physical processes. The function 'enter order to magnetic tape' is an example of a physical function which performs nothing more than a state change, that is not logical processing; it should not be carried forward to the logical DFDs.

Finally, all of the remaining functions should be renamed, if necessary, to accurately describe the logical processing. Some examples are given below:

Function descriptions

Physical	*Logical*
Write out order on pink form	Receive order
Update ledger card to reflect the payment of an invoice	Allocate payment to invoice
Type order report	Produce order analysis

Create the current logical data flow diagrams
The current physical DFDs have so far been modified by renaming the data flows, except those to and from data stores, by the removal of time dependencies and by the removal or renaming of functions. The current logical DFDs can now be created by removing the physical data stores and incorporating the logical data stores.

This is a relatively simple activity. First, the data flows to and from data store should be examined. These data flows were named using one or more entity names. By reference to the logical data store entity cross-reference produced by task 1.5, the logical data store containing the named entity can be established. The appropriate logical data store can therefore be entered on to the logical DFD to provide a source or destination for the data flow.

Secondly, all the data flows not contributing inputs or outputs to the system should be examined. Frequently the logical name chosen for a data flow is an entity name. This data flow should be redrawn to reflect an insert into the appropriate logical data store and a subsequent read of the data store, replacing the direct flow of data between the functions. Figure 4.40 shows examples of both types of modification.

Physical data stores M2 and M3 have been replaced by one logical data store L1, order. The data store then serves both functions 1.6 and 1.7 as well as providing information for the warehouse. Note also that function 1.5 has been removed as a purely physical function.

Note also that the responsibility section of the function rectangle is left blank on the logical DFDs.

The final step within task 1.5 is the revision and review of the newly produced current logical DFDs.

The logicalisation task should be undertaken on the lowest level of DFD produced. The changes introduced on the lower levels should be reflected level by level on the higher levels. This will generally require the higher levels to be completely redrawn using the boundaries of the lower levels as function rectangles. High levels are constructed bottom up.

The removal of functions as a result of logicalisation often reduces a DFD to very few functions or even a single function. This means that the decomposition may require a second examination. Lower-level DFDs may be combined and the appropriate changes made at the higher levels. In this way a new set of DFDs is produced incorporating all levels of decomposition.

The current logical DFDs provide a user's view of what the system currently does, not how the system currently operates. It shows logical data flows, logical data stores and logical functions. This set of DFDs will form the basis of the requirements specification.

Summary of task 1.5
The current logical DFDs are a vital part of the documentation and the methodology. These logical DFDs will be used to develop, in stage 2, the required logical DFDs. This set of diagrams represents a major part of the requirements specification, one of the most vital documents in any development project.

Task 1.5 comprises four simple steps:

Step 1: logicalise the data flows
Step 2: remove physical time dependencies
Step 3: logicalise the functions
Step 4: logicalise the data stores

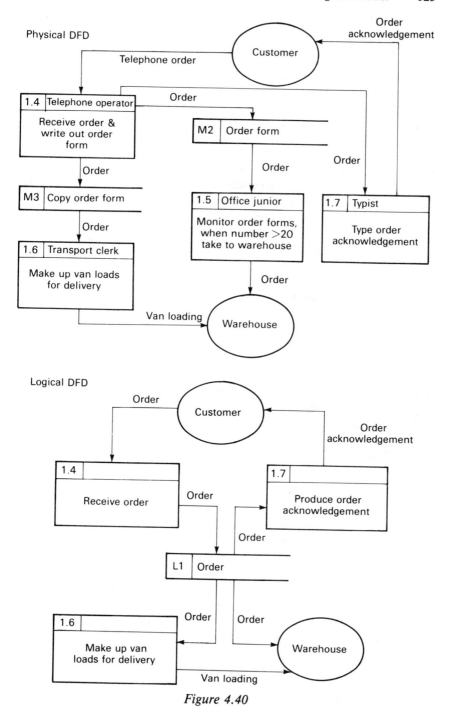

Figure 4.40

4.4   Section 3: Creation of the problems and requirements list

4.4.1   Task 1.6:   Create the problems and requirements list

This final task in stage 1 produces the third output from the stage, the problems and requirements list.

The list is compiled by reference to the investigation notes, and by analysis of the DFDs and entity models. A simple format is used for the list, see Figure 4.41. The format includes a description of the problem or requirement, the initials of the originator of the problem or requirement and a solution reference. At this stage the solution reference is not used; this will be added when the required system has been specified to show that solutions have been incorporated into the new system.

Problems with the current system and requirements for the new system should be part of any information-gathering techniques used during task 1.1. Interviewing is perhaps the most productive technique for establishing problems and requirements. Problems are also revealed during the construction of the DFDs and the entity model, particularly during the several tasks forming the sequence of events leading to the final current logical DFDs.

An example of a problem revealed during modelling could be the number of separate instances of similar processing or similar or identical data stores. Some of these problems can be removed during the construction of the current logical DFDs; these are associated with physical problems. Logical problems will not be removed. These logic problems need to be recorded on the problems and requirements list so that in stage 2 they can be removed when the logic is optimised.

Figure 4.41 shows some examples of problems and requirements for the X-ray system.

4.5   Stage 1 summary

Stage 1, Analysis, comprises perhaps the most difficult set of tasks. They are all concerned with gaining a thorough understanding of the current system. This understanding is researched and documented to form the basis of the vital document, the specification of requirements to be produced during stage 2. One of the common problems of systems analysis is the temptation to become involved in minute detail before a good understanding of the system is obtained. The methodology described for analysis in this chapter attempts to prevent this descent into detail by providing top down modelling techniques.

What is vital to stage 1 is that it is the analysis stage. It is the stage where the understanding is reached by an iterative process of investigate and model. The initial models will therefore not be correct; they will represent

PROBLEM/REQUIREMENTS LIST

SYSTEM: *X-RAY MANAGEMENT*	DATE:
AUTHOR: *G.CUTTS*	PAGE: *1* of *1*

No.	Problem/requirement	Init.	Solution reference
1.	X-ray films and reports can be located in several places. This makes tracing of films and reports difficult in emergency situations. (Problem)	File Clerk	
2.	There is no system to ensure patients are seen by radiographers in appointment sequence. The sequence tends to be arrival sequence. (Problem)	Radio-grapher	
3.	A report showing the number and type of X-ray films produced each day. (Requirement)	Radiologist	
4.	A facility to reproduce efficiently standard reports such as 'no fracture seen'. (Requirement)	Radiologist	

Figure 4.41

the best understanding at the point of modelling. Task 1.1, investigation of the current system, and tasks 1.2 and 1.3, the creation of the current physical DFDs and the current entity model, should be regarded as an iterative set of tasks. High-level investigation should be followed by a first attempt at modelling, then detail should be added to the models by subsequent iterations of investigate and model. The modelling processes should progress until both the current physical DFDs and the current entity model have been agreed with the user.

Task 1.4, create the data store entity cross-references, contributes towards task 1.5 where the current physical DFDs are converted, by a series of simple steps, to current logical DFDs. The diagrams are logicalised to reflect what the system does, not how the system is currently implemented. The activity of extracting the logic of the existing system is one of the major benefits of the methodology.

The final task in stage 1, task 1.6, creates a list of problems with the existing system and a list of requirements for the new system. The problems and requirements are extracted from the investigation notes and from the DFDs and entity model. The analysis of the investigation notes to produce the models will reveal problems with the current system such as duplicate data stores and processing.

Stage 1 is complete when the user review of the output from it is completed and agreed. The output documents are a set of current logical DFDs, an entity model and a list of problems and requirements.

5

Specification of requirements

5.1 Introduction

Chapter 5 describes the second stage of SSADM, the specification of requirements (Figure 5.1). The stage uses the logical models produced by stage 1, together with the problems and requirements list, to produce a logical requirements specification. This will specify what the new system is required to do, not how it should be implemented.

Tasks 2.1 and 2.2, creation of the required logical DFDs and the required entity model, provide the highest level specification. They may be created by modification of the current logical DFDs and the current entity model. Modifications are made to reflect the requirements listed during stage 1, task 1.6, and to provide solutions to the problems listed as part of the same task. The required logical DFDs and the required entity model may alternatively be created from the list of requirements and from the detailed knowledge of what the current system accomplishes without reference to the current logical DFDs. Tasks 2.1 and 2.2 are often linked under the heading of optimisation, improvement and development of the logical model.

The remaining tasks add detail to the model, as well as providing a third view of it in the form of an entity function matrix and entity life histories. These tasks document the function descriptions, the entity descriptions, the input/output and data flow descriptions as well as providing a third view of the system.

The full specification of requirements comprises seven sets of documentation:

(1) The required logical DFDs—task 2.1
(2) A revised entity model—task 2.2
(3) Entity descriptions—task 2.3
(4) Input, output and data flow descriptions—task 2.4
(5) Function descriptions—task 2.5

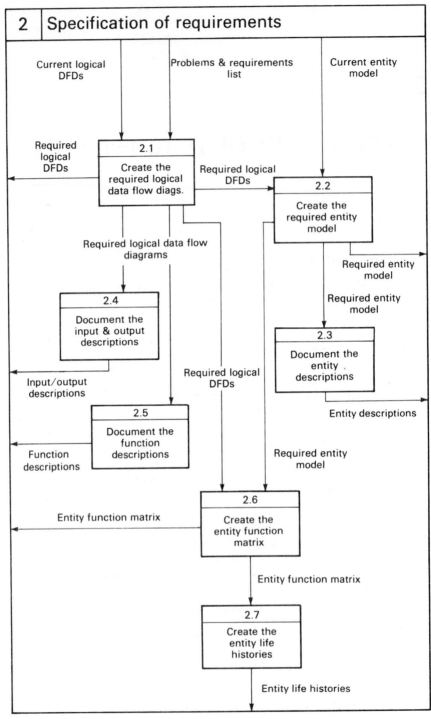

| 2 | Specification of requirements |

Current logical DFDs

Problems & requirements list

Current entity model

Required logical DFDs

2.1 Create the required logical data flow diags.

Required logical DFDs

2.2 Create the required entity model

Required logical data flow diagrams

Required entity model

2.4 Document the input & output descriptions

Required entity model

2.3 Document the entity descriptions

Input/output descriptions

Required logical DFDs

2.5 Document the function descriptions

Entity descriptions

Function descriptions

Required entity model

2.6 Create the entity function matrix

Entity function matrix

Entity function matrix

2.7 Create the entity life histories

Entity life histories

Figure 5.1

(6) The entity function matrix—task 2.6
(7) Entity life histories—task 2.7

Stage 4, logical data design, will use the entity model, entity descriptions and input/output descriptions to produce the final logical data design. Stage 5, logical process design, will use the required DFDs, the entity function matrix, the entity life histories, the function descriptions and the logical data design to produce the logical process catalogue and a set of logical process outlines.

Stage 2 therefore commences by optimisation, improvement and development of the logical model and concludes by providing a detailed logical requirements specification.

Chapter 5 comprises three sections:

Section 1: Creation of the required logical model
Section 2: Detailed documentation of the required logical model
Section 3: Validation of the model

5.2 Section 1: Creation of the required logical model

5.2.1 Task 2.1: Create the required logical data flow diagrams

SSADM made considerable use of DFDs in stage 1. During stage 1 they were used to provide a view of the current system, understandable by the user. They provided a method of documenting the current system. Physical DFDs provided a method of testing the completeness of understanding against the observed actual system. Logical DFDs provided a method of documenting what the system accomplished, an abstraction of the logic of the current system.

Task 2.1 will again use DFDs to document logic; the logic of the required system, what the new system is required to accomplish. Instead of testing the completeness of understanding against the actual system, the completeness of understanding against the requirements for the new system is tested.

Data flow diagrams still provide a user's view of the system. In this case, the required logical DFDs provide a view of what the new system will accomplish, not how, at this stage, it will be implemented.

Task 2.1 creates the required logical DFDs. These may be produced by modification of the current DFDs. Alternatively, they may be produced by consideration of the existing and new requirements without reference to the logic of the current system.

The objective of task 2.1 is to eliminate the problems associated with the current system and to incorporate the requirements for the new system.

Figure 5.2 shows a current logical DFD with modifications to provide a new management planning report. It is therefore a required logical model. The modifications are shown using dotted structures.

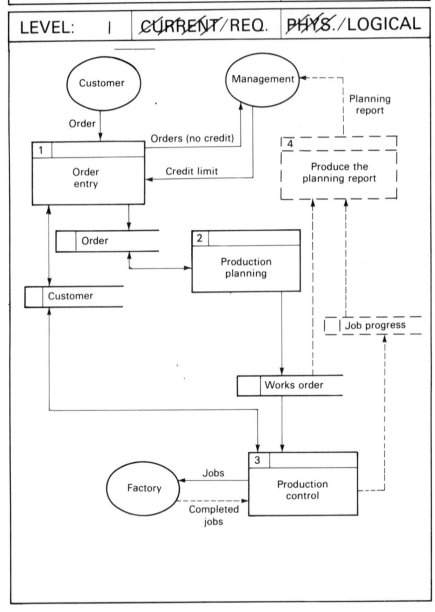

DATA FLOW DIAGRAM

SYSTEM: CHAPTER 5 EXAMPLE	DATE:
AUTHOR: G. CUTTS	PAGE: 1 of 1

LEVEL: 1	~~CURRENT~~/REQ.	~~PHYS.~~/LOGICAL

Customer

Management

Order

Orders (no credit)

Planning report

1 Order entry

Credit limit

4 Produce the planning report

Order

2 Production planning

Customer

Job progress

Works order

3 Production control

Factory

Jobs

Completed jobs

Figure 5.2

The modifications comprise a new function, new data flows, a new data store and the revision of an existing function. Modifications will typically comprise new functions and data stores, and revision of existing data stores and functions. Each of these modifications may result in new or revised data flows.

Figures 5.3 and 5.5 show a complete DFD before and after modification. Figure 5.3 shows the current view and Figure 5.5 the required view, after modification. Modifications were made to provide solutions to the problems, and to provide the requirements documented on the problems and requirements list, Figure 5.4.

Note that the problems and requirements list has been updated to include solution references.

Problem 1 is solved by the inclusion of a new data store, L4, revision to functions 2 and 3 and by a new function 5. Function 3, stock check, is enhanced to include the insertion of the delivery note into a new data store L4, delivery. Function 5, record delivery success, simply modifies the delivery inserted during function 3 to indicate that a satisfactory delivery has taken place. Finally, function 2 requires enhancement to read the new data store, to access delivery information and to include this information on the management report.

Requirements 2 and 3 both require function 4, produce invoice, to be amended.

The invoice price depends upon both the customer and the product. A new entity called price is therefore required as a link between customers and products. The entity price should be added to the entity model. A new logical data store should be created for the entity or the new entity should be added into an existing logical data store. In Figure 5.5, the entity price has been incorporated into logical data store L3, product.

The invoice price is obtained from the price entity within the logical data store L3, see Figure 5.5.

Function 4, produce invoice, references data store L4, delivery. Deliveries are marked to indicate a satisfactory delivery has taken place by new function 5. Invoices may therefore only be produced for deliveries so marked, satisfying requirement 3 on the problems and requirements list.

Figure 5.5, therefore, shows a required logical DFD which has been developed by modification of the current logical DFD. The decomposition into functions which was considered when the current DFDs were developed still exists. Some aspects from the current physical system, for example, current departments or sections as functions, still exist on the required logical DFDs.

This may be a major disadvantage with the method of developing required logical DFDs. It may be a major advantage in that the final design may preserve an existing department's or section's major functional responsibilities. A statement to that effect in the 'terms of reference' is not uncommon.

DATA FLOW DIAGRAM

SYSTEM: EXAMPLE	DATE:
AUTHOR: G. CUTTS	PAGE: 1 of 1

LEVEL: 2	CURRENT/~~REQ~~ ~~PHYS~~//LOGICAL

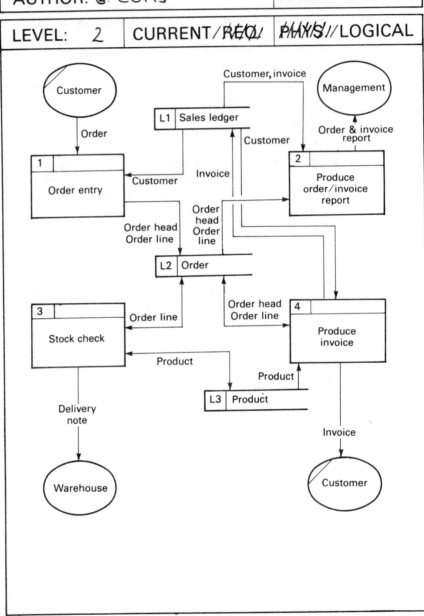

Figure 5.3

PROBLEM/REQUIREMENTS LIST

SYSTEM: EXAMPLE	DATE:
AUTHOR: G. CUTTS	PAGE: I of I

No.	Problem/requirement	Init.	Solution reference
1.	Management require the order/invoice report extended to include details of the delivery note produced for each order line. The report should also include evidence that the delivery has taken place. This is to overcome the problem of lost deliveries. There is evidence of goods being lost in transit. Two copies of the delivery note should be produced, one copy being signed by the customer and returned to the company by the delivery driver.	Sales Manager	Functions 2 3 & 5 Data store L4
2.	It is required to introduce a flexible pricing structure whereby the price of each product may vary according to a customer.	Sales Manager	Additional Entity Price
3.	Invoices should not be generated until a satisfactory delivery has taken place. The current system allows invoices to be generated after production of a delivery note which does not guarantee despatch from the warehouse.	Chief Accountant	Function 4

Figure 5.4

DATA FLOW DIAGRAM

SYSTEM: EXAMPLE	DATE:
AUTHOR: G. CUTTS	PAGE: 1 of 1

LEVEL: 1	~~CURRENT~~/REQ.	~~PHYS.~~/LOGICAL

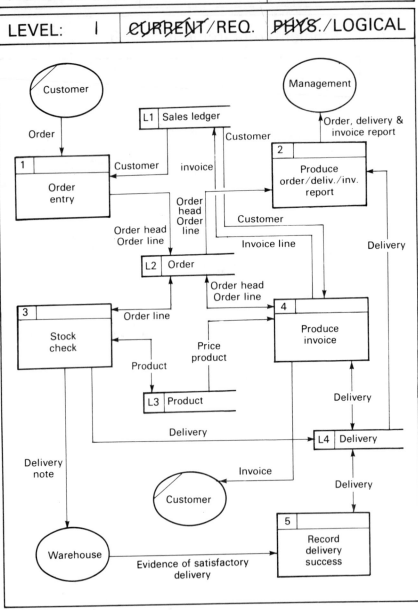

Figure 5.5

Using the current logical model as a base for the required logical model may also be a major disadvantage. Responsibilities may have been allocated in the current system to serve operational needs. The decomposition into departments and sections may therefore exhibit little logic.

The alternative method of developing the required logical DFDs allows the analyst to commence with a list of requirements and to develop a set of DFDs to satisfy them. The DFDs need not be influenced by any aspects of the current system.

The decomposition of DFDs into functions and sub-functions can be based completely according to the rules of coupling and cohesion. Each decomposition must seek to produce highly cohesive functions, which represent one set of system-related activities, loosely coupled to other functions, that is with a minimum number of inter-function data flows.

One method of obtaining high cohesion and loose coupling is by bottom up development. A DFD should be produced at the lowest level showing all of the primitive functions. Functions should then be grouped to form the levels of decomposition required to assist the understandability of DFDs. Figure 5.6 shows a large DFD divided into functional areas.

The required logical DFDs may therefore be developed without being influenced by the current system.

If the system being developed is entirely new and no current system exists, then this may be the only method of development of the required logical DFDs.

The required logical DFDs are transformed into required physical DFDs in stage 3. Several required physical DFD sets may be produced to represent different implementation or business options.

For many systems, the required logical DFDs can be eliminated. The required physical DFDs can be created to satisfy the requirements. There is some merging of the tasks within stages 2 and 3.

5.2.2   Task 2.2: Create the required entity model

The entity model, which resulted from stage 1, modelled the generic underlying structure of the data and data relationships associated with the current system. The creation of the required logical DFDs during the previous task may well introduce new entities into the model. It is also possible for entity descriptions to be modified and for entities to be deleted. The addition, deletion and modification of entities needs to be reflected in the entity model. The changes made to the DFDs however, are not entity additions, deletions and modifications; they are additions, deletions and modifications to logical data stores on the DFDs.

Stage 1, task 1.4 transformed the entity model into a set of logical data stores. What is required now is the reverse process: the transformation of the new logical data stores into a revision of the entity model. The data store

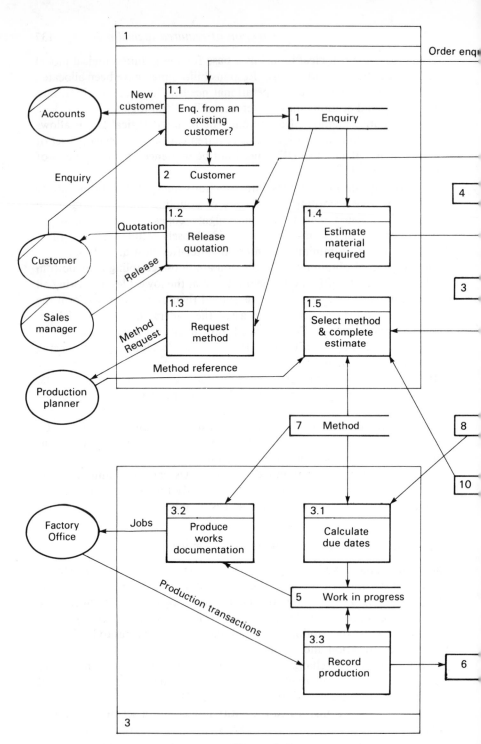

Figure 5.6

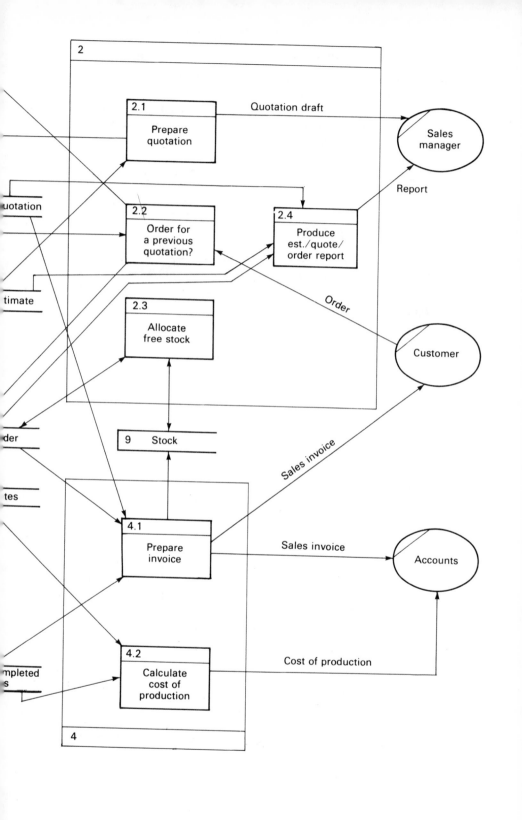

2

2.1 Prepare quotation

Quotation draft

Sales manager

Report

uotation

2.2 Order for a previous quotation?

2.4 Produce est./quote/ order report

timate

2.3 Allocate free stock

Order

Customer

der

9 Stock

tes

Sales invoice

4.1 Prepare invoice

Sales invoice

Accounts

mpleted s

4.2 Calculate cost of production

Cost of production

4

entity cross-reference will require revision due to the new entities created. The new entities should then be added to the entity model.

Appropriate relationships should be generated and a revised entity model created for further refinement in stage 4. The new data store added to Figure 5.3, delivery, shown on Figure 5.5 results in modification to the data store entity cross-reference and the entity model.

Figure 5.7 shows the original entity model and Figure 5.8 the revised entity model.

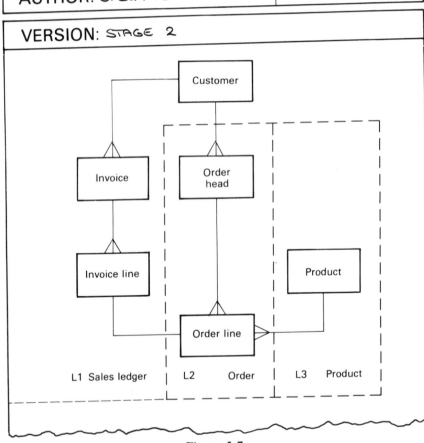

Figure 5.7

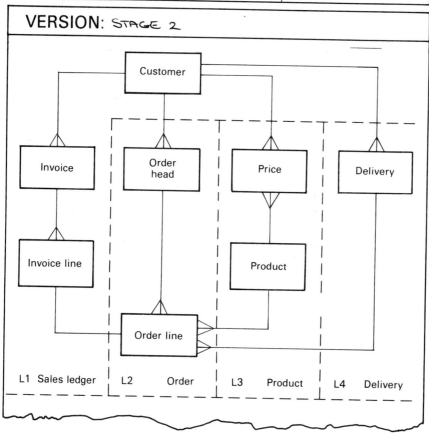

ENTITY MODEL

SYSTEM: *CHAPTER 5 EXAMPLE*	DATE:
AUTHOR: *G. CUTTS*	PAGE: *1* of *1*

VERSION: *STAGE 2*

Figure 5.8

There now exists a price entity between customer and product. A customer has many prices, one for each product, and a product has many prices, one for each customer. A new entity price, accessed by function 4, produce invoice, is introduced.

A new entity, delivery, has also been introduced. Customers receive many deliveries, each delivery comprises many order lines; however, an order line can only have one delivery (no part deliveries) and be to one customer.

5.3   Section 2: Detailed documentation of the required logical model

5.3.1   Task 2.3: Document the entity descriptions

An entity description comprises a list of attributes. For example, the customer entity may have the following attributes: name, address, delivery address, credit limit, telephone number, date of last order etc. The entity descriptions should be completed in as much detail as possible, as part of the specification of requirements.

Task 2.3 should not be considered to be the sole task where entity descriptions are considered. It is the task that brings together all of the data collected on attributes to produce the formal documentation. From the moment that entities are introduced, task 1.3, entity descriptions, should be considered. Examine the physical data store entity cross-reference shown in Figure 5.9.

Three physical data stores (credit limit, name and address, and part of sales ledger) are cross-referenced with the entity, customer. The conclusion from this is that the customer entity must contain the combined data items or attributes from all of the physical data stores. The customer entity must include, as a minimum, credit limit, name, and address as attributes.

This process is slightly more difficult when a physical data store is cross-referenced with a number of entities. Figure 5.10 shows a sales statement. The cross-reference of the data store, sales statement, with the entity model is shown in Figure 5.11.

Each data item on the sales statement should be allocated to one of the entities and will therefore become an attribute of one of the entities. The current data store data items should be listed and, by reference to the data store entity cross-reference, allocated to an entity. A typical allocation is shown in Figure 5.12.

This method will work for all entities identified during stage 1, analysis. Attributes may have been added during stage 2, task 2.2, to satisfy a new requirement. In this case, an attribute list for the new entity can be created to satisfy the new requirement. Figure 5.7 included a new entity, price; the attributes might be:

customer number
product code
selling price
date of last price change

The entity descriptions created should be in business terms; technical detail will be added during stage 6. The entity descriptions will also be validated in stage 4.

A typical entity description is shown in Figure 5.13.

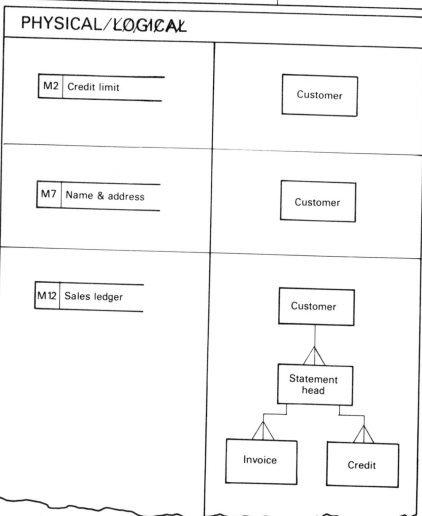

DATA STORE/ENTITY X REF.

SYSTEM: *CHAPTER 5· EXAMPLE*   DATE:

AUTHOR: *G. CUTTS*   PAGE: *I* of   *I*

PHYSICAL/~~LOGICAL~~

Figure 5.9

STATEMENT

Customer: A. Jones   J4719
                          21 West Street
                          Cardiff

Month ending: 31 Jan 1986

Date	Tran. Type	Reference	Credit	Debit
31/12/85		Brought forward		71.00
3/1/86	Inv.	I4719		10.00
4/1/86	Inv.	I4737		15.00
10/1/86	Payment	Cheque 474198	60.00	
12/1/86	Inv.	I5179		17.00
15/1/86	Inv.	I5711		19.00
21/1/86	Inv.	I5800		21.00
30/1/86	Credit	CR2/I5179	17.00	
	Total			76.00
	1 month			65.00
	2 months			11.00
	Prior			—

Figure 5.10

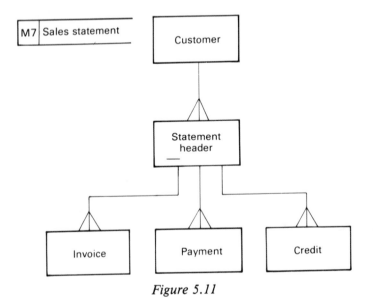

Figure 5.11

Entity	Attribute list	
Customer	Customer	Number
		Name
		Address
Statement header	Month ending date	
	Value b/f	
	Value c/f (total)	
	Value 1 (1 month)	
	Value 2 (2 months)	
	Value 3 (prior)	
Invoice	Invoice date	
	Invoice number	
	Value	
Credit	Credit date	
	Credit note number	
	Credit reference	
	Value	
Payment	Payment date	
	Payment type	
	Payment reference	
	Value	

Figure 5.12

Note that at this stage only the data item and comment column have entries. Round brackets (delivery address) indicate that an attribute value need not be present; the attribute is optional.

5.3.2   Task 2.4: Document the system input, system output and data flow description

The required logical DFDs comprise logical data stores, input and output data flows, internal data flow and functions. The previous task produced the detailed documentation of the entities. The logical data store entity cross-reference, together with the entity descriptions, effectively document the logical data stores. This task, task 2.4, documents the data flows: input, output and internal.

For existing data flows, the task is relatively simple. For example, the data flow sales statement probably corresponds to a document which is already in existence. The data items on the sales statement can be listed, discussed with the user and documented on the appropriate form. The user may add or delete data items from the list.

The sales statement, Figure 5.10, is documented as shown in Figure 5.14. Square brackets, [ ], show alternative attributes or groups of attributes and the vertical bar indicates a repeating group of attributes.

Many of the data flows are particular occurrences of an entity and will be named with the entity name on the DFDs. These data flows have already

ENTITY DESCRIPTION

SYSTEM: *CHAPTER 5 EXAMPLE*	DATE:
AUTHOR: *J. CUTTS*	PAGE: *1* of *1*

NAME: *CUSTOMER*

NARRATIVE: All customers attibutes not related to a specific order.

Key	Data item	Format	Len.	Comment
	Customer Number			
	Name			
	Address			5 lines
	(Delivery Address)			5 lines
	Credit Limit			
	(Date of last order)			
	Area			
	(Discount)			
	(Salesman's reference)			
	Method of delivery			

VOLUMETRICS

ENTITY SIZE	
No. OF OCCURRENCES	
TOTAL	

Figure 5.13

INPUT OUTPUT DESCRIPTION

SYSTEM: *CHAPTER 5 EXAMPLE*	DATE:
AUTHOR: *G. CUTTS*	PAGE: *1* of *1*

NAME: *SALES STATEMENT*

NARRATIVE: *This output documents all invoices, credit notes, and payments posted to the sales ledger during the month.*

Key	Data item	Format	Len.	Comment
	Customer number			
	Name			
	Address			
	Statement date			
	Value brought forward			Previous month's carried forward
	Value carried forward			To next month
	Value owing 1 month			
	Value owing 2 months			
	Value owing prior			
	Transaction type			Invoice, payment or credit
	Date of transaction			
	Invoice number			
	Payment type, reference			
	Credit note number, reference			
	Value			
	Credit/debit			

Figure 5.14

been documented during task 2.3. Some will comprise several entities; again, these data flows have been documented.

Task 2.4 therefore completes the documentation of all data within the required system, data flows and data stores.

This task is perhaps one of the most important ones. It is this task which documents, for the user and the designer, the input to the system and the output produced by the system: the user interface. It may be necessary at this stage to prototype some sample physical input forms, output report and screen formats to assist the user specification task. Indeed, it might be politically expedient, at this stage, to devote major effort into obtaining agreement on the exact requirements for input and output, via the design of the physical system's input and output.

Task 2.4 can therefore become one of the more visible tasks to the user, where the user can become deeply involved. The user will eventually be asked to agree the requirements specification. The approach of the users will often be to satisfy themselves that the input and output is satisfactory leaving the detail to the systems analysts and designers.

5.3.3   Task 2.5: Document the function descriptions

A function description is required for every primitive function on the required logical DFDs, that is, every function that is not further decomposed. The number of levels of decomposition produced during stage 2 should have ensured that all primitive functions can be documented concisely, completely and unambiguously.

The input and output for each function will have been documented by tasks 2.3 and 2.4; it is the detailed processing that is now required to be documented. Many techniques may be used to document the processing including pseudo-code, structured English, decision tables and decision trees. These are techniques well known to the analyst; examples of each are given in Figure 5.15. They all provide the detailed documentation of the function also shown in Figure 5.15.

The function descriptions must be in business terms. It will be the user who will agree the specification at the end of stage 2, and the user will generally only understand function descriptions which are written in business terms.

The method used for the function descriptions must suit the user. If the user presented much of the current processing by tables, then decision trees and tables may be appropriate. If the user has experience of computing systems and algorithm specification, then pseudo-code might be appropriate.

Stage 2 produces a specification of requirements documenting what is required of the system. The user must review and agree the specification; it must, therefore, be in a language acceptable to and understandable by the user.

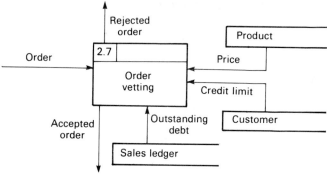

Pseudo-code

Compute order value: = order qty. × price each
Obtain credit limit
Obtain outstanding debt
Compute credit remaining: = credit limit − (order value + outstanding debt)

if credit remaining ≥ 0
    then accept order
    else if special clearance obtained
        then accept order
        else reject order.

Structured English

IF order value + outstanding debt less than credit limit
    THEN accept order
        ELSE IF special clearance obtained
        THEN accept order
        ELSE reject order.

Decision tree

Order value + outstanding debt less than credit limit?

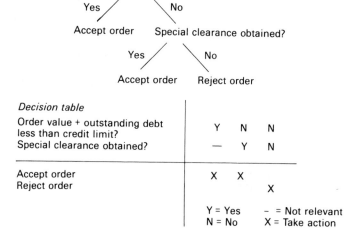

Decision table

Order value + outstanding debt less than credit limit?	Y	N	N
Special clearance obtained?	—	Y	N
Accept order	X	X	
Reject order			X

Y = Yes   − = Not relevant
N = No   X = Take action

Figure 5.15

5.4 Section 3: Validation of the model

5.4.1   Task 2.6: Create the entity function matrix

The entity function matrix provides a third view of the system, a dynamic view. It charts the effect, in time, of functions on entities. Data flow diagrams and entity models do not provide a view which involves time. They provide a view of the data flow, the data and of the data structure, with no reference to time. The entity function matrix and the entity life histories, task 2.7, include the effect of time. They document events in time, and their effect on the data. The sequence of events is important at this stage, not their real timing.

This third view of the system allows questions such as the following to be answered:

● Does each entity have a function which inserts it and a function which deletes it?
● Is each entity accessed after being inserted?
● Which entities are referenced by a function?

The major questions to be answered are:

● Does each entity possess a complete life?
● Does each function behave properly?

Functions form the columns of the entity function matrix, entities the rows. The matrix outline is therefore created by listing all the functions and all the entities within the system.

The required logical DFDs provide the source of the function list. Each primitive function, that is functions which are not further decomposed, becomes a column. The retention of the function's DFD number on the matrix provides a useful cross-reference. The entity model from task 2.2 provides the list of entities. Figure 5.16 shows the skeleton matrix for the system documented in Figures 5.5 and 5.8, the required logical DFD and the entity model, respectively.

The entities within the matrix may contain one or more of the following letters:

blank   the function has no effect on the entity
I   the function INSERTS the entity into the database
M   the function MODIFIES the entity
R   the function READS the entity
D   the function DELETES the entity

Figure 5.17 shows the entity function matrix for the system shown in Figures 5.5 and 5.8.

ENTITY/FUNCTION MATRIX

SYSTEM: CHAPTER 5 EXAMPLE	DATE:
AUTHOR: G. CUTTS	PAGE: 1 of 1

Entity name / Function name	1 Order entry	2 Produce order/deliv./inv. report	3 Stock check	4 Produce invoice	5 Record delivery success						
Customer											
Invoice											
Invoice line											
Order head											
Order line											
Price											
Product											
Delivery											

Figure 5.16

The entries are made by reference to the DFDs. All data flows between functions and data stores result in one or more entries into the matrix.

The following paragraph refers to Figures 5.5 and 5.17.

Function 1, order entry, reads the entity, customer, since the arrow points from the data store to the function. Function 1 also inserts the entities, order head and order line, since the arrow points to the data store. A double-pointed arrow indicates reading and writing, a modification of the

ENTITY/FUNCTION MATRIX

SYSTEM: CHAPTER 5 EXAMPLE	DATE:
AUTHOR: G. CUTTS	PAGE: 1 of 1

Entity name \ Function name	1 Order entity	2 Produce order/ deliv./inv. report	3 Stock check	4 Product invoice	5 Record delivery success								
Customer	R			R									
Invoice				I									
Invoice line				I									
Order head	I	R		M									
Order line	I	R	M	M									
Price				R									
Product			M	R									
Delivery		R	I	M	M								

Figure 5.17

entity. The modification may be a genuine modification or one with a null write representing a deletion of the entity occurrence.

Some functions may perform more complicated processing; entries such as I/M are therefore possible.

Entity life
Each row of the matrix shows the life of an entity. It shows which functions

insert the entity, which functions read or modify it, and which functions delete it. Each row should comprise at least one I (insert), one R (read) or M (modify) and one D (delete).

Entities such as customer and supplier exist in a system so that orders, deliveries and invoices can be inserted, processed and deleted. Very often the function which inserts the entity customer or supplier is overlooked during investigation and analysis. It is an exception rather than ongoing processing. There will therefore be no documented insert function on the DFDs. The entity row in the matrix will comprise reads, R, and modifies, M, but no I, insert. Such omissions need to be corrected.

Similarly the function in the current system which removes customer entities out of the physical data store may well not have been documented. Indeed, such a function may never take place, the data store being allowed to grow indefinitely. This situation will be shown up in the entity function matrix by the absence of a D, delete, within an entity row.

If a row comprises a single I and a single D, then questions need to be asked regarding the need for the entity. Is it inserted, never accessed, and then deleted?

Multiple occurrences of I or D also require further investigation. If an entity can be inserted by more than one function, there must be a distinct possibility of inconsistency between the two functions. Figure 5.18 shows an entity row with two I insert functions.

Function 1.3, create new product entity, results from a management decision to stock and sell a new product. When deliveries of stock arrive they are recorded in the system by function 1.4 which modifies the quantity in stock. If a delivery of stock is made for which no product entity exists,

	1.3 Create new product entity	1.4 Record delivery into stock	2.1 Record delivery to customer	4.3 Discontinue product
Product	I	I/M	M	D

Figure 5.18

then function 1.4 automatically inserts the entity. This prevents the transaction being rejected, saving time and effort. However, it also creates an
entity occurrence for every wrongly coded delivery note, resulting in a total
loss of control of the database. Function 1.4 should therefore be allowed
only to modify existing occurrences, rejecting transactions for which no

ENTITY/FUNCTION MATRIX

SYSTEM: CHAPTER 5 EXAMPLE	DATE:
AUTHOR: G. CUTTS	PAGE: 1 of 1

Entity name \ Function name	1 Order entry	2 Produce order/deliv./inv. report	3 Stock check	4 Produce invoice	5 Record delivery success		6 Customer maintenance	7 Product maintenance	8 Price tables maintenance		
Customer	R			R			I/M /D				
Invoice				I							
Invoice line				I							
Order head	I	R		M/D							
Order line	I	R	M	M/D							
Price				R					I/M /D		
Product			M	R				I/M /D			
Delivery		R	I	M/D	M						

Figure 5.19

entity occurrence exists. Function 1.4 should therefore be allowed modification status but not insert status.

Multiple Ds, delete entries, are also possible. The provision of multiple functions which can delete an entity occurrence leads to auditing problems. Multiple deletes and inserts require careful investigation with subsequent reduction to single entry only, if possible.

The entity lives shown in Figure 5.17 need careful investigation. Three new maintenance functions are required, function 6, customer maintenance, function 7, product maintenance, and function 8, price table maintenance. Each of these functions will insert, modify and delete entity occurrences.

The entities invoice and invoice line are only inserted. This is satisfactory in this system, since the entities are further processed by a sales accounting system. The remaining entities order head, order line and delivery may be deleted from the system when all the deliveries for an order have been invoiced. Function 4 will therefore be allowed to delete entities order head, order line and delivery subject to the above criteria. Each entity now possesses a complete life.

Figure 5.19 shows a revised entity function matrix.

Three new functions have emerged and one has been amended. These new functions need to be added into the required logical DFDs to complete the documentation.

5.4.2 Task 2.7: Create the entity life histories

Each row of the entity function matrix provided a list of functions with its effect on an entity. The entity function matrix cannot show for every entity the sequence of functions, nor can it show the effect of abnormal events. Entity life histories are drawn to chart the sequence of functions in an entity's life and to identify and chart the effect of abnormal events. Each abnormal event requires a function to process the event.

Diagram conventions

There are several diagram conventions for entity life histories. The convention first illustrated is based on the theory of Petri nets. Four structures are used for entity life histories when based on Petri nets, Figure 5.20.

The ellipse is used as a diagrammatic start and end symbol. It is annotated with the entity name.

The square is used for a function. The function name is written into the square and the function DFD number is written into the box in the bottom right corner of the square. Its effect on the entity is written into the bottom left box. The first function after the start oval must be the insertion of the entity into the database.

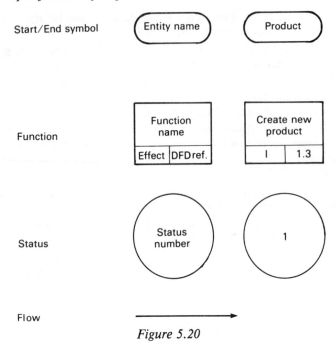

Figure 5.20

The circle is used to show the status of the entity. Circles are simply numbered.

Arrows indicate the transition from one status to another by the action of a function.

Figure 5.21 shows an entity life history.

The entity order is inserted into the database by function 1.1, order entry. The order then takes on the status 1. It is modified by functions 3.2, produce delivery note, and 3.3, invoice, then deleted by function 4.7, receive payment of invoice. Note that function 3.2 cannot take place unless the status of the order is 1, that is, an order exists. After function 3.2, the status is set to 2. Similarly, function 3.3, invoice, has a 'valid previous' status of 2 and a 'set to' status of 3 and function 4.7, receive payment of invoice, has a 'valid previous' status of 2 and no 'set to' status.

Functions which insert, modify or delete entities are shown on the entity life history. All of these functions modify the entity status; functions which only read do not modify the status.

Simple life

Many entities have simple lives. An occurrence of an entity is inserted, read, perhaps many times, and eventually deleted, Figure 5.22. Note that since read functions do not affect an entity's status, they are not shown on the entity life history.

ENTITY LIFE HISTORY

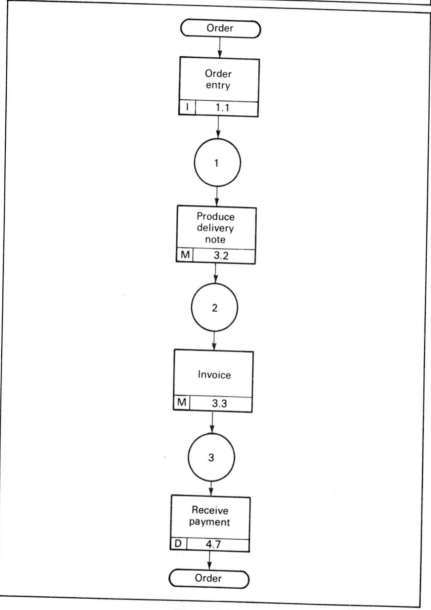

Figure 5.21

ENTITY LIFE HISTORY

SYSTEM: *SIMPLE LIFE*	DATE:
AUTHOR: *G. CUTTS*	PAGE: of

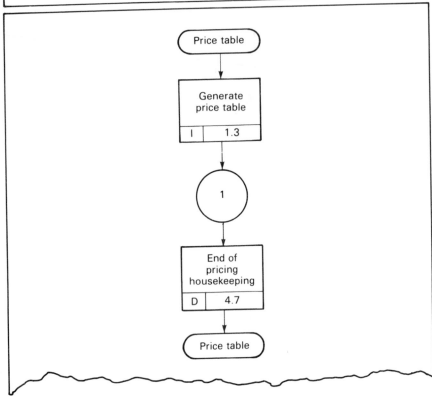

Figure 5.22

A minor extension of this simple life is shown in Figure 5.21. The entity, order, is inserted, modified to show the quantity delivered by the function, produce delivery note, further modified to indicate that an invoice has been produced by the function, invoice, and finally deleted by the function, receive payment.

Only one delivery is allowed against each order if the entity, order, has the life history, Figure 5.21. Multiple deliveries are allowed in Figure 5.23.

The function, produce invoice for delivery, re-sets the status to 1, which allows the function, produce delivery note, to execute. However, when the status of the order entity is set to 1, two functions can occur, produce

ENTITY LIFE HISTORY

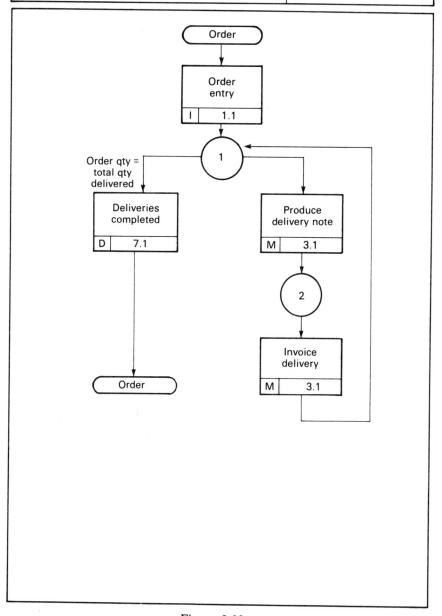

Figure 5.23

delivery note, and deliveries completed. The choice of function to execute can only be made based on further information, for example, the total quantity delivered to date. The entity life history can indicate choice, by simple annotation of the arcs. Note also that the order cannot be deleted if a delivery note exists which has not been invoiced since the status would be 2 preventing the function, deliveries completed, from executing.

Figure 5.24 shows an entity life history for the entity, order, where there exists a requirement to show separately the first and last deliveries.

Function 2.1, produce first delivery note, is very slightly different to functions 2.2, produce delivery note, and 2.3, produce last delivery note. They differ only in wording, 'this is your first/a/your last delivery'. The status indicators now provide more information concerning the entity.

Status 1 order accepted, no deliveries made
   2 order accepted, 1 or more deliveries made, last not invoiced
   3 order accepted, 1 or more deliveries made, and invoiced
   4 order accepted, all deliveries made, last not invoiced

Diagram structures

Three structures have been introduced, sequence, selection, and iteration. Figure 5.25 shows these simple constructs.

The diagram structures, which equate to standard programming structures, provide an excellent relationship with process design. Data design and process design therefore possess a common approach. The structures also allow entity life histories to be developed top down, a proven, well-understood fashion.

Concurrent functions

Sequence, selection and iteration only allow functions to execute in sequence, that is, one function followed by another. There are many functions where sequence is not important; functions may execute concurrently.

The entity, customer account, may be modified to record deliveries and invoices raised against the account concurrently with modification to record the total value of payments received, Figure 5.26.

The easiest way of handling the status indicators is to create a separate one for each of the concurrent lives. It is important to understand that this entity life is different from that shown in Figure 5.27, since with the concurrent lives, payments may be received when the B status is set to 2. This is not possible in Figure 5.27.

The introduction of a second status indicator creates a status vector, a generalisation of the simple status indicator. The status vector, Figure 5.26,

ENTITY LIFE HISTORY

SYSTEM: SEPARATE 1st & last DELIVERIES	DATE:
AUTHOR: G. CUTTS	PAGE: 1 of 1

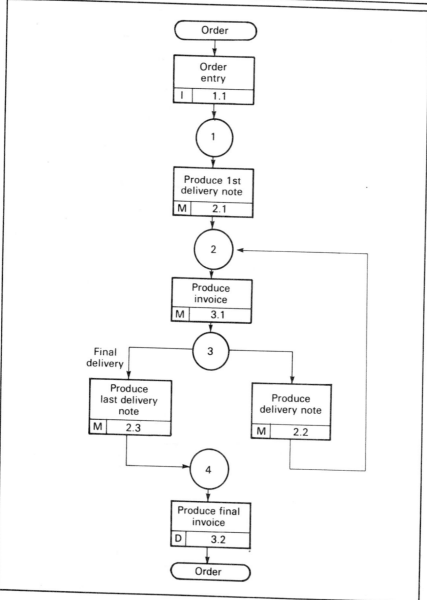

Figure 5.24

Sequence

Selection

Iteration

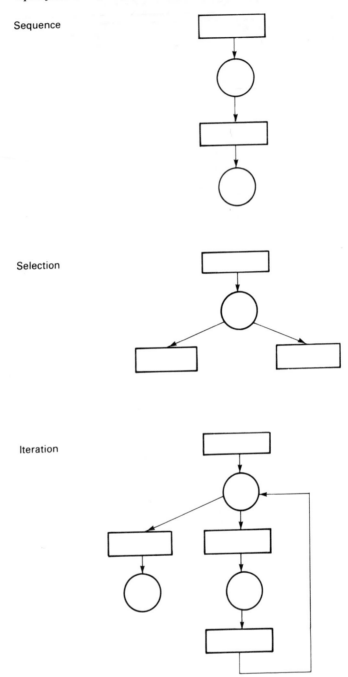

Figure 5.25

ENTITY LIFE HISTORY

SYSTEM: CHAPTER 5 EXAMPLE	DATE:
AUTHOR: B. CUTTS	PAGE: 1 of 1

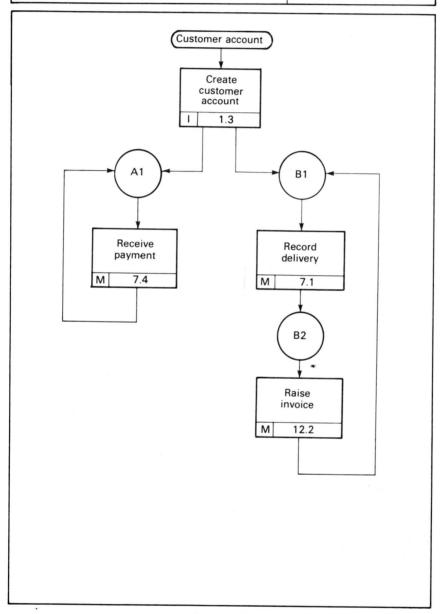

Figure 5.26

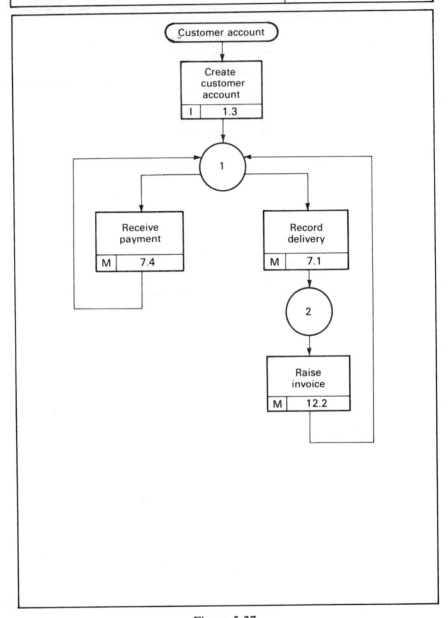

Figure 5.27

has the following interpretation:

> A B
> Status vector ⟨1 1⟩ Account created, functions 7.1 & 7.4 may execute concurrently
> ⟨1 2⟩ Account created, functions 12.2 & 7.4 may execute concurrently

It could be argued that no payment should be received until the first invoice has been issued; this could be easily incorporated into the entity life history.

Entities may therefore have concurrent lives, shown using the diagram construct shown in Figure 5.28.

Each individually executing entity life may use sequence, selection and iteration constructs and, of course, be developed using top down design techniques.

The conclusion of concurrently executing lives does not require any new construct. The selection construct with identical criteria applied to all lives is sufficient. All lives must provide an input into the function.

Where more than two lives exist, concurrency may be gradually reduced. Figure 5.29 shows a possible life history for the entity customer account.

A choice of functions can take place when, and only when, the status vector is ⟨1 1⟩. Either functions 7.1 and 7.4 may execute singly, or concurrently, or function 1.4 may execute, if the total of payments received equals the total invoice value. The choice does not mean that function 1.4 must execute when the criterion is satisfied, only that it may execute.

Abnormal lives

The documentation of standard lives for each entity is followed by careful analysis of each life for abnormal but possible situations. For example, 'what happens to customer accounts where payment is never received?' In most cases, arcs are required to allow premature deletion of an entity due to a variety of reasons.

The status points to be linked to the deletion activity require careful choice, as not all status points should be linked. For example, if a customer account is being closed because of bad debts, all deliveries should still be invoiced for accounting purposes before the account is closed. Status ⟨1 2⟩, Figure 5.26, should, therefore, not be linked to the account closing function.

All choice arcs should be annotated. These abnormal life arcs require choice between continuing with the normal life or executing some abnormal termination. They should therefore be annotated with the choice criterion. Figure 5.30 shows an abnormal termination arc.

The account can only be closed when the status is 3. Status 3 may be reached from status 1, when there is no debt, via a normal closure route, or from status 2, when there are payments outstanding. In this case, status 3 is only reached via the function, 12.2, claim insurance. The function, claim insurance, would probably have been identified during stage 1, analysis, and would therefore be recorded on the DFDs. This is not always the case with abnormal terminations, resulting in the identification of new functions. These new functions should be recorded on the required logical DFDs, to keep the documentation up to date.

Complete life

The construction of an entity life history ensures that each entity possesses a complete life. Each occurrence of the entity in the database must be at some appropriate stage in its life, the stage being represented by the status indicator or status vector.

Moreover, each complete life possesses a beginning, a normal life, a possible abnormal life, and a series of functions which always lead to an end to the life. Entity occurrences are inserted, behave properly and are eventually deleted from the database. The designer of the database can be assured that the functions specified by the system act upon entities within the database in a prescribed and controlled fashion.

The inclusion of the status as an attribute of the entity provides some of the control. Each entity occurrence will have associated with that occur-

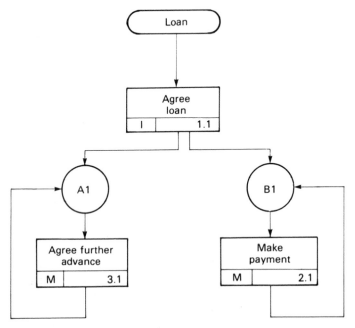

Figure 5.28 Concurrent lives

ENTITY LIFE HISTORY

SYSTEM: *CHAPTER 5 EXAMPLE*

DATE:

AUTHOR: *G. CUTTS*

PAGE: I of I

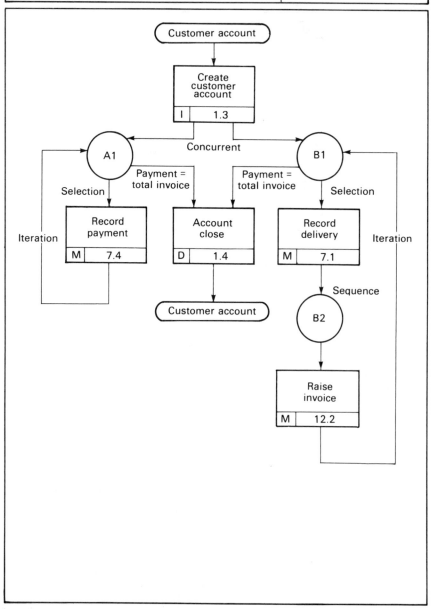

Figure 5.29

ENTITY LIFE HISTORY

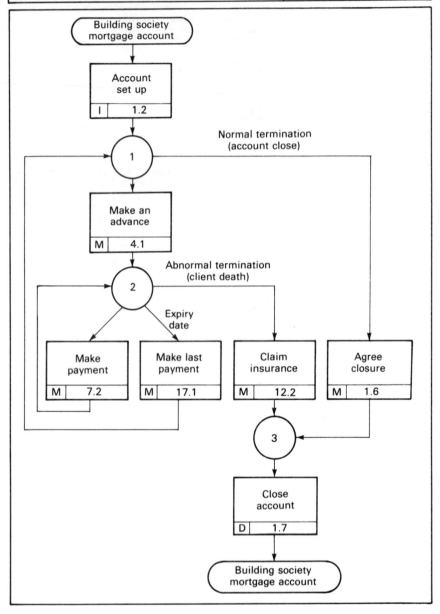

Figure 5.30

rence the status. This instantly limits the number of valid processes which may have an effect on the entity. Each process specification will first test the entity status before execution, setting the new status after successful completion of processing. Entity statuses are therefore important in stage 5, logical process design.

Petri net convention
The entity life history convention using Petri nets enables the dynamic concept of an entity life history to be modelled by the movement of tokens.

A Petri net is made up of places, the circles or states on the entity life histories, and transitions, the functions on the entity life histories. A marked Petri net includes the idea of tokens which reside on the places.

Figure 5.31 shows a Petri net; Figure 5.32 shows a marking of the Petri net.

The initial marking, Figure 5.32, shows a token on place a, with zero tokens on all the other places.

Using Petri net terminology, transition 1 may now occur; it possesses a token on all of its input places. A token on place 'a' represents a state of the entity life history where the only valid function which may execute is function 1.

A successful occurrence of transition 1, that is, successful execution of function 1, removes the token from place 'a' and places it on place 'b'. The 'valid previous' and 'set to' statuses for each function within the entity life history is represented by the position and movement of the tokens. Figure 5.33 shows the marking or status after function 1 has successfully executed.

Function 2 or 3 may now execute as both have a token on their input places. Note that this construct models choice or if... then.... Either functions 2 and 4 execute or functions 3 and 5. Figure 5.34 shows the movement of tokens for execution of functions 2 and 4.

When a transition occurs or a function executes, a token is placed on all output places. Petri nets may therefore be used to model parallel execution, Figure 5.35.

The successful execution of function 1 removes the token from place 'a' and inserts tokens on to all the output places, 'b' and 'c', Figure 5.36.

Functions 2 and 3 are now enabled and may execute in parallel. The status is given for each entity life history by the position of the tokens. Essentially this is a vector with one entry for each place. The marking of Figure 5.35 is

1
0
0
0
0

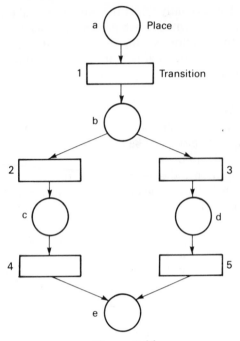

Figure 5.31

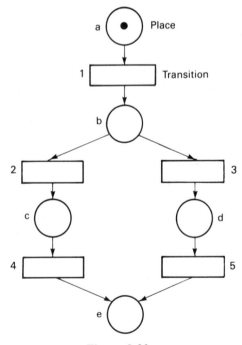

Figure 5.32

and the marking of Figure 5.36 is

0
1
1
0
0

This mathematical representation of the marking may be enhanced by one of the Petri net. Two matrices can represent a Petri net, a pre-condition matrix (Figure 5.37) and a post-condition matrix (Figure 5.38).

Read each column of the matrix as follows. For function 1 to execute, there must be a token on place 'a', the 'valid previous' status for function 1, obtained from the pre-condition matrix.

After successful completion of function 1, tokens must be inserted on places 'b' and 'c', the 'set to' status for function 1, obtained from the post-condition matrix. This mathematical format for entity life histories provides a convenient storage method.

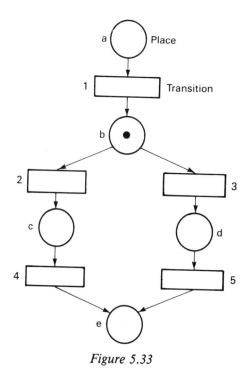

Figure 5.33

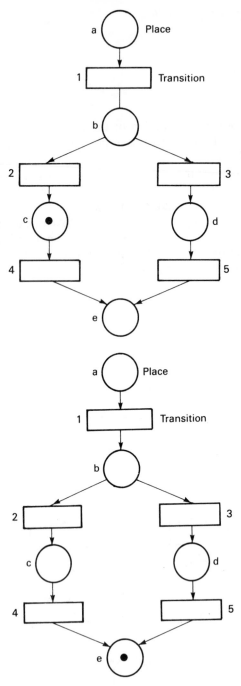

Figure 5.34

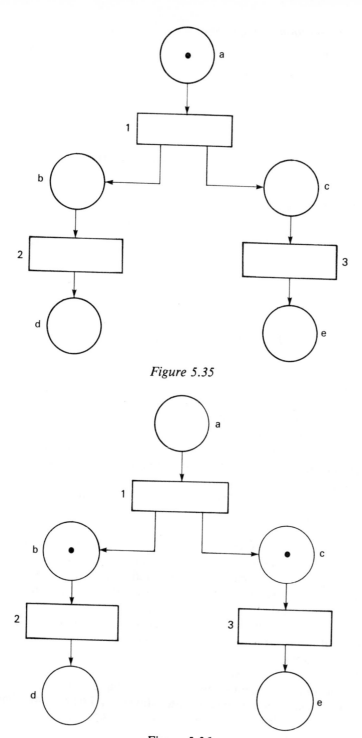

Figure 5.35

Figure 5.36

Function	1	2	3
Place			
a	I	O	O
b	O	I	O
c	O	O	I
d	O	O	O
e	O	O	O

Figure 5.37 Pre-condition matrix

Function Place	1	2	3
a	O	O	O
b	I	O	O
c	I	O	O
d	O	I	O
e	O	O	I

Figure 5.38 Post-condition matrix

Hierarchical convention

Other conventions for entity life histories are based on hierarchical and network constructs. Figure 5.39 shows an entity life history using the hierarchical constructs.

It is equivalent to Figure 5.21. The 'valid previous' and 'set to' statuses for each function are shown either side a solidus, e.g. 2/3, where the 'valid previous' status is 2 and the 'set to' status is 3.

The asterisk notation is used to indicate iteration. Figure 5.40 is therefore equivalent to Figure 5.23 where iterations of functions 2.1 and 3.1 are allowed.

The constructs in Figures 5.39 and 5.40 show sequence and iteration. Selection is achieved using the circle notation to represent an optional function. An optional null function is also required. Figure 5.41 shows an order being inserted either via order entry or via a function which generates orders to satisfy a previously negotiated contract.

Abnormal lives are shown using selection and a notation using Q and R for quit and resume. Figure 5.42 shows a possible order cancellation. The entity life history may quit at the functions indicated and resume with the cancellation of the order. Alternatively, if the order is processed normally, then the possible cancellation null function should be chosen.

The final construct required is also shown in Figure 5.42. Parallel horizontal lines indicate that functions 3.1 and 3.2 may execute in any sequence or in parallel.

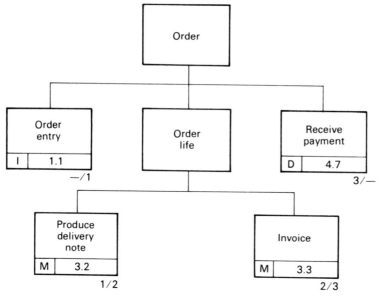

Figure 5.39

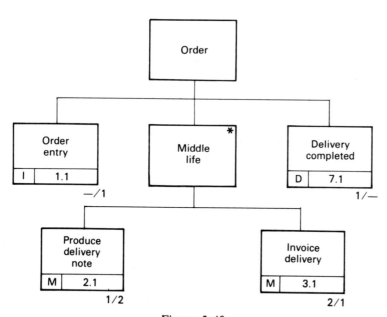

Figure 5.40

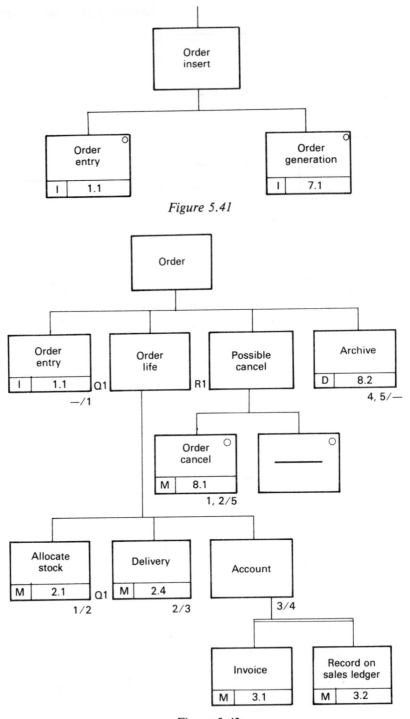

Figure 5.41

Figure 5.42

Network convention

Network entity life histories are based on the diagram conventions, shown in Figure 5.43.

The equivalent entity life histories to Figures 5.21 and 5.23 are shown in Figures 5.44 and 5.45.

The status indicator is dealt with in exactly the same fashion as the hierarchical entity life histories. The asterisk is used either within a box (Figure 5.45) or within an individual modify circle to represent zero or many iterations of the box or circle.

Selection is achieved by simply following the arcs on the network (Figure 5.46) and parallel functions are shown using the box notation (Figure 5.47).

Abnormal lives are easily added using the arcs in a similar fashion to those arcs used by the Petri net approach.

5.5 Stage 2 summary

The specification of requirements comprises seven tasks which may be divided into three sections.

Tasks 2.1 and 2.2 develop the required logical model. The output from this initial section are the required logical DFDs and a required entity

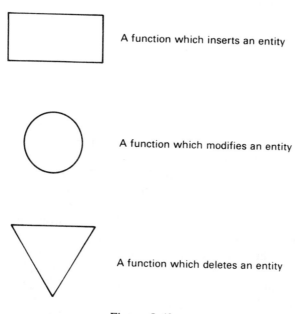

A function which inserts an entity

A function which modifies an entity

A function which deletes an entity

Figure 5.43

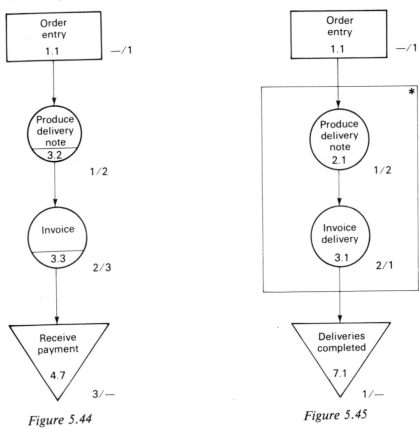

Figure 5.44   *Figure 5.45*

model. Solutions to problems with the current system and requirements for the new system should be incorporated into the required logical models.

Tasks 2.3, 2.4 and 2.5 provide the detailed documentation for the specification of requirements. These tasks document the entities, the data flows, the input, the output and the functions.

The final section comprises tasks 2.6 and 2.7. These tasks, which create the entity function matrix and the entity life histories, provide a third view of the system, a dynamic view, showing the effect of functions on entities. This view tests the completeness of the DFDs by charting the documented functions for each entity. The entity life history can then be analysed to determine if additional functions, or modifications to functions, are necessary in order to ensure that the entity has a complete life in all circumstances.

Any additional functions or modifications to functions must be documented on the required logical DFDs. It may be necessary to return to tasks 2.1 to 2.5 to bring the documentation up to date.

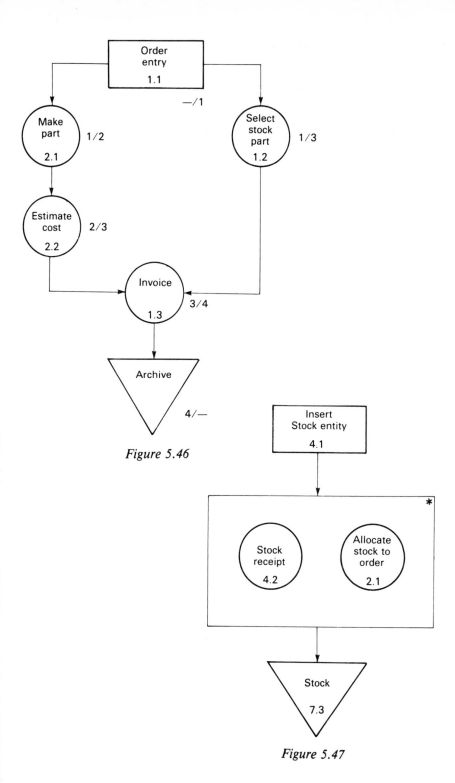

Figure 5.46

Figure 5.47

The specification of requirements, which must now be reviewed and accepted by the user, comprises the seven sets of documents.

Stage 3 will use the required logical DFDs to postulate implementation or business options and to select an option for implementation.

Stage 4 will use the entity model, the entity descriptions, the input descriptions and the output descriptions to undertake logical data design.

Stage 5 will use the function descriptions, the entity function matrix, the entity life histories and the logical data design to undertake logical process design.

6

Selection of a system option (for further development)

6.1 Introduction

Chapter six, selection of a system option for further development, describes the third stage of SSADM, Figure 6.1. The prime input to stage 3 is the required logical DFDs; however, many of the other pieces of documentation from stage 2, the specification of requirements, will act as useful reference documents. The objective of stage 3 is to produce a set of required physical DFDs, a high-level specification of how the new system will be implemented.

The required logical DFDs represented a solution to the system problems as well as incorporating the logical requirements for the new system. Stage 3's objective is to produce a set of physical DFDs which represent the required system having taken due account of all the constraints including hardware, software and people available. A new physical system is required which offers a best fit with the requirements, the hardware, the software and the user, and is achievable within the resources available for further development and implementation.

Stage 3 provides a formal link between the feasibility study findings, the terms of reference for the project, the developed specification of requirements and the system to be designed and implemented.

There are three tasks within stage 3. Task 3.1 postulates a number of system options together with a cost–benefit analysis for each option, task 3.2 makes a selection of one of the options, and task 3.3 sets some additional constraints on the design for the selected option. This option is then developed into a detailed logical design by stages 4 and 5.

6.2 Task 3.1: Postulate system options

Figure 6.2 shows a level 1 required logical DFD.

The responsibility box, associated with each function, was not used on the logical DFDs. This box is used in stage 3 to indicate how the processing

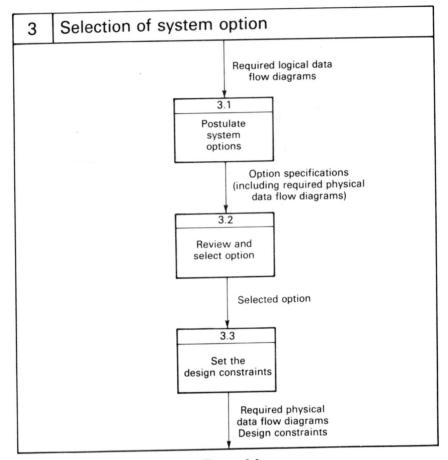

Figure 6.1

represented by each function box will be implemented. Options for the completion of the box are therefore words such as: computer, sales office, depot, warehouse etc. Indeed, with each of the options, further detail could be added such as on-line computer or batch computer.

The initial exercise is carried out using the level 1 DFD, the highest level. It is possible that at this level, a function might be part clerical and part computer. Entries such as warehouse/computer are acceptable with the level 2 DFD being used to indicate exactly which sub-functions are to be implemented via a computer and which sub-functions will be carried out by staff in the warehouse.

Figures 6.3, 6.4 and 6.5 show three possible system solutions.

The solution in Figure 6.3 makes the maximum use of the computer with all functions on it.

DATA FLOW DIAGRAM

SYSTEM: EXAMPLE	DATE:
AUTHOR: G. CUTTS	PAGE: I of I
LEVEL: I ~~CURRENT~~/REQ.	~~PHYS.~~/LOGICAL

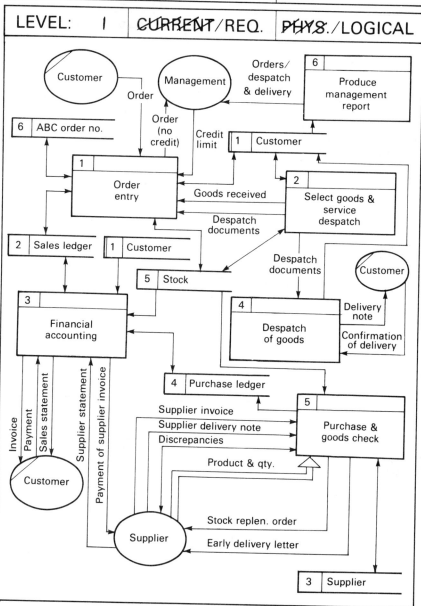

Figure 6.2

DATA FLOW DIAGRAM

SYSTEM: EXAMPLE	DATE:
AUTHOR: G. CUTTS	PAGE: 1 of 1

LEVEL: 1	~~CURRENT~~/REQ.	PHYS./~~LOGICAL~~

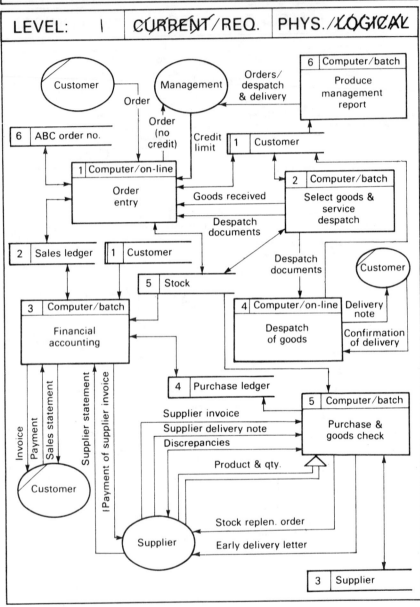

Figure 6.3

DATA FLOW DIAGRAM

SYSTEM: EXAMPLE	DATE:
AUTHOR: G. CUTTS	PAGE: 1 of 1

LEVEL:	CURRENT/REQ.	PHYS./LOGICAL

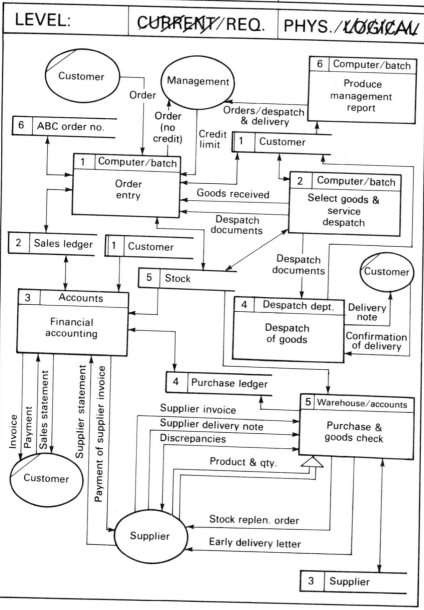

Figure 6.4

DATA FLOW DIAGRAM

SYSTEM: EXAMPLE	DATE:
AUTHOR: G. CUTTS	PAGE: 1 of 1

LEVEL: 1	~~CURRENT~~/REQ.	PHYS./~~LOGICAL~~

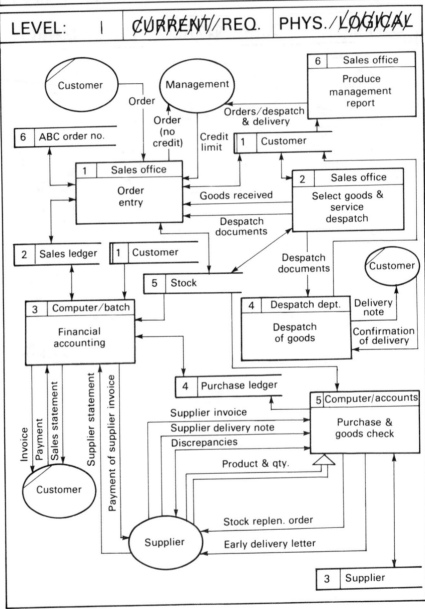

Figure 6.5

The solution in Figure 6.4 uses the computer for functions dealing with orders and customers.

The solution in Figure 6.5 uses the computer for financial functions only.

6.2.1 The computer system boundary

For each option, the boundary of the computer system can be established. All functions for which the responsibility is computer are inside the boundary. If a level 1 function has a joint computer/clerical responsibility, e.g. Figure 6.5, function 5, then the boundary may be determined by including some of the functions from the appropriate level 2 DFD.

Figure 6.6 shows option 3, Figure 6.5, in more detail. Function 5, where the responsibility was shared between computer and accounts, is decomposed to show exact responsibilities using the level 2 DFD.

All functions, and their sub-functions, marked 'computer' are considered to be inside the boundary of the required new system. The inclusion of functions within the boundary is therefore straightforward, but the inclusion of data stores is not so easy. If a data store is excluded, then any interaction with that, now, manually maintained data store and the computer must be via input or output documents. Alternatively, if a data store is included, then any interaction with non-computer functions must be via input or output documents.

The number of data flows each data store possesses with functions inside and outside the boundary is one guide to whether the data store should be included or excluded. A second guide is the maintenance of the data store. If the transactions which maintain a data store are within the system, then the data store should be within the system. A third guide is the problems and requirements list. If it is necessary to provide a computer data store to solve a stated problem or meet a new requirement, then the data store should be included inside the boundary.

The boundary of the computer system can now be fully agreed and the new physical functions, data stores, input and output documented.

Each option will have different system functions, data stores, input and output. In general, therefore, each option will have a different impact on the problems and requirements list. The impact on the list must be documented as part of the option specification.

Figure 6.7 shows two possible boundaries.

Function 5, which will be implemented as a manual process, requires information from data store 5. With the outer boundary, a computer function is required to provide the information, either as an on-line enquiry function or as a computer report. In this case a daily report is appropriate, a new function, produce daily low stock report, is required. This is an additional output from the system, which will of course affect the total cost of

DATA FLOW DIAGRAM

SYSTEM: A B C	DATE:
AUTHOR: G. CUTTS	PAGE: 1 of 1

LEVEL: 2	~~CURRENT~~/REQ.	PHYS./~~LOGICAL~~

TITLE: PURCHASE & GOODS CHECK

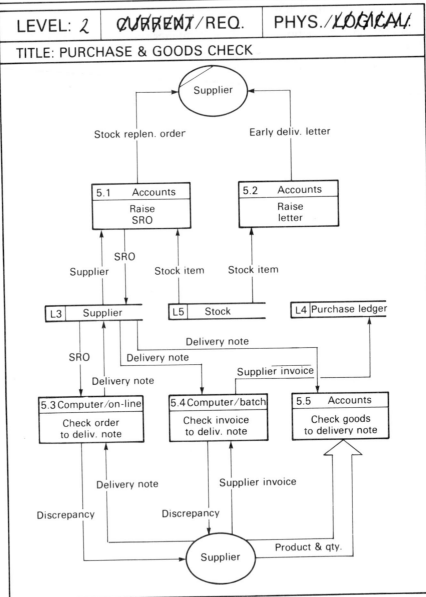

Figure 6.6 Purchase and goods check

DATA FLOW DIAGRAM

SYSTEM: EXAMPLE

DATE:

AUTHOR: G. CUTTS

PAGE: 1 of 1

LEVEL: 1 | CURRENT/REQ. | PHYS./LOGICAL

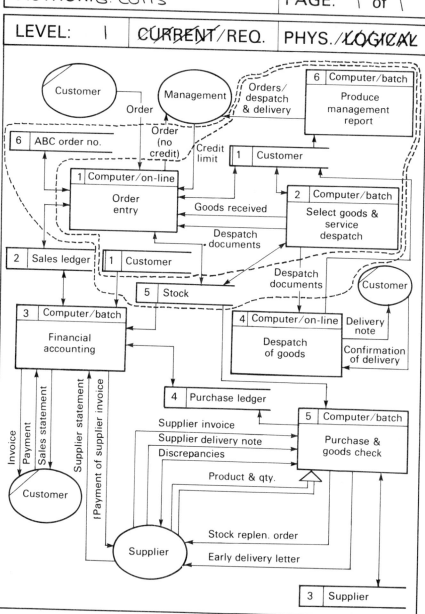

Figure 6.7

implementing the option. This new function and output must be added to the existing documentation.

Data store 6 provides the next order number to be used as a unique key for orders received. There are two options shown. Option 1, the inner boundary, would require the computer to print the last used number. At the start of the next run, the number could be input via parameter to the program. Option 2 would require the program to store the number at the completion of processing and to retrieve it at the start of the next run.

Part of the option specification is therefore a set of required physical DFDs. The diagrams form one of the inputs to task 3.2, option selection.

6.2.2   Constraints

All of the required physical systems postulated must adhere to all of the constraints of the project. Decisions on hardware, software, people, timescales, costs etc. which were not specified as part of the project terms of reference or as part of the feasibility study report must now be taken. Some of the system constraints will have emerged during the detailed investigation and modelling tasks. Mandatory reports, mandatory on-line facilities and minimum response times are examples of constraints which emerge during detailed investigation. These constraints should be documented as part of the requirements list produced during stage 1.

In general terms, however, very few projects enjoy a free choice of hardware, software, people, development timescales etc. These constraints represent decisions taken very often before the commencement of the project. Projects have to be implemented on currently available hardware, with existing software and people, and with development timescales imposed by management. This is the real environment of many projects.

Constraints which must be considered include the resources available for further development, costs and timescales, mandatory requirements, logical and physical; and the required service levels, response times and performance levels.

6.2.3   Implementation considerations

The responsibility box, on the required physical DFDs, developed at the start of task 3.1, specified for each function how it will be implemented: on-line, batch or manual.

This is just one of the considerations regarding the planned implementation. Other implementation decisions need to be taken before the detailed design stages may commence.

Decisions need to be taken regarding the hardware and software to be used. For example, 'Is a package to be used for part or all of the system?' 'Does the software provide sophisticated database management facilities?'

'Will the system be centralised or distributed?' 'What is the total available on-line disk capacity?' 'What method of data communication will be used?'

Decisions taken on issues such as these will have an impact on the design stages. Decisions taken on many of the issues will impact the user. The user must therefore be involved in the discussions on the user interface, and on organisational and staffing issues.

The final areas for detailed consideration before any option is selected are the design and implementation methods to be employed throughout the remainder of the project.

The constraints must be observed by all the postulated options. Consideration of implementation matters may well result in different decisions for each option. The effect of the decisions taken must be carefully documented and presented to task 3.2 as part of the option specification.

The option specification comprises a set of physical DFDs and a narrative addressing implementation issues.

6.2.4 Outline sizing

The selection of hardware may well be influenced by the total amount of on-line disk capacity required. An estimate of the disk capacity can be obtained by simple processing of the entity model. The entity model shown in Figure 6.8 has been annotated with figures to show the maximum number of occurrences of each entity. All data is retained in the system for six months. For example, an aircraft makes two flights per day, seven days per week. Twenty-six weeks' data is held within the system. Within the system, each aircraft has data on $2 \times 7 \times 26 = 364$ flights.

Approximately, then, there are:

30 aircraft each making 364 flights	= 11,000 flights
100 airports each with 55 flights in and out	= 11,000 flights
11,000 flights each with 100 bookings	= 1,100,000 bookings
1,000,000 passengers each making, on average, 1.1 bookings	= 1,100,000 bookings

The next task is to estimate the size of each entity. For example, the passenger entity may have name and address as attributes, giving a size of 250 bytes, say.

The total disk capacity required for system data can be easily calculated.

Entity name	No. of entity occurrences	Entity size	Total space required
Aircraft	30	100	3,000
Airport	100	300	30,000
Flight	11,000	100	1,100,000
Booking	1,100,000	50	55,000,000
Passenger	1,000,000	250	250,000,000
		Total required	306,133,000

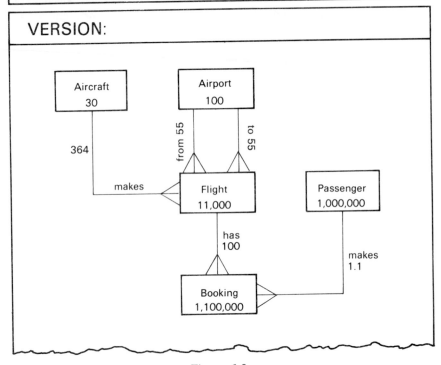

Figure 6.8

The total space required is just over 3×10^8 bytes plus an allowance for system software. This may be too large. It may be necessary, therefore, to reduce the number of passenger records maintained on-line, for example.

6.2.5 Supporting narrative

The options specification may require further narrative to make it acceptable to the users. The physical DFDs may need to be enhanced with descriptions of the environment and the system. The environment description should address both technical and social issues. The technical descriptions should provide an overview of the hardware and software to aid the user's understanding and therefore to support the decisions documented as part of the implementation considerations. The social description should provide an overview of the user's operational environment to further the user's understanding and to provide a basis for discussion of the implementation considerations.

Both narratives should refer to existing documentation whenever possible. They should not provide a narrative of existing documents. Documents which should be referenced include the required physical DFDs, the hardware and software vendor manuals plus any relevant internal standards, such as project control standards, methods standards, or performance standards.

The option specification requires two further items: an impact analysis, specifically addressing the impact on the problems and requirements list of the option, and an option cost–benefit analysis.

The impact analysis should document precisely for each problem how, in the new system, the problem is overcome. Many problems are removed when the current physical DFDs are transformed to the current logical diagrams. That is, many of the problems that users describe are associated with the current implementation. There is a tendency, however, to re-introduce problems of a physical nature when transforming the required logical DFD to the required physical. Problems of duplicated data stores and physical functions emerge. It is important, therefore, to describe precisely how, in real terms, each problem is solved in the new system.

The impact analysis should also document how each of the requirements is implemented in the new system.

The ratio of computer functions to manual functions and the number of computer files will determine the costs for the design and implementation of the system. They will also determine the costs of hardware, software, training, operation and future modification and maintenance. A very good estimate of the future cost of continuing the project can therefore be calculated.

Further, by reference to the impact analysis and the technical and social descriptions, the benefits to the organisation of the project can be established.

A cost–benefit analysis can therefore be undertaken for each option.

An option specification comprises a set of required physical DFDs; a narrative describing technical aspects, social aspects and implementation considerations; an impact analysis; and a cost–benefit analysis.

The effort required to produce an option specification is therefore considerable, even if it can be based upon a good feasibility report. Two or three options only should be developed to this advanced stage. A high-level selection process is required to eliminate all of the options which are technically or socially unacceptable. This can be done by careful study of the required physical DFDs. Six or seven options can be postulated using DFDs with two or three being selected for detailed analysis.

6.3 Task 3.2: Select the required option

The selection process chooses between a number of options, selecting one for continued development. The selection should be carried out by the user, advised and guided by the project team.

Four sets of documentation assist the decision-making process: the physical DFDs, the narrative, the impact analysis and the cost–benefit analysis.

All of the options should meet the constraints set out in the terms of reference and in the feasibility study report. Typical constraints would be on resources available for the development; hardware, software and staff; and on the timescale for development, say, within six months of the commencement of the project. The selection process is very much therefore between implementation or business options.

That is,

What processing will be manual?
What will be on-line?
What will be batch?
Which data stores will be computer files?
What will be the impact on the user's operation?

One method of involving users and senior management in the selection process is to prepare a presentation. This should present the logical specification followed by overviews of each of the options. The overviews should concentrate on how, in each case, the logical specification would be implemented. This initial part of the presentation should concentrate on educating the users on the options. The second part should concentrate on providing sufficient information to allow the user, assisted by the project team, to select one of the options.

The major items to be included within the presentation are the impact analysis and the cost–benefit analysis.

A possible consequence of the presentation may be that no decision is reached. The project team must then be available for follow-up advice and guidance during the decision-making process. They must also be available to rework options for minor changes, to combine options and to develop further options as directed by the user senior management.

With all decision-making processing, no decision is the easiest. It is the responsibility of the project team to record the user's requests and management decisions so that the user can be guided towards the selection of an original or reworked option for further development.

6.4 Task 3.3: Set the design constraints

Many of the constraints on the design have been specified as part of the option specification. The new system input, output, files and functions are identified on the required physical DFDs. The hardware and software available are described in the narrative and the resources available for the design and implementation are documented as part of the cost–benefit analysis. All of these constraints must be adhered to during the detailed design.

There are, however, other design considerations. The design must meet standards on security, recovery and privacy. It must adhere to any installation standards and it must provide for efficient audit and control.

If installation standards exist, then it is sufficient to state that the design must meet those standards. If no standards exist, the required level of security, recovery and privacy must be specified before stages 4 and 5 commence.

6.5   Stage 3 summary

Stage 3 is not a reworking of the feasibility study. It is a further investigation into the options available for implementation within the constraints already set out in the terms of reference and the feasibility study. Constraints such as the budget, the hardware and software available and the people available must be honoured if set out in the feasibility study documentation.

All options postulated must adhere to these constraints.

Stage 3 is an investigation and specification of various implementation options. Each option specifies a different physical interpretation of the stage 2 logical specification of requirements. Stage 3 also includes the selection of an option for the design stages and the setting of constraints on the design.

Selection of the system option is perhaps the most important stage. This involves the user in a detailed examination of the specification of requirements in the form of implementation options. The selection of one of the options by the user is, in effect, acceptance by the user of the specification of requirements, which contributes a major milestone in any project.

7

Logical data design

7.1 Introduction

Chapter 7 describes the fourth stage of SSADM. Stage 4 uses the required physical DFDs, the entity model and the entity descriptions from stage 2, and the input/output descriptions, to produce a logical entity model and a revised set of entity descriptions. The logical entity model will form the basis for the physical file or database design and the revised entity descriptions will form the basis for the record descriptions.

Figure 7.1 shows the tasks for stage 4.

7.2 Task 4.1: Select data structures

The normalisation task, while relatively straightforward, can be time-consuming. Careful selection of data structures, as candidates for normalisation, is therefore necessary. Sufficient data structures need to be analysed to ensure the resultant entity model is complete. Normalisation should be considered as a further process in the refinement of the entity model, not a technique to produce the final version. All of the techniques used in the construction of the final entity model can be used to further refine the model. If additional data structures are created during the later stages of the project, then normalisation can be performed on the new data structures resulting in yet further refinement of the entity model.

It is important to identify the major data structures. These will include:

(1) output documents/screen content;
(2) input documents/screen content.

In many cases it is only necessary to analyse the output documents and screen content as this represents the data necessary to be stored by the system. A list of data structures can be easily obtained from the level 1 required physical DFD, the system's input and output. It is particularly important

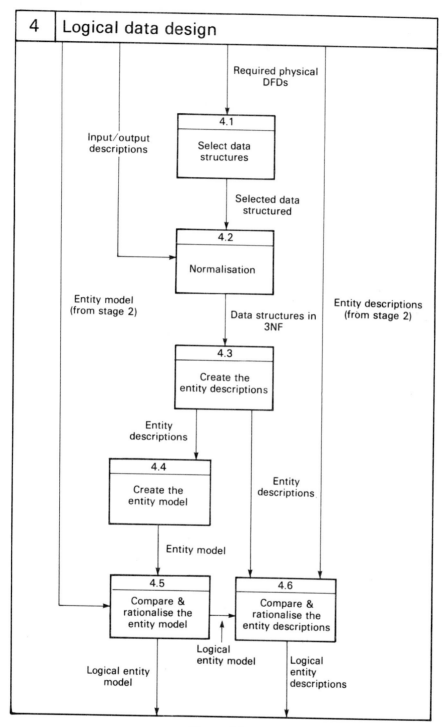

| 4 | Logical data design |

Required physical DFDs

4.1

Select data structures

Input/output descriptions

Selected data structured

4.2

Normalisation

Entity model (from stage 2)

Entity descriptions (from stage 2)

Data structures in 3NF

4.3

Create the entity descriptions

Entity descriptions

4.4

Create the entity model

Entity descriptions

Entity model

4.5

Compare & rationalise the entity model

4.6

Compare & rationalise the entity descriptions

Logical entity model

Logical entity model

Logical entity descriptions

Figure 7.1

Order	Customer number
	Customer order number
	Customer address
	International Standard Book Number
	Title
	Author
	Price each
	Quantity ordered

Figure 7.2

to include output which was not in the original system. Entities and relationships necessary to generate new output may not have been included in the entity model which was constructed as part of systems analysis since this essentially was a documentation of the data structures supporting the current system.

The first sub-task of the normalisation task involves listing all the fields on a data structure. Figure 7.2 gives a list of fields on a sales order document for textbooks; Figure 7.3 gives a list of fields on a new customer agreement form; note that the fields in Figure 7.3 are a subset of the fields in Figure 7.2 so there is nothing to be gained by applying the normalisation process to the new customer agreement form. Similarly, the textbook data structure (Figure 7.4) may be eliminated from the normalisation task.

Task 4.1 yields a set of data structures as candidates for task 4.2, normalisation. The deliverable item from task 4.1 is therefore a list of candidate data structures for normalisation.

New customer	Customer number
	Customer address

Figure 7.3

Textbook	International Standard Book Number
	Title
	Author
	Price each

Figure 7.4

7.3   Task 4.2: Normalisation

Normalisation consists of four sub-tasks. It is a technique for transforming complex data structures into simple tables which form the basis of the third normal form entity model.

Normalisation sub-tasks
4.2.1   Convert the un-normalised data structures into first normal form (1NF).
4.2.2   Convert each of the data structures generated in 1NF into second normal form (2NF).
4.2.3   Convert each of the 2NF data structures into third normal form (3NF).
4.2.4   Validate the 3NF data structures.

Each sub-task is illustrated using examples.

Representation of data structures
Figure 7.5 shows, in table format, a data structure representing orders for fruit. The table contains three rows each providing details of a given customer's order. Because of the problem of representing rows of varying length on a single line, it is more usual to present the table as shown in Figure 7.6, which still comprises three rows.

A thorough understanding of the data is necessary before the process of normalisation can be successfully undertaken.

Customer number	Customer name	Product number	Product name	Qty.	Price	Product number	Product name	Qty.	Price
J27	Jones	A01	Apples	10	2.00	B14	Bananas	12	3.00
A12	Allen	B14	Bananas	50	3.00	P16	Pears	20	1.50
WO1	Williams	A01	Apples	20	2.00				

Figure 7.5

Customer number	Customer name	Product number	Product name	Qty.	Price
J27	Jones	A01	Apples	10	2.00
		B14	Bananas	12	3.00
A12	Allen	B14	Bananas	50	3.00
		P16	Pears	20	1.50
WO1	Williams	A01	Apples	20	2.00

Figure 7.6

Hidden meaning

In Figure 7.6 the rows are organised in priority sequence. Apples and bananas will be supplied to Jones before Allen and finally Williams. This is very common with manually completed lists, the orders to be supplied first are sorted to the head of the list. Normalisation considers only the logic of the data structure, not the physical presentation. To ensure the information contained in the physical presentation of the data is not lost, an extra column, priority, must be added. For example, the sequence of products within each row may reflect priority, or delivery sequence. The relative positions of rows and columns must not conceal information about the data structures.

Meaningless data names

Figure 7.7 gives a set of column headings, many of which are ambiguous.

The headings must be unique and meaningful for a proper understanding of the data. Figure 7.8 represents the data structure after further discussion with the user.

Each column is now uniquely defined. A thorough understanding of the data is vital to the task of normalisation.

Name	Date	Port	Port	Time
Spirit	14 July 87	Calais	Dover	14.00
Herald	14 July 87	Dover	Dunkirk	10.00

Figure 7.7

Vessel name	Date of sailing	Port from	Port to	Departure time (local)
Spirit	14 July 87	Calais	Dover	14.00
Herald	14 July 87	Dover	Dunkirk	10.00

Figure 7.8

7.3.1   Sub-task 4.2.1: First normal form (1NF)

The first sub-task of normalisation is to remove the groups of repeated data within an un-normalised data structure.

Unique keys must be selected for the complete data structure and for each group of repeated data. Selection of keys is necessary for the normalisation process; however, the process will work for any correctly chosen key. While the process will work for any chosen key, it is sensible to choose one that will be usable as part of the final design.

Choosing a key
(1) Any key chosen must be unique, that is it must uniquely identify a row.
(2) If a choice of keys is possible, lengthy keys and alphanumeric keys should be avoided.

A unique key for the order data structure (Figure 7.6) could be the customer number. This assumes that customers only have one order outstanding at any point in time. In this case, a single attribute provides the key (a simple key). This is not always possible and in some cases a compound key has to be formed from two or more attributes.

If the restriction on outstanding orders was not possible, then a key formed by two attributes would be necessary. A candidate key in this case would be the customer number linked with the date of the order.

In Figure 7.9 it is necessary to choose a compound key formed by the course code and the subject. Both attributes are required to uniquely identify a row.

A simple method of marking the key is by underlining.

Having chosen a key, 1NF is created by removing all groups of repeating attributes. A group can be anything from one attribute to very many. Start by listing in a single column the column headings. Figure 7.10 provides a list of column headings for the data structures shown in Figure 7.6. Note that repeated groups of attributes are marked by a vertical bar and optional attributes are shown enclosed by round brackets ( ).

If a key has not already been chosen for the repeating groups, it should now be chosen. In this case, product number seems an appropriate choice. First normal form is then created by performing the transformation shown by the arrows (Figure 7.11). Two data structures are created, the second structure having several occurrences in the database.

Course code	Subject	Lecturer ID.	Time allocated	Qualification	Number on course
Comp. Stud.	Systems	GC	90	HND	60
Comp. Stud.	Prog.	DS	100	HND	60
Comp. Stud.	Bus. stud.	WW	60	HND	60
Inf. Tech.	Electronics	KE	60	B.Sc.	50
Inf. Tech.	Systems	GC	90	B.Sc.	50
Inf. Tech.	Prog.	DS	90	B.Sc.	50

Figure 7.9

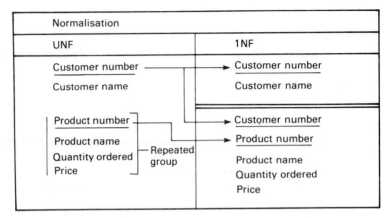

Figure 7.10   *Figure 7.11*

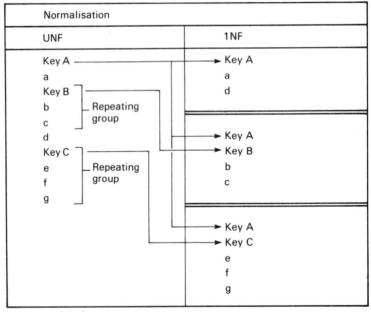

a to g are data items

Figure 7.12

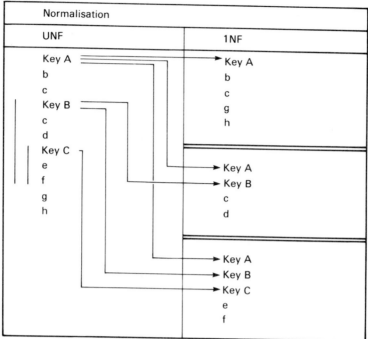

a to h are data items

Figure 7.13

With a simple repeated group as in Figure 7.10, the conversion to 1NF is relatively easy. It is possible, however, to have nested repeating groups or more than one repeating group. The appropriate transformations are shown in Figures 7.12 and 7.13.

7.3.2   Sub-task 4.2.2: Second normal form (2NF)

The sub-task of moving from 1NF to 2NF only applies to data structures with compound keys. Data structures with a simple key in 1NF are automatically in 2NF.

The process requires that each attribute is examined to determine if it is dependent on the whole of the compound key or only part of the compound key. Attributes which only depend upon part of the compound key are shown using arrows, Figure 7.14.

Part name and price only depend on the part itself, not on the customer number. The quantity ordered depends upon the specific part on this order where we have identified it by the customer number.

Three data structures result—Figure 7.15. The attributes which only

Normalisation	
1NF	2NF
Customer number Customer name	Customer number Customer name
Customer number Part number ◄───────┐ Part name ──────────┤ Qty. ordered Price ──────────────┘	Customer number Part number Qty. ordered
	Part number Part name Price

Figure 7.14   *Figure 7.15*

depend on the part number have been extracted to create a third data structure. This leaves only quantity ordered in the second data structure.

7.3.3   Sub-task 4.2.3: Third normal form (3NF)

The sub-task conversion from 2NF to 3NF is similar to the conversion from 1NF to 2NF. Instead of examining the relationship between non-key attributes and attributes in the key, the relationships between pairs of non-key attributes and between pairs of key attributes are established.

Figure 7.16 shows a relationship in 2NF. (Customers only book one holiday at a time.)

The arrows, Figure 7.16, show the relationship between the non-key attributes. Ask 'is attribute A dependent on attribute B or vice versa?' This question must be repeated for all the non-key attribute pairs, and the key attribute pairs.

Extraction of the inter-data dependency creates two relationships in 3NF, Figure 7.17. The hotel address and number of rooms in the hotel do not change from holiday booking to holiday booking.

Hotel code is now a key to a new relationship. Since this attribute, hotel code, appears in the first relationship, it is marked by an asterisk and called a foreign key.

The choice of hotel number as the key for the new relationship was obvious and trivial. This is not always the case and careful examination of the real data may be necessary.

The data structure, Figure 7.18, is in 2NF, but not in 3NF since a relationship exists between job title and salary scale. The 3NF relations are either those shown in Figure 7.19 or those shown in Figure 7.20.

Normalisation	
2NF	3NF
<u>Customer number</u> Customer name Address Hotel code ← Hotel address —— Number of rooms —— Date of holiday Number of nights	<u>Customer number</u> Customer name Address Hotel code* Date of holiday Number of nights
	<u>Hotel code</u> Hotel address Number of rooms

Figure 7.16 Figure 7.17

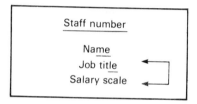

Figure 7.18

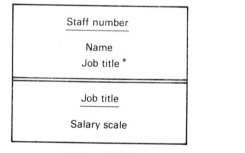

Figure 7.19

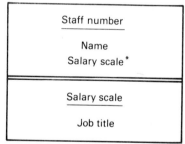

Figure 7.20

The key to the second data structure salary scale/job title needs to be established.

A diagram, Figure 7.21, helps to establish which attribute should be the key.

For each job title there exists only one salary scale, but for each salary

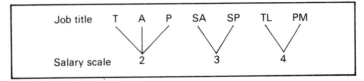

Figure 7.21

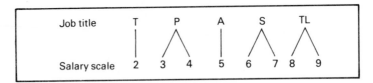

Figure 7.22

scale a range of job titles are possible. Job title therefore becomes the key and Figure 7.19 the 3NF representation.

Alternatively, if the diagram, Figure 7.22, had resulted, then Figure 7.20 would be the correct 3NF representation.

7.3.4   Sub-task 4.2.4: Validation of the 3NF data structures

The normalisation task is based on sound mathematical principles; however, knowledge of the data and the application of common sense contribute good practice.

It is good practice to validate in detail each 3NF data structure to eradicate errors in processing and to discover obscure dependencies.

Errors in the normalisation task can be established by asking the questions: 'For each unique value of the total key can each attribute possess one, and only one value?' and 'Is the value of each attribute directly dependent upon the key or keys?'

For example, the value for discount code, Figure 7.23, can possess only one value for a particular order and product. The answer to the first question is 'Yes'.

| Order number |
| Product code |
| Discount code |

Figure 7.23

Customer code
Discount code

Figure 7.24

However, by further investigation, it can be established that the discount code depends upon the customer identified by customer code. All orders for all products for any given customer have the same discount code. This data structure is therefore replaced by that shown in Figure 7.24, assuming that a data structure already exists linking customer code and order numbers. The answer to the second question would have been 'No'.

The section describing sub-task 4.2.1, first normal form, required that a key be chosen for each of the data structures. This key could be either a simple key or one made up from several simple keys, a compound key. The selection of a key is not always straightforward and often it is necessary to use a composite key or a generated key. A further problem sometimes exists where the key does not exist as a data attribute but is implied by the existence of some other attribute or attributes. Composite keys, generated keys and implied keys must be considered during task 4.2, normalisation.

7.3.5 Keys

Composite keys
Simple keys and compound keys made up of more than one simple key have already been defined. Composite keys are keys made up of two or more attributes where one or more attributes of the key are not simple keys in their own right. Very often a second attribute has to be included to create a unique key.

For example, the key, book number/chapter number, is a composite key since the attribute chapter number has no meaning without its associated book number. Figure 7.25 provides data on equipment in a school, a school inventory.

Equipment code	Description	Identification numbers	Date required
D	Desk	1–100	1/10/80
D	Desk	200–300	1/10/81
C	Chair	1–100	1/10/80
C	Chair	200–300	1/10/81

Figure 7.25

To be able to uniquely identify an individual chair or desk, a composite key equipment code/identification number is required, written:

$$\left\{ \begin{array}{l} \text{equipment code} \\ \text{identification number} \end{array} \right\}$$

In this case, identification number is not unique. Note that composite keys are shown enclosed by curly brackets.

Generated keys

Situations arise where it is necessary to generate a composite key. Consider the data structure, order, in Figure 7.26.

Orders, Figure 7.26, are not unique. Customer A47 has ordered ten of product number 210 on three occasions. A further attribute is required to provide a unique key; this could be date of order, time of order or more simply a sequence number for orders received from a given customer. The composite key, customer number/sequence number, provides a unique but generated composite key, Figure 7.27.

Customer number	Product number	Qty. ordered
A47	210	10
J21	479	15
A47	479	70
A47	210	10
A47	210	10
W15	298	5

Figure 7.26

Customer number Sequence number	Product number	Qty. ordered
A47/1	210	10
J21/1	479	15
A47/2	479	70
A47/3	210	10
A47/4	210	10
W15/1	298	5

Figure 7.27

Implied keys

Figure 7.28 shows a data structure for staff with their project allocation.

There is only an indirect dependency between project charge rate, project code and staff number. The project charge rate actually depends on the staff grade and the project type. The 3NF data structure should be replaced by Figure 7.29, where the project code and staff number are replaced by their implied keys. In this case it is assumed a staff data structure links staff numbers to staff grades and a project data structure links project code to project type.

All staff of a given grade on a specific project type attract the same charge rate.

Normalisation	
UNF	3NF
Staff number Name Project code Project charge code	Staff number Name Staff number Project code Project charge rate

Figure 7.28

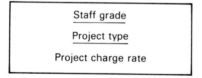

Figure 7.29

Aliases

Very often different descriptions for an identical attribute exist. Aliases should be documented as they are discovered to assist the task of merging data structures before creating the entity model in stage 4.

The keys for the two data structures, Figure 7.30, were identified during the normalisation task. However, during systems analysis an alias was documented whereby internal order numbers correspond on a one-to-one basis with quotation numbers. The keys are therefore identical and the data structures should be merged.

Quotation number	Internal order number
Customer name	Customer code
Project number	Customer name
Quoted price	Product number
	Quantity ordered
	Delivery date

Figure 7.30

Key only data structures

The task of normalisation may occasionally yield a key only data structure in the third normal form. The data structure, Figure 7.31, represents all the projects worked on by staff members.

The tests, represented in Figures 7.21 and 7.22, should be carried out to determine transitive dependencies between keys.

'For each staff number is there only one project number?'   No
'For each project number is there only one staff number?'   No

Normalisation	
UNF	1NF
Staff number	Staff number
Name	Name
Grade	Grade
Project number	Staff number
Project name	Project number ◄┐
	Project name ──┘
2NF & 3NF	
Staff number	
Name	
Grade	
Staff number	
Project number	
Project number	
Project name	

Figure 7.31

Neither of the attributes can therefore become the key and the key only data structure must be retained.

Task 4.2 may therefore create a large number of data structures in third normal form.

7.4 Task 4.3: Create the entity descriptions

Task 4.3 takes all the data structures in third normal form and merges all those with identical keys. This creates a set of entity descriptions from which the entity model is created.

Only data structures with identical keys may be merged. Merging is a very simple task accomplished by first establishing all of the different keys, and secondly listing all of the attributes for each key.

Figure 7.32 shows a number of third normal form data structures.

Customer number	Product number
Name	Depot number
Address	Qty. allocated
Product number	Product number
Depot number	Depot number
Qty. in stock	Location reference
Re-order qty.	Storage type
Customer number	Customer number
(delivery address)	Credit code
	Area code
	Representative

Figure 7.32

Customer number	Product number
Name	Depot number
Address	Location reference
(delivery address)	Storage type
Credit code	Qty. in stock
Area code	Re-order qty.
Representative	Qty. allocated

Figure 7.33

There are only two different keys, the simple key, customer number, and the compound key, product number/depot number. All attributes are listed under their appropriate key, Figure 7.33.

The result is the identification of two entities along with their entity descriptions.

Occasionally, merging of data structures may not be appropriate. For example, consider Figure 7.34, a merged data structure obtained from two original data structures, Figure 7.35.

In this case, only 5 per cent of quotations result in orders. A considerable amount of space could be saved by not merging the data structures. This is because there would be zero occurrences of the order data structure in 95 per cent of the cases.

The process of merging can introduce new data dependencies. Sub-task 4.2.4, validate, should be re-applied to the newly formed data structures.

Task 4.3 therefore identifies and provides for each entity an entity description.

Works order number	Works order number
Customer number	Customer number
Drawing number	Drawing number
Enquiry reference	Enquiry reference
enquiry data	enquiry data
• • •	• • •
Quotation reference	Quotation reference
quotation data	quotation data
• • •	• • •
Order number	
order data	Works order number
•	Order number
•	order data
•	• • •
production data	production data
• • •	• • •

Figure 7.34   *Figure 7.35*

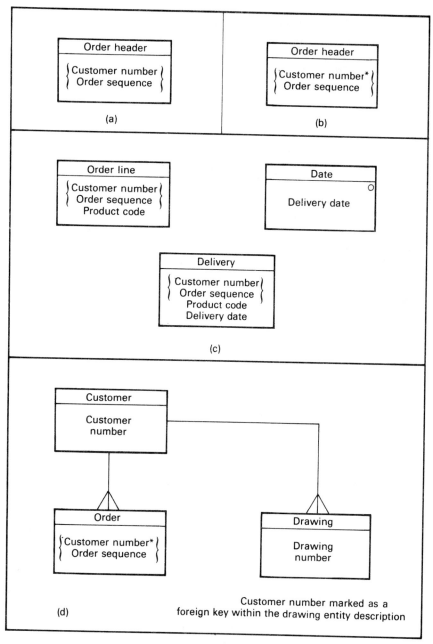

Figure 7.36

7.5   Task 4.4: Create the entity model

The task of constructing an entity model from the entity descriptions is very straightforward and comprises five simple steps.

Step 1 introduces the entities on to the entity model by drawing, for each entity description, a rectangle. The rectangle is annotated with the entity name and the entity key is written inside it, Figure 7.36(a). The entity is named order header and the key is a composite key customer number/order sequence.

Some of the entities may have entire keys which are composite keys. Each of the stand-alone simple keys within the composite key should be marked as a foreign key, Figure 7.36(b). This is step 2 and will allow relationships to be established at step 4. This step is only applied to entities whose entire key is a composite key.

Step 3 requires that all compound keys are examined to ensure that an entity exists for each simple or composite key within the compound key. If an entity does not exist, then an entity should be created with the appropriate key. The newly created entity should be marked as an operational owner, Figure 7.36(c).

Step 4 introduces relationships between entities. All entities with compound keys become members and must be connected to their owners. An owner relationship must exist for each element of the compound key,

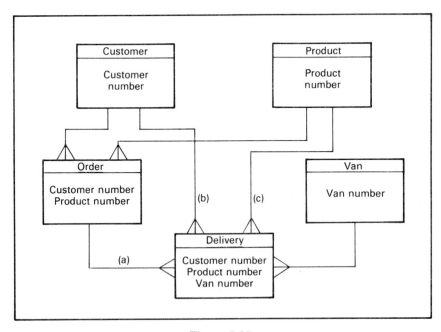

Figure 7.37

although it is acceptable to connect compound keys to compound keys at a lower level. The relationship may therefore be via an entity with a compound key itself, to the owners, see Figure 7.37. In this case, relationship (a) provides the owner keys customer number and product number, relationships (b) and (c) are therefore not required.

The final step is to introduce relationships connecting all foreign keys to their owners. Foreign keys may be found within the entity description, or as a result of step 2, Figure 7.36(d).

As each relationship is introduced, its degree must be determined and entered on to the entity model.

By applying these simple rules, an entity model is built, bottom up, from the third normal form merged data structures.

7.6 Task 4.5: Create the logical entity model

The construction of the logical entity model from the stage 2 and stage 4 entity models again follows a number of steps, four in total. Each step is straightforward.

The initial step creates the first entities on the logical entity model by entering on to it all of the operational owners from the stage 2 entity model. These operational owners were created to satisfy a specific user requirement and it is likely therefore that they will be required as access routes into the database.

Operational owners from the stage 4 entity model result from missing elements of compound keys and key only data structures. These operational owners should only be entered on to the logical entity model if there are sound reasons for doing so emanating from the user requirements.

Comparison of all remaining entities and insertion of further entities on to the logical entity model comprises step 2. It may be necessary to compare the entity descriptions at this step to identify logical aliases in entity names. Differences should be resolved by reference to the user requirements and all the entities inserted on to the logical entity model.

Step 3 now refers to relationships and commences with a comparison of all of them. Differences are again resolved by reference to the user requirements and the relationships are inserted on to the logical entity model. The relationships will be further validated in stage 5.

The final step is to enter volumetric data on to the logical entity model. The number of logical occurrences of each entity should be determined and the entity box annotated as in Figure 7.38.

It may be necessary to estimate a minimum, maximum and expected growth rate. The numbers of occurrences may be added to the entity descriptions so that the entity description forms may be completed in task 4.6. Secondly, for each relationship the average number of dependencies

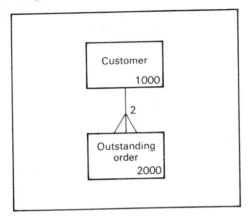

Figure 7.38

should be added to the logical model. Figure 7.38 shows a relationship between customer and order. The figure 2 should be interpreted as follows:

1000 customer entities have on average two orders outstanding, giving 2000 current outstanding order entities.

7.7   Task 4.6: Create the logical entity descriptions

The final task in stage 4 produces the logical entity descriptions by simple comparison of the entity descriptions from stages 2 and 4.

Differences are usually minor and resolution of them easy. However, at this task it is possible to enhance the entity descriptions to include the entity size and the average number of occurrences. Thus the total amount of storage required for each entity can be calculated by simple arithmetic.

7.8   Stage 4 summary

The base technique employed during stage 4, logical data design, is the process of normalisation. Normalisation of data structures is necessary to ensure data structures represented, in their simplest form, are presented to the physical design stage, and to remove the possibility of loss of data integrity.

Re-examine Figure 7.10, a data structure for orders which is in UNF. Figure 7.39 adds some data to the structure.

If a new customer negotiates an account, the unnormalised structure cannot record it until the customer places an order. Similarly, when the order for Frost is met, the information regarding Frost as a customer will be lost along with the product data regarding Nuts. These are insertion and deletion problems with unnormalised data structures. Update problems also

Customer number	Name	Product number	Name	Qty.	Price
J2741	James	A273	Screws	100	1.00
		B147	Bolts	50	2.00
W1798	Waters	B147	Bolts	10	2.00
F1001	Frost	L110	Nuts	100	0.50
		A273	Screws	10	1.00

Figure 7.39

exist, for example if the price of Bolts is modified, then multiple update of the data structure is necessary since the price of Bolts is recorded with each order for them.

The representation of data in third normal form overcomes insertion, deletion and update problems of this kind. Data structures are held in their simplest form and all duplication of data removed. The 3NF representation

Normalisation	
UNF	**1NF**
Customer number	Customer number
Customer name	Customer name
Product number	Customer number
Product name	Product number
Qty.	Product name
Price	Qty.
	Price
2NF	**3NF**
Customer number	
Customer name	
	Identical to 2NF
Customer number	
Product number	
Qty.	
Product number	
Product name	
Price	

Figure 7.40

Customer number	Name
J2741	James
W1798	Waters
F1001	Frost

Product number	Name	Price
A273	Screws	1.00
B147	Bolts	2.00
L110	Nuts	0.50

Customer number	Product number	Qty.
J2741	A273	100
J2741	B147	50
W1798	B147	10
F1001	L110	100
F1001	A273	10

Figure 7.41

of the data structure in Figure 7.39 is shown in Figures 7.40 and 7.41. Note that the problems described are eliminated.

The six tasks of logical data design, stage 4:

4.1   Selection of data structures for normalisation.
4.2   Normalisation of each of the selected data structures using
    4.2.1   Conversion of un-normalised data structures to first normal form including choice of appropriate keys.
    4.2.2   Conversion of data structures in first normal form to second normal form.
    4.2.3   Conversion of data structures in second normal form to third normal form.
    4.2.4   Validation of the third normal form data structures.
4.3   Merging of third normal form data structures with identical keys to create entities and the entity descriptions.
4.4   A simple set of sub-tasks then transforms the entity descriptions into an entity model.
4.5   The entity model created during systems analysis is compared with the entity model from task 4.4, differences are resolved and the logical entity model is output to stage 5.

4.6 The entity descriptions again created during the systems analysis stages are compared with the entity descriptions from task 4.3. Anomalies are removed and a set of logical entity descriptions are output to stage 5.

8

Logical process design

8.1 Introduction

Chapter 8 describes the fifth stage of SSADM, shown in Figure 8.1. Stage 5 uses the entity function matrix, the entity life histories and the function descriptions from stage 2; the required physical DFDs from stage 3; and the logical entity model and logical entity descriptions from stage 4. These inputs are transformed into logical process outlines during stage 5.

Stage 5 commences with a review of the stage 2 documentation. The documents need to be updated to reflect the implementation option chosen at stage 3 and the results of the logical data design stage. The second task enters all of the required functions from the required physical DFDs into the process catalogue. All functions which have common processing requirements are collected together, to form a process. Each process is then expanded into a detailed process outline, the third task, by reference to the entity function matrix, the entity life histories, the function descriptions, the logical entity model and the logical entity descriptions.

The logical process outlines from stage 5, together with the logical entity model and logical entity descriptions from stage 4, form the input to stage 6, physical design. The conclusion of stage 5 marks the boundary between logical design and physical design. Stage 6 must consider the target hardware, software and people. Effectively, therefore, the outputs from stages 4 and 5 form a complete logical design specification.

8.2 Task 5.1: Review the stage 2 documentation

The entity function matrix, the entity life histories and the function descriptions from stage 2 may require updating to reflect decisions taken during stage 3, and changes to the entity descriptions and entity model, as a result of stage 4.

During stage 3, new functions may be inserted and existing functions

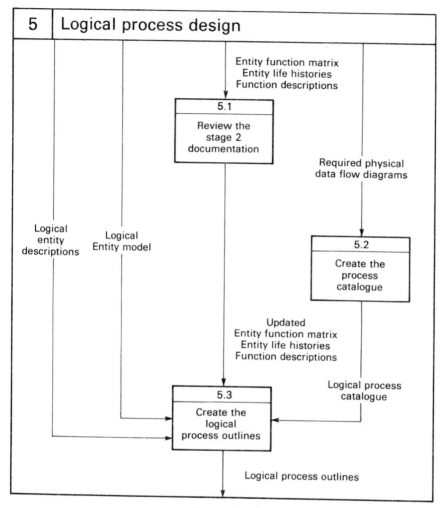

Figure 8.1

modified or even deleted. Other functions may have had their responsibility box completed to indicate non-computer processing. The entity function matrix will require additional columns, modified columns and the removal of columns to reflect the changes in the processing requirements.

This first step within task 5.1 is to bring the entity function matrix up to date with the required physical DFDs from stage 3.

Stage 4, logical data design, very often produces new entities as well as modification or even deletion of existing entities. The second step within task 5.1 is to bring the entity function matrix up to date with the logical entity model. The entity function matrix must have a new row added for

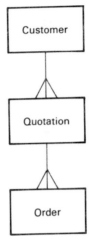

Figure 8.2 Entity model (from stage 2)

each new entity with the effects of functions on that entity charted. In addition, an entity life history must be constructed for each new entity.

The addition of new entities on to the entity function matrix is a relatively easy process. More problems are encountered if entities are merged or divided as part of logical data design.

Figure 8.2 shows a section of an entity model from stage 2. Figure 8.3 shows the same section of the logical entity model from stage 4. Note that there is one new entity and a merging of two entities. The new entity, product, has emerged during stage 4 and has been included on the logical entity model. The entities quotation and order on the stage 2 entity model have been merged into one entity, order, on the logical entity model. This results from merging data structures with identical keys during stage 4.

The entity function matrix, Figure 8.4, shows the three entities from Figure 8.2.

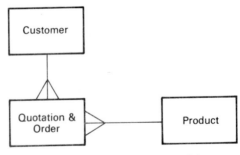

Figure 8.3 Logical entity model

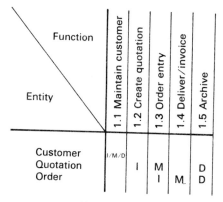

Figure 8.4

The entity descriptions for quotation and order are shown in Figure 8.5. In third normal form, four data structures result. Quotation numbers are unique. The four data structures are shown in Figure 8.6.

The order entity key, after the first three steps of the normalisation task,

---

Quotation

UNF, 1NF, 2NF	3NF
Quotation no.	Quotation no.
Customer no. ◄──	Customer no.*
Customer name ──┘	Product code*
Product code ◄──	Quoted price
Product description ──┘	
Quoted price	Customer no.
	Customer name
	Product code
	Product description

Order

UNF, 1NF, 2NF	3NF
{ Customer no. } ──	Quotation no.
{ Order no. } ──	Customer no.*
Quotation no. ◄──┘	Order no.
Qty. ordered	Qty. ordered

Figure 8.5

Quotation:	Quotation no. Customer number* Product code* Quoted price	Customer:	Customer number Customer name
Product:	Product code Product description	Order:	Quotation number Customer number* Order number Quantity ordered

Figure 8.6

is a compound key comprising a composite key, customer number/order number, and a simple key, quotation number. The final validation of the data structure revealed that the composite key customer number/order number was dependent upon the quotation number. The simple key, quotation number, therefore became the key to both the quotation entity and the order entity.

The entities quotation and order were therefore merged in the construction of the logical entity model, Figure 8.3.

The updated entity function matrix must merge the two existing rows, quotation and order, from Figure 8.3. The new matrix must also have a new row for the product entity together with a new function column, function 1.6, to maintain the product entity. Figure 8.7 shows the updated entity function matrix. Note also the reading of the product entity by functions 1.2, 1.3 and 1.4.

The entity life histories for the order and quotation entities need to be redrawn as one entity life history. In this case it is likely that the two histories will follow in sequence since orders always follow quotations, that

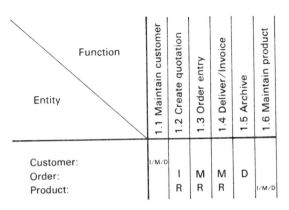

Entity \ Function	1.1 Maintain customer	1.2 Create quotation	1.3 Order entry	1.4 Deliver/Invoice	1.5 Archive	1.6 Maintain product
Customer:	I/M/D					
Order:		I	M	M	D	
Product:		R	R	R		I/M/D

Figure 8.7

is, if an order is received. A new entity life history is required for the product entity.

Finally, all the status indicators should be reviewed. These form a very important integrity check during processing. They are therefore carefully recorded on the logical process outlines during task 5.3.

8.3 Task 5.2: Create the process catalogue

The required physical DFDs, selected by the user during stage 3, indicate, for each function, a mode of processing. The mode might be simply on-line or batch. The mode may be further divided into on-line update, on-line enquiry, batch report or batch update and further by time period and data access requirements.

The mode may be batch update weekly or batch update daily or batch update weekly stock file or batch update weekly sales ledger. The mode represents the exact resources required by the process.

A catalogue of processing modes can be established with each function being posted to one mode in the catalogue.

Very often the level 2 DFDs represent functions which do not comprise more than one mode of processing. It is these functions which can therefore be posted to the catalogue.

The process catalogue, Figure 8.9, resulted from the posting of functions represented on the level 2 required physical DFD, Figure 8.8.

All of the functions that have the responsibility box completed indicating computer processing are entered into the logical process catalogue. The catalogue therefore provides a complete list of all required computer processing. As each function is entered into the process catalogue, the designer should check that the function is fully understood and documented since it is that documentation which will form the basis of the process outlines.

The objective of posting functions into the process catalogue is to identify groupings of functions which may become programs or program modules. If the processing modes chosen are simply on-line and batch, then perhaps two programs would result, one on-line and one batch. The decision tree below shows a more practical set of processing modes.

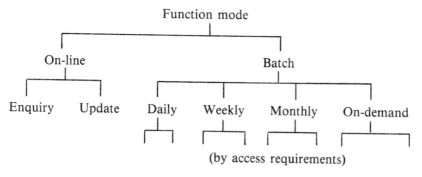

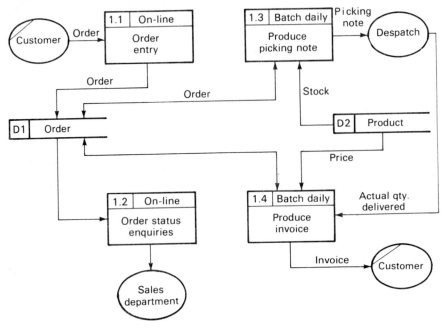

Figure 8.8 Level 2

Mode/process no.	Function reference	Name
On-line enquiry 1	1.2	Order status enquiry
On-line update 2	1.1	Order entry
Batch update-daily 3	1.3 1.4	Produce picking note Produce invoice

Figure 8.9 Logical process catalogue

The catalogue modes may therefore be:

on-line enquiry
on-line update
batch daily sales area
batch daily product area
batch weekly
batch monthly sales area
batch monthly product area

where sales and product are areas of the database.

8.4   Task 5.3: Create the logical process outlines

The updated entity function matrix, entity life histories, logical function descriptions together with the logical entity model, logical entity descriptions and the logical process catalogue comprise the input to task 5.3, creation of the logical process outlines. The logical process outlines will be used during stage 6 to create program specifications.

Only processes listed in the process catalogue require logical process outlines. All processes that are to remain manual will have been excluded from the catalogue.

The creation of logical process outlines adds the fine processing detail including the processing of entities to the set of function descriptions for the process.

A process outline is both detailed and logical.

A logical process outline should be created for each on-line function. The logical process outlines will be linked to process complete transactions during stage 6.

A logical process outline should be created for each batch process. A process may therefore combine a number of functions all of which share the same timescales and the same resource requirements.

The two above statements constitute the rules for the relationship between logical process outlines and functions. These rules follow on from the posting of functions into the process catalogue. There are, however, other considerations which may influence the number of logical process outlines produced.

Many current target systems provide software to link programs or modules to be able to process a complete transaction. The design of the dialogue from screen formats through processing is therefore dependent upon the target system. In this instance, a logical process outline should be produced for each on-line function. The functions should then be linked during stage 6 to form transaction processing routines.

An alternative is to define the dialogue during this stage, stage 5. Each transaction can be identified as an input to an on-line function. Its route through the required physical DFDs can be traced, thus linking the input to one or more functions and its output. These functions may be linked together as the processing for one transaction and a logical process outline created for its processing. Great care must be taken to ensure common functions are identified and not reproduced in many logical process outlines.

The only potential problem with batch logical process outlines is the size. If very many functions are catalogued as batch daily requiring access to a particular area of the database, then some further splitting may be necessary and appropriate.

The logical process catalogue, Figure 8.9, would therefore result in one batch update, daily, process outline. This is reasonable since both functions are batch daily and require access to the orders and products data stores. It could be argued, however, that since the two functions access different orders, and that since function 1.3 updates the product data store and function 1.4 only references the data store, then two logical process outlines should result.

As the methodology progresses nearer and nearer to the production of physical specifications, which depend upon a knowledge of the target hardware and software, so the methodology becomes much more guidelines rather than rules. The grouping of functions into processes is an example of a guideline rather than an exact rule.

Each process outline comprises a process outline heading and a number of operation entries. The heading provides documentation of the complete process including the process number, a process name, the process mode, its frequency, the volume of transactions plus a brief description of the processing.

Operation entries may take many forms. Operations may perform the modification of an entity, validate some input, format some output or perform a calculation. For each operation, the documentation should include some or all of the following: operation number, the name of the entity affected by the operation, the 'valid previous' and 'set to' status indicators for the entity, any input or output or error handling plus a detailed description of the processing associated with the operation.

Figure 8.10 shows a blank process outline form.

Each process will affect a number of entities. The entities affected by a process and the effect on the entity can be obtained by reading down a column on the entity function matrix. A column of an entity function matrix is shown in Figure 8.11.

The function, produce invoice, reads contract, modifies order line, modifies stock, and inserts an invoice and invoice line, although at this stage the sequence of effects on the entities cannot be determined. This is made clear by reference to the logical function description.

Further, by reference to the entity life histories the entity statuses that must exist for the functions to execute validly may be determined. Secondly, again from the entity life histories, the 'set to' status on completion of successful processing may be determined. An extract of the entity life history for the entity order line is shown in Figure 8.12.

The order line entity must have status 3 for the function, produce invoice, to be valid. Further, after the function has completed successfully, the status should be set to 4. This will allow a subsequent function to archive the order line.

The effect on each entity by the function can be described by the operation Read, Insert, Modify or Delete and the status indicators 'valid previous' and 'set to'.

The entities affected by the process should be identified from the entity

LOGICAL PROCESS OUTLINE

SYSTEM:	DATE:
AUTHOR:	PAGE: of

PROCESS No: NAME:

MODE: FREQUENCY: VOLUME:

BRIEF DESCRIPTION:

DFD Functions.

ENTITY NAME										
EFFECT										
VALID PREV.										
SET TO										

Op. no.	Entity Name	Effect	Status Ind. Valid prev.	Set to	Description Narrative	Ref.	I/O ref.	Error ref.

Figure 8.10

	2.5 Produce invoice
Contract	R
Order line	M
Stock	M
Invoice	I
Invoice line	I

Figure 8.11

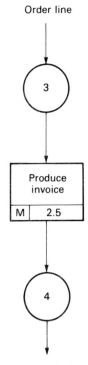

Figure 8.12

function matrix, perhaps by reading down several function columns. For each entity affected, the entity life history should be examined to determine the 'valid previous' and 'set to' statuses for each of the functions within the process. This information is extracted as a first step towards the completion of a logical process outline.

The extract is a number of columns from the entity function matrix, enhanced with status information from the appropriate entity life histories. It provides a concise reference of the process's effect on the entities, a vital section of the process outline.

This concise reference is included as part of the logical process outline itself, Figure 8.13.

The detail of each operation's processing may be expressed in English, structured English, decision tables or trees, pseudo-code or some appropriate combination of techniques. A simple example of each technique is provided later.

In describing processing in detail, error conditions must be considered. Here again, the updated entity life histories are important as they document the effect on each entity of abnormal events.

Returning to the process produce invoice, the logical function description from stage 2 was: 'For all advice notes produce an invoice line. If it is the first invoice line enter an invoice header. Prices are obtained either from the

LOGICAL PROCESS OUTLINE

SYSTEM: *SALES ACCOUNTING*	DATE:
AUTHOR: *G. CUTTS*	PAGE: *1* of *2*

PROCESS No: *1*   **NAME:** *PRODUCE INVOICE*

MODE: *BATCH*   **FREQUENCY:** *WEEKLY* **VOLUME:**

BRIEF DESCRIPTION: *Insert invoice & invoice lines into the database for all delivery notes created during the previous week. Note the invoice is not printed by the process.*

ENTITY NAME	Contract	Order line	Stock	Invoice	Invoice line	
EFFECT	R	M	M	I	I	
VALID PREV.	—	3	1	—	—	
SET TO	—	4	1	1	1	

Figure 8.13

LOGICAL PROCESS OUTLINE

SYSTEM: *SALES ACCOUNTING*	DATE:
AUTHOR: *G. CUTTS*	PAGE: *1* of *2*

PROCESS No: *1*   NAME: *PRODUCE INVOICE*

MODE: *BATCH*   FREQUENCY: *WEEKLY* VOLUME:

BRIEF DESCRIPTION: *Insert invoice & invoice lines in to the database for all delivery notes created during the previous week. Note the invoice is not printed by the process.*

ENTITY NAME	Contract	Order line	Stock	Invoice	Invoice line	
EFFECT	R	M	M	I	I	
VALID PREV.	—	3	1	—	—	
SET TO	—	4	1	1	1	

	Entity Name	Effect	Status Ind. Valid prev.	Set to
	Order line	M	3	4
	Stock	M	1	1
	Contract	R		

Figure 8.14

LOGICAL PROCESS OUTLINE

PROCESS No: *1*	NAME: *PRODUCE INVOICE*
MODE: *BATCH*	FREQUENCY: *WEEKLY* VOLUME:

BRIEF DESCRIPTION: *Insert invoice & invoice lines in to the database for all delivery notes created during the previous week. Note the invoice is not printed by the process.*

ENTITY NAME	Contract	Order line	Stock	Invoice	Invoice line	
EFFECT	R	M	M	I	I	
VALID PREV.	—	3	1	—	—	
SET TO	—	4	1	1	1	

	Entity Name	Effect	Status Ind. Valid prev.	Set to
	Invoice	I	—	1
	Invoice line	I	—	1

LOGICAL PROCESS OUTLINE

SYSTEM: *SALES ACCOUNTING*	DATE:
AUTHOR: *G. CUTTS*	PAGE: *1* of *2*

PROCESS No: *1*   NAME: *PRODUCE INVOICE*

MODE: *BATCH*   FREQUENCY: *WEEKLY* VOLUME:

BRIEF DESCRIPTION: *Insert invoice & invoice lines in to the database for all delivery notes created during the previous week. Note the invoice is not printed by the process.*

ENTITY NAME	Contract	Order line	Stock	Invoice	Invoice line	
EFFECT	R	M	M	I	I	
VALID PREV.	—	3	1	—	—	
SET TO	—	4	1	1	1	

Op. no.	Entity Name	Effect	Status Ind Valid prev.	Status Ind Set to	Description Narrative	Ref.	I/O ref.	Error ref.
1					Read the advice note details & validate the input fields.	V10	I100	
					If validation error reject.			E100
2	Order line	M	3	4	Obtain the relevant Order line. If not found reject the advice note			E200
					If found but status indicator errors then reject the advice note.			E300
					Modify the order line status to indicate Order Line despatched.			
3	Stock	M	1	1	Obtain the relevant stock item.			
					If not found report error.			E210
					If found but status indicator. errors then error.			E310
					Extract the stock item price.			
					Modify the entity to de-allocate the stock & also to decrement the qty. on hand.			
4	Contract	R			Read the relevant contract for all order lines stating a contract number.			
					If not found error.			E220
					continued			

Figure 8.15

LOGICAL PROCESS OUTLINE

SYSTEM: *SALES ACCOUNTING*	DATE:
AUTHOR: *G. CUTTS*	PAGE: *2* of *2*

PROCESS No: *1*	NAME: *PRODUCE INVOICE*	

MODE: *BATCH* **FREQUENCY:** *WEEKLY* **VOLUME:**

BRIEF DESCRIPTION: *Insert invoice & invoice lines in to the database for all delivery notes created during the previous week. Note the invoice is not printed by the process.*

ENTITY NAME	Contract	Order line	Stock	Invoice	Invoice line	
EFFECT	R	M	M	I	I	
VALID PREV.	—	3	1	—	—	
SET TO	—	4	1	1	1	

Op. no.	Entity Name	Effect	Status Ind. Valid prev.	Set to	Description Narrative	Ref.	I/O ref.	Error ref.
5					Extract the contract price. If not contract use the price from the stock item entity. Calculate the invoice line value = quantity delivered (delivery note) x price.			
6	Invoice	I	—	1	If this is the first advice note for a given customer insert an invoice entity into the database.			
	Invoice line	I	—	1	Insert an invoice line entity into the database.			

contract entity or the stock entity. Update the stock entity to record the quantity despatched.'

The initial logical process outline for produce invoice is shown in Figure 8.14. This initial logical process outline is constructed by using the logical function descriptions to sequence the entries in the reference section of the process outline.

The processing to handle the effect on the entities must now be described together with any intermediate processing such as calculation of the invoice value, the handling of error conditions and the validation of input documents.

The specification of error processing is often more complicated than the specification of standard processing. The use of error references in logical process outlines removes the necessity to include detailed error processing within the body of the standard process description. All error processing can be collated and specified separately in an error processing logical process outline. An example of the use of an error reference is shown in Figure 8.15.

The description refers to error reference E100 where a description of the error processing can be found. This process outline will eventually be programmed with a call to the error processing module, reference E100.

To complete the process outline, reference needs to be made to any system input or output. An operation such as print sales statement will involve access to several entities as well as producing the printed sales statement. A complete specification of the input or output format within the process is not necessary, a reference to the format is required. A column input/output reference is included on the process outline document. Figure 8.15 shows an input reference. Input reference I100 contains the physical format of an advice note.

Note that the error references have a leading significant digit. The one hundred series represents validation errors, the two hundred series represents database errors and the three hundred series status indicator errors. Strictly speaking, the error references E210 and E310 refer to entity not found in this specific case. It is good practice to check the status indicator before any operation on an entity, with the exception of read.

Reference V10 provides the detailed validation rules for the advice note.

Where the narrative description is insufficient to provide the exact detail, reference may be made to a more detailed description. This may be in the form of a decisions table or tree, it may be an algorithm specified in pseudo-code or it may be a set of validation rules. This reference is shown along with the narrative description of the operation. Figure 8.15 includes a reference V10 to the validation rules for an advice note input in format I100.

A logical process outline may therefore reference other logical process outlines, for common routines and for error processing; input and output formats; and documents supporting the narrative description of an operation; for validation or detailed calculation rules.

A set of logical process outlines with supporting documentation is the major deliverable from stage 5.

8.4.1 Specifying process logic

The detailed processing for each operation on a logical process outline may be expressed in English, structured English, decision tables or trees, pseudo-code or some appropriate combination of techniques.

The specification of process logic will very often make reference to entities and attributes of entities. Care should be taken to ensure all entity names are identical to the names on the logical entity model. Similar care should be taken to ensure all attribute names are identical to the names used in the logical entity descriptions.

One convention for attribute naming is to use the dot notation, e.g. customer.credit-limit where credit-limit is an attribute of the entity customer.

8.5 Stage 5 summary

Stage 5 is the final logical stage before physical design. It produces the logical process outlines to add to the logical entity model and logical entity descriptions from stage 4. These three sets of documents form the complete logical specification and are the final set of documents to be independent of hardware, software and people considerations.

There are three tasks within stage 5. Task 5.1 reviews the entity life histories, the entity function matrix and the function descriptions, produced during stage 2, against the logical entity model produced during stage 4, and the selected required DFDs, produced during stage 3.

The DFDs represent the required processing and the mode of processing. The functions are posted to a logical process catalogue, task 5.2. This documents, for each function, its processing mode, batch or on-line. All functions remaining manual are excluded from the catalogue. The catalogue is then used by task 5.3 to provide a list of processes for which logical process outlines should be created.

The logical function descriptions described, in business terminology, the detailed processing for each function. These are now transformed, in task 5.3, into logical process outlines. The effect on each entity is documented by reference to the entity life histories and reference is made to validation and error processing rules.

Finally, the logical process outlines are validated against the user's view of the system, the selected required physical DFDs, and against the system view, the logical entity model, by the stage 4 and 5 user review.

9

Physical design

9.1 Introduction

Chapter 9 describes the sixth stage of SSADM, physical design, shown in Figure 9.1. Stage 6 uses the logical process outlines, the logical entity model and the logical entity descriptions to create a complete, detailed, physical design specification. The design specification comprises a file or database specification, a set of program specifications, an implementation plan, an operations manual and a user manual.

The input to stage 6 is the logical design specification. This is independent of the target hardware or software. Stage 6 transforms the logical specification into the physical specification by taking into account the constraints imposed by the target system. The output from stage 6 is therefore installation dependent.

Moreover the design must adhere to objective measures of performance and resource usage. The tasks within stage 6 must provide for performance and resource usage estimation, with the opportunity for design tuning, if the objectives are not met.

9.2 Task 6.1: Specify the physical files or database

The objective of this task is to create the physical specification of the files or database and the physical specification of the records and record content.

The initial step is to annotate the logical entity model with a series of arrows to show the entry points into the model. These arrows will lead to index tables or indexed files allowing direct access to the data. Operational owners indicate entry points identified during the analysis stages.

Figure 9.2 shows a logical entity model with entry points marked by arrows. Note that all entities at the head of a hierarchy and all those with operational owners must be entry points.

The entry points marked on the customer, product and supplier entities

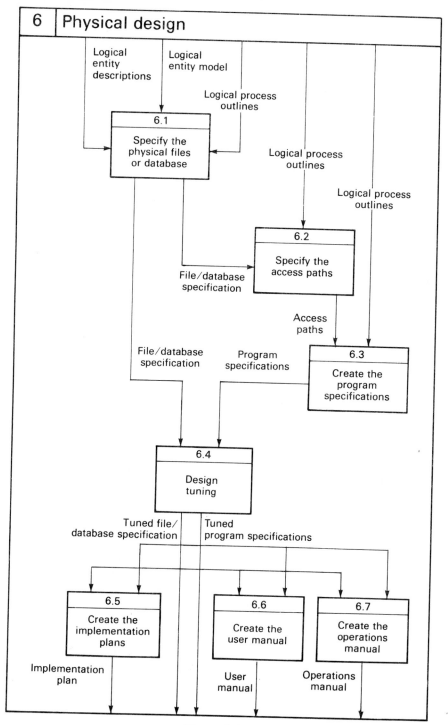

Figure 9.1

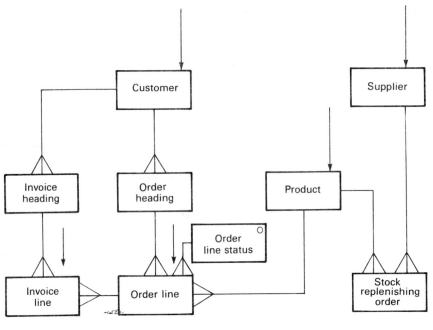

Figure 9.2

result from the entities being at the head of a hierarchy. The entry point on order line results from the operational owner, order line status.

The entry point on the invoice line entity results from a requirement to satisfy a process outline. The process outline stated: "Read all of the invoice lines inserted into the system over the past week and produce a report of the total invoice value delivered each day." Note that an invoice line represents a delivery against an order line.

Entry points may result, therefore, from the requirements of a process outline. All of the process outlines must be validated against the logical entity model to determine the entry points required. Many of the entry points required by the process outlines will have been indicated already since the entities will either be at the head of a hierarchy or be linked to an operational owner.

Subsequent steps in task 6.1 depend on the target system. A set of guidelines for creating the physical specification should be constructed for each target system. Some examples are given below. These examples are given as an indication of the task involved when conversion is required to indexed sequential files or to an IDMS schema. The examples are not intended to be an exact set of rules.

9.2.1 Conversion to indexed sequential files

The guidelines for creating a set of indexed sequential files follow a similar route to that used to create logical files in stage two. The guidelines are explained by reference to the logical entity model shown in Figure 9.2.

Commence a new file for each entity at the head of a hierarchy. Three initial files result from Figure 9.2, a customer file, a product file and a supplier file. Follow the relationships from the entities already placed in a file to determine the member entities.

The member entity may be treated in one of three ways:
(i)   the entity may become a repeating group within the owner member entity record
(ii) the entity may become a separate record type in the owner member entity file
(iii) the entity may create a new file.

Some entities, for example, the stock replenishment order, have a choice of owner entity file for ways (i) and (ii) above. If way (i) is chosen then either a fixed maximum number of repeats must be decided or variable record lengths must be used.

Figure 9.2 has many member entities related to the owner entities, customer, product and supplier. Reference to the process outlines indicate that the stock replenishment order entity is processed on-line with product entities. For this reason stock replenishment orders are included as a separate record type in the product file.

File	Record types	Key
Customer	Customer	Customer code
Supplier	Supplier	Supplier code
Product	Product	Product number
	Stock replenishment order	Product number/supplier code
Order	Order heading	Customer code/order reference
Order line	Order line	Customer code/order reference/product number*
Invoice	Invoice heading	Customer code/invoice number
	Invoice line	Customer code/invoice number/delivery note number**

* Order line status is included as an attribute of the entity Order line.

**Order reference and Product number are included as attributes of Invoice line.

Figure 9.3

The customer entity possesses two members, order heading and invoice heading. Since there are many repeat orders and therefore invoices in this system, way 3 is chosen for both cases. The invoice heading entity and order heading entity will create new files, effectively making them into hierarchy heads.

The ratio of invoice headings to invoice lines is high whereas the ratio of order headings to order lines is very low, sometimes one to one. The overhead of processing invoice headings when accessing invoice lines only is therefore low and for that reason the invoice line entities are included in the invoice heading file. Order lines are located in their own file.

The final file specification is shown in Figure 9.3. Each key is obtained from the logical entity descriptions. Note that the access points shown on the logical entity model are preserved.

9.2.2   Conversion to an IDMS schema

The conversion step is relatively straightforward.

For each entity on the logical entity model, three parameters must be specified, since entities become records in IDMS. The three parameters are:

Entity or record name	A unique name to be used in the IDMS schema
Record identifier	A unique number to identify the record type
Location mode	The storage method

Generally, there are two choices of location mode, CALC and VIA. With location mode CALC, the record key is randomised to derive a page

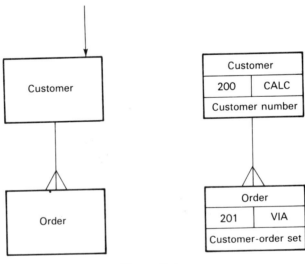

Figure 9.4

number where the record will be stored. The record will occupy the first available line in the page and is linked to the CALC set for the page. This means the record may be accessed directly. Entities with location mode VIA an owner record require the record to be stored as near as possible to the current occurrence of its owner. This allows member records to be clustered around their owners and access is generally but not exclusively via their owner. An owner–member relationship is called a set.

Figure 9.4 shows two entities and their IDMS record identifiers.

The CALC location mode is used for all entities marked as entry points into the database. Where an entity can be 'located via' more than one owner, the choice may be made by reference to processing requirements. This is similar to the choice made for the stock replenishment order in the previous example.

The IDMS record identifiers for the logical entity model, shown in Figure 9.2, are:

Logical entity	*Record name*	*No.*	*Location mode*	*Access key or set*
Customer	CUST	200	CALC	CUSTOMER-CODE
Product	PROD	201	CALC	PRODUCT-NUMBER
Supplier	SUPP	202	CALC	SUPPLIER-CODE
Stock replenishment order	SRO	203	VIA	PROD-SRO SET
Order heading	OHEAD	204	VIA	CUST-OHEAD SET
Order line*	ORD	205	CALC	ORD-LINE-STATUS
Invoice heading	IHEAD	206	VIA	CUST-IHEAD SET
Invoice line*	INV	207	CALC	DATE-OF-DELIV

* Because of the chosen access key, directly related to the processing, duplicate entity occurrences are likely which are uniquely identified by the attributes or fields within the entity.

For each relationship, six parameters must be specified. The term set is used for a relationship in IDMS.

Set name	A unique name that will be used in the IDMS schema.
Set order	This determines where a new member will be linked in the set and thus determines the sequence of member records.
Data name	This is only required for sorted members. It is the data name within the record for sequencing the members.
Pointers	A definition of the links required between owners to members and members to members.
Membership rules	This allows the specification of a storage class and is necessary for optional links.
Duplicates	This is only required for sorted members and provides a definition of the processing required if duplicate keys exist.

There are seven relationships in Figure 9.2. The PROD-SRO relationship might be specified as:

Set-name	PROD-SRO
Set-order	LAST
Data-name	—
Pointers	NEXT
Membership rules	MANDATORY AUTOMATIC
Duplicates	NOT ALLOWED

This short example is not intended to provide any of the detail of using IDMS; it serves only to show that guidelines can be constructed for converting from the logical entity model to an IDMS schema.

In both cases, entities have become records, either as record types within an indexed sequential file or as IDMS records. The logical entity description forms the basis of the record descriptions.

The additional information required to convert a logical entity description into a record description is the physical data relating to each attribute's size and format. The entity description form contains columns for this data, which have not been completed up to this point. Volumetric data is also required to enable the file size to be calculated from the record size.

Some careful arrangement of attributes is necessary if more than one record type is required on a file. Record type indicators are required along with a common key position and format. Each record must include a status field to hold the current status value from the entity life histories.

9.3   Task 6.2: Specify the access paths

The objective of this task is to specify, for every entity operation, on every logical process outline, the access path for the entity. Each process outline is processed in turn, against the physical file or database specification.

The logical process outline will state the entity name, the effect, the 'valid previous' status and the 'set to' status. The method of access must state exactly how the effect is achieved on the named entity.

Figure 9.5 shows an extract from a logical process outline; only those operations which affect an entity are shown.

Figure 9.6 shows the access paths using the indexed sequential files.

Figure 9.7 shows the access paths using IDMS.

Note that Figures 9.6 and 9.7 are dependent upon the hardware and software of the target system.

9.4   Task 6.3: Specify the programs

The program specifications form part of the documentation handed over from the development team to the implementation team. Specifically a

Operation no.	Entity name	Effect	Description
			Repeat the following processing for all order lines.
1	Order line	R	Check the Order-lines status. If the status = delivered then next-order line (operation 1) else (operations 2-7)
2	Product	R	If qty. ordered > qty. on hand then (operation 3) else (operations 4-7)
3	Order line	M	Change status to pending
4	Product	M	Subtract qty. order from qty. on hand
5	Order line	M	Change status to delivered
6	Invoice heading	R	If there exists an Invoice heading then (operation 8) else (operations 7-8)
7	Invoice heading	I	Create an Invoice heading
8	Invoice line	I	Create an Invoice line

Figure 9.5

program specification should provide a clear, complete, correct and unambiguous description of a program to enable a programmer to design, code and test the program.

The format of program specifications is installation dependent. A minimum program specification should comprise:

the program number and name
an overview or short description
the data access required
input, output and screen formats
menu and dialogue design and formats
the processing required

9.4.1 On-line programs

The logical process outlines together with the physical access paths provide

Operation no.	Entity name	Effect	Access path
1	Order line	R	Read (next)
2	Product	R	Set the access key to the product number from the order line Search & read
3	Order line	M	Rewrite (of previous read)
4	Product	M	Rewrite (of previous read)
5	Order line	M	Rewrite (of previous read)
6	Invoice heading	R	Set the access key to customer code from the order line and invoice number to this week's number Search & read
7	Invoice heading	I	Set access key to customer code from the order line and invoice number to this week's number Write (an invoice heading)
8	Invoice line	I	Set access key to customer code from the order line, invoice number to this week's number and delivery note number to that from the input Write (an invoice line)

Figure 9.6

the substantial element of the physical program specification. Logical process outlines reference input and output, documented during stage 2, the specification of requirements. Screen designs, report designs, menus and dialogue designs are required to complete the program specifications.

Many target systems will possess software for screen and report design and documentation; some will possess software for menu and dialogue design. The creation and execution of menu screens is becoming available on many systems. The final on-line program specification will therefore comprise:

the logical process outline
the access paths
screen designs, validation rules and error messages
report layouts
the menu and dialogue designs

Operation no.	Entity name	Effect	Access path
1	Order line	R	Set the access key, order line status to delivered Obtain first (for 1st access only) Obtain next (for subsequent access)
2	Product	R	Set the access key, product number, to the product number from the order line Obtain calc.
3	Order line	M	Store (of previous obtain)
4	Product	M	Store (of previous obtain)
5	Order line	M	Store (of previous obtain)
6	Invoice heading	R	Set the access key for the Customer entity to the customer code from the order line Find (the customer) Obtain first Ihead in Cust-Ihead set while there exists invoice headings and invoice heading not found If invoice-number = this week's number then invoice heading found else obtain next Ihead in Cust-Ihead set
7	Invoice heading	I	Set invoice number to this week Store Ihead
8	Invoice line	I	Set delivery note number to input number Store Iline

Figure 9.7

as a set of individual documents or in a represented format conforming to the installation standards.

The only step required to complete the on-line program specifications is the identification of common processing. Any common processing not identified during the production of the logical process outlines should be extracted from the program specifications and collected into a common module specification.

9.4.2 Batch programs

Many batch programs, such as the on-request production of standard reports, are free standing. Very often there exists a necessary or preferred sequence of execution of batch programs. Sequencing may be necessary to extract information, prior to sorting and printing. Similarly, it may be

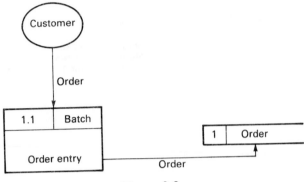

Figure 9.8

necessary to execute a file update program prior to using the file for the production of reports. The sequencing of programs into batch run flows can be determined by reference to the required physical DFDs.

The definition and sequencing of batch programs inevitably leads to the identification of temporary files and transaction files. For example, if the section of the DFDs shown in Figure 9.8 is transformed into a batch program sequence, the program sequence shown in Figure 9.9 may result.

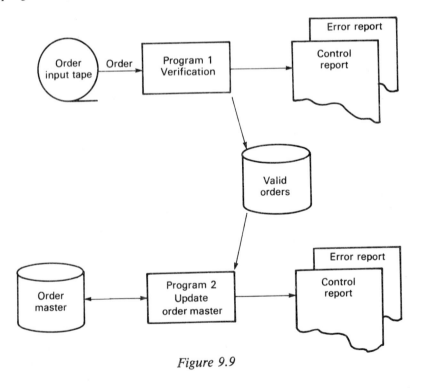

Figure 9.9

Program 2 results from a logical process outline; program 1 requires its processing to be defined.

Program specifications, which enable batches of data to be processed, need not necessarily result from logical process outlines; they result from the definition of batch run flows. In this case, program 1 simply verifies the accuracy of the data preparation; the order entry validation defined by function 1.1 on the DFD is translated into a logical process outline and then into a program specification.

The final batch program specifications will comprise:

the logical process outline or a description of the processing required
the access paths (possibly including temporary or transaction files)
input and report layouts

The batch run flows will be documented in task 6.7, creation of the operations manual.

9.5   Task 6.4: Design tuning

Design tuning is necessary to ensure the performance and resource usage objectives are met.

Performance objectives include batch run times, transaction response times and recovery times. The associated issues of security and privacy, which both affect performance, are also included. Resource objectives include direct access device space and device utilisation.

The objectives were specified during stage 3. These objectives now require to be developed into a set of detailed physical objectives against which the final system can be measured.

Resource objectives are generally easier to specify than performance objectives. The amount of direct access space and the number of devices, e.g. terminals, is very often fixed for a particular system.

This task requires that the performance of the major on-line and batch programs be calculated in order to check if the design objectives have been met. If they have not been met, design modifications may be necessary to ensure they are met. If objectives are shown to be not achievable, then modifications to them may be necessary. In either case, the reworking of earlier stages and tasks will result.

Design tuning is not a self-contained task; it is the calculation of the expected performance and resource utilisation for the current system desigı , and the comparison of the results against the design objectives.

The utilisation of resources is easier to calculate than system performance. The calculation of batch run times and response times are particularly difficult. It is often necessary to involve the hardware and software suppliers to provide performance figures. In many situations, the only reliable figures result from actual measurement of the system performance.

Design tuning is not just a task which iterates through earlier development stages; it is a task to which the implementation team should return as the implementation progresses and more actual figures on performance and utilisation become available.

9.5.1 Ways of improving performance

If the performance of the system as calculated or as observed does not meet the objectives, then ways of improving it may have to be found. The simple introduction of more hardware may not solve the problem. The design itself may require modification.

The design of the files or database should be examined in detail. Changes to the indexing methods, file and record sizes and page size, are all examples of detailed changes which may affect performance. Other changes include the duplication of data to allow concurrent access and the reduction of the amount of data held on-line to reduce the on-line storage requirements. Many changes do not affect the user's requirements, many will.

A reduction in the level of service offered to the user by the new system may be the only way to improve the performance. The removal of direct access by alternate keys to files, the alteration of direct access to extract, sort and print and the change from on-line to batch mode are examples of reduced service levels. These changes will improve the performance of remaining on-line modules.

Task 6.4 is the final task relating to the data and program specifications before the specifications are handed over to the implementation team. Design tuning therefore provides an opportunity for the development team to review their design against the system objectives before detailed implementation work commences. Errors and potential problems identified at this stage are easier and less expensive to correct than errors detected during program testing, system testing, user testing or live operation.

9.6   Task 6.5: Create the implementation plan

The development team should have gained valuable knowledge of the system and the user during the development stages. The team should therefore prepare a detailed implementation plan, based on their experience, to hand over to the implementation team.

Implementation includes the design, writing and testing of the programs, system testing, user testing, changeover, review and preparation for maintenance and modification.

The method by which plans are constructed and presented is again installation dependent. Some installations use sophisticated planning and monitoring software, others use simple bar charts.

All methodologies should provide a starting point for the next phase of the project. The implementation plan should provide a planning starting point for the implementation phase.

9.7 Task 6.6: Create the user manual

The user manual should provide the system user with sufficient information to be able to use and control the system in an efficient manner. The manual defines the interface between the new computer system and the manual system.

Data flow diagrams are one way of describing activities external to the computer system. Figure 9.10 shows a level 1 required physical DFD.

The external entities may be exploded into their own level 2 DFDs, each diagram using the standard DFD conventions of external entity, data store, data flow and, in this case, manual function.

Figures 9.11 and 9.12 provide examples of level 2 DFDs for the customer external entity and the warehouse external entity.

Figure 9.11 describes the method of input for orders received from customers. The sequence of functions is easily identified from the diagram. Each function now needs to be described in detail if it is to be included in the user manual. In the example function C2, the review of order received by the sales manager could well be excluded from the user manual. Function C4 is the only function which directly interacts with the computer system and is therefore the only one which must be described in the user manual.

The user manual must describe the procedure for the input of orders, for example, the use of menus and the choice of screen format. It must also describe the error messages and the methods of error correction. Further, in this example, since the input of orders is closely related to process C3, batch orders for on-line data entry, then the user manual should describe batching and control procedures.

Many installations have their own format for user manuals. In these cases, DFDs may be used as a technique to assist in the completion of the user manual.

Figure 9.12 describes the user of an output report, in this case the picking list. Function W1 is the first to receive output from the computer; procedures for requesting a re-run of the print generation programs should be described in the event of error or loss. Note also that function W4 involves input to the computer system. This function again requires careful description, this time describing the procedures for batch input and error correction.

The topics covered by the user manual described using DFDs cover the input and output procedures. There are many other areas of interest to the user. These should be described in further sections within the user manual

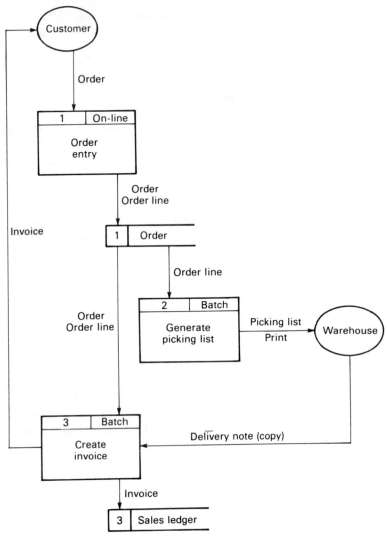

Figure 9.10 Level 1 required physical DFD

and include:

the days and times when the program should be available

procedures for start up and close down of the system, for example logging on and off via password identification

procedures for back up in the event of system failure either manual or via some other computer system

procedures for recovery after a failure

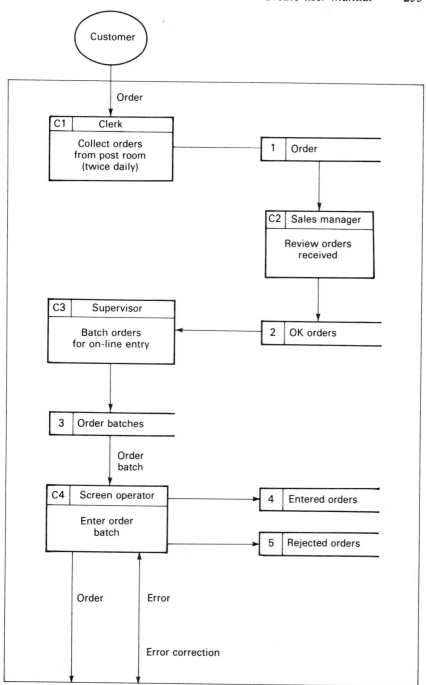

Figure 9.11 Level 2 required physical DFD

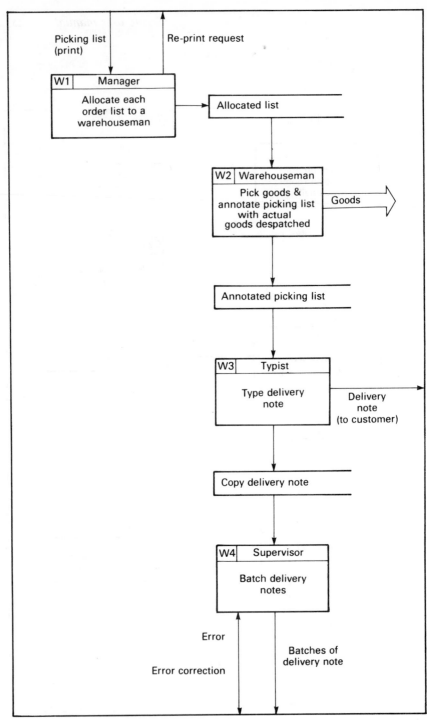

Figure 9.12 Level 2 required physical DFD

9.8   Task 6.7: Create the operations manual

The operations manual provides the detailed technical documentation of the operational requirements. Many of the sections are common to the user manual and the same techniques should be employed. Detailed documentation of such items as the batch run flows, the files required for on-line programs and the data control and data preparation procedures are included in the operations manual.

The format of the operations manual will again be installation dependent. Further, many sections of the manual may not be able to be completed at this time. However, the development team should hand over to the installation team a manual completed up to an agreed point.

The operating schedule and requirements are the prime documents completed by this task. Typically for each on-line program, the manual should include:

the days and times when the program should be available
the set up and the close down requirements for the program
the resource requirements in terms of direct access space and memory space including the files or database areas required
the instructions covering any non-standard processing, e.g. recovery from system failure

9.9   Stage 6 summary

Stage 6 concludes SSADM. The final output from the stage being:

a physical files or database specification
a set of program specifications
an implementation plan
an operations manual
a user manual

along with the system documentation produced by all the stages of the structured systems analysis and design methodology.

The completion of the physical design concludes the work of the analysts and designers. The project is now handed over to an implementation team which might have no common membership with the team of analysts and designers. The completion of stage 6 represents, therefore, a major milestone in the project.

The implementation team will wish to study the system specification in great detail. An initial walkthrough of the specification with representatives of both teams provides an ideal vehicle for education of the implementation team and for a detailed review of the specification.

Part 3 Case Study

10

SKC stage 1: analysis

10.1 Introduction

The Silent Kitchen Company manufactures complete dishes, such as coq-au-vin, which are sealed in plastic bags for sale to restaurants. The restaurant simply places the bagged meal in a microwave oven prior to serving. In this way, even small restaurants can offer a large à la carte menu at reasonable prices.

Customers of the Silent Kitchen Company (SKC) send their orders to the sales department. Orders are acknowledged and transcribed on to pink order forms. Each dish on an order is transcribed on to a separate form. Each order may therefore be for one or more dishes. Customers may also enter into contracts with sales. A contract form is sent to the customer who signs the form and returns it to sales. A contract is for one dish only, and offers it at a discount for an undertaking by the customer to purchase a fixed quantity over a fixed period. Customers may have many contracts. Orders may therefore contain some dishes quoting a contract price. A copy of all contract forms are sent to accounts for invoice pricing. All other invoices are priced from a price list prepared by the kitchen staff. Sales receive a daily stock list from the kitchen of dishes available for sale.

Accounts perform the invoicing and sales ledger functions. Invoices are sent to customers when a copy of the delivery note is received from the kitchen. Accounts also prepare credit notes for returned dishes and provide for sales a weekly stop list of customers who have exceeded their credit limit. Accounts vet and authorise new customers and send the details of all of them to sales so that they may update their wall chart. Accounts send statements to customers and record payments received from customers.

The kitchen, apart from performing the obvious function, deal with pink order forms, the daily stock list, delivery notes and returned dishes. For each dish returned by a customer, the kitchen staff prepare a returned dish notification form for accounts. When a delivery of ingredients is received, the kitchen staff send an ingredients received note to accounts and prepare an ingredients received list for purchasing. This is to allow purchasing to check the invoice received from the supplier against the actual ingredients received. When any ingredient is running short, a low ingredient card is prepared and sent to purchasing who raise a purchase order on the supplier. Purchasing handle all the purchase ledger transactions.

A computer-assisted system is required initially for the sales and accounting functions. SSADM is to be used to design a new system.

10.2 Interview transcript—sales manager responsible for the sales office

The first task each morning for me is to check how many signed contracts have arrived in the post. This is my major function negotiating contracts with customers. For each new signed contract a copy is made for accounts and the original is filed on the contracts file.

When orders are received quoting a contract price, the contracts clerk retrieves the contract from the file, records on it the quantity ordered and returns it to the file. Each contract is negotiated for only one dish, an order therefore may reference several contracts if it is for more than one dish.

All orders are checked against the weekly stop list for creditworthiness by a junior clerk. They are then placed on an orders outstanding pile.

The manageress, apart from looking after the typing pool, is responsible for checking whether dishes are available to meet the outstanding orders. All pending orders are checked first each day against the stock list. If there is sufficient stock for all the dishes on the order, then the order is transcribed on to a number of pink order forms. The pink order forms create the dishes or order lines for despatch pile. If there is insufficient stock, then the complete order is returned to the pending orders pile. When all pending orders have been checked, today's orders are checked in the same fashion.

Each day then a number of order lines are placed in the ready to despatch pile. The typing pool then prepare an order acknowledgement for the customer and a typed version of the pink form for the kitchen. Names and addresses are extracted from a name and address wall chart kept up to date by a junior clerk from information supplied by accounts.

10.3 Interview transcript—chief accountant responsible for accounting

My two major functions as chief accountant are the authorisation of new customer accounts and of credit notes.

When a potential customer applies for an account, they are vetted for creditworthiness. If satisfactory references are received, their name and address, and credit status are added to the sales ledger and notification of a new customer is sent to sales.

Credit note authorisations result from the return of dishes for a variety of reasons. I raise a credit authorisation slip which goes to a typist who types a credit note. The credit note itself is sent to the customer and the credit is recorded on the sales ledger.

We also receive copies of delivery notes from the kitchen. For each delivery note, an invoice is typed and sent to the customer. Full details of the invoice are typed on to a ledger sheet. Payments are recorded on the ledger sheets by a clerk. We keep one sheet per customer; these sheets comprise the sales ledger.

Invoice pricing is tricky. Two files are needed, a standard price list for standard orders and the contracts file for orders against a contract. The standard price list is provided weekly by the kitchen staff.

Every week each sales ledger sheet is examined to identify customers who have overstepped their credit limit. A stop list is compiled and sent to sales. Finally, at the end of every month all the sales ledger sheets are photocopied and the copies sent to our customers in the form of a sales statement.

The kitchen staff send us ingredient received notes but we have no use for them.

These notes and interview transcripts comprise part of the output from stage 1, task 1.1, investigation.

At this early stage in the project, a brief introduction and two interviews, the understanding of SKC's current system can only be at a high level. The exact detail of how some functions are carried out has not been investigated or documented.

It is possible, from the investigation notes, to construct the document flow, a level 1 current physical DFD, level 2 current physical DFDs for sales and accounting, and the entity model.

It is necessary to make some assumptions. List your assumptions while constructing the diagrams, then compare your diagrams with those provided, to ascertain if similar assumptions were made.

10.4 SKC: Current physical data flow diagrams, task 1.2

Figure 10.1 Document flow diagram
Figure 10.2 Level 1 DFD
Figure 10.3 Level 2 DFD, sales
Figure 10.4 Level 2 DFD, accounts

DATA FLOW DIAGRAM

SYSTEM: *SKC – SALES & ACCOUNTING*	DATE:
AUTHOR: *G. CUTTS*	PAGE: / of /

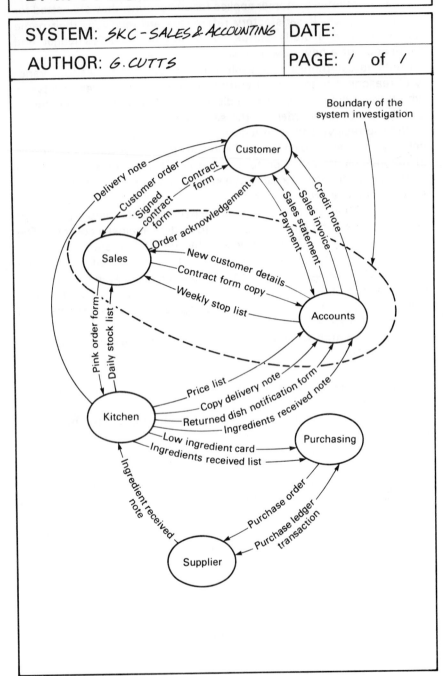

Figure 10.1

DATA FLOW DIAGRAM

SYSTEM: SKC - SALES & ACCOUNTING

DATE:

AUTHOR: G. CUTTS

PAGE: 1 of 3

LEVEL: 1 | CURRENT/~~REQ~~. | PHYS./~~LOGICAL~~:

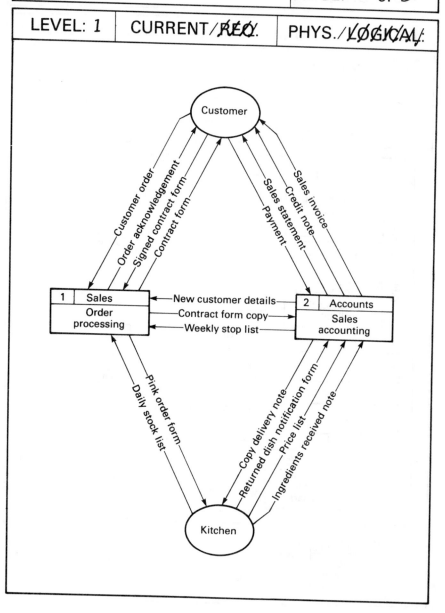

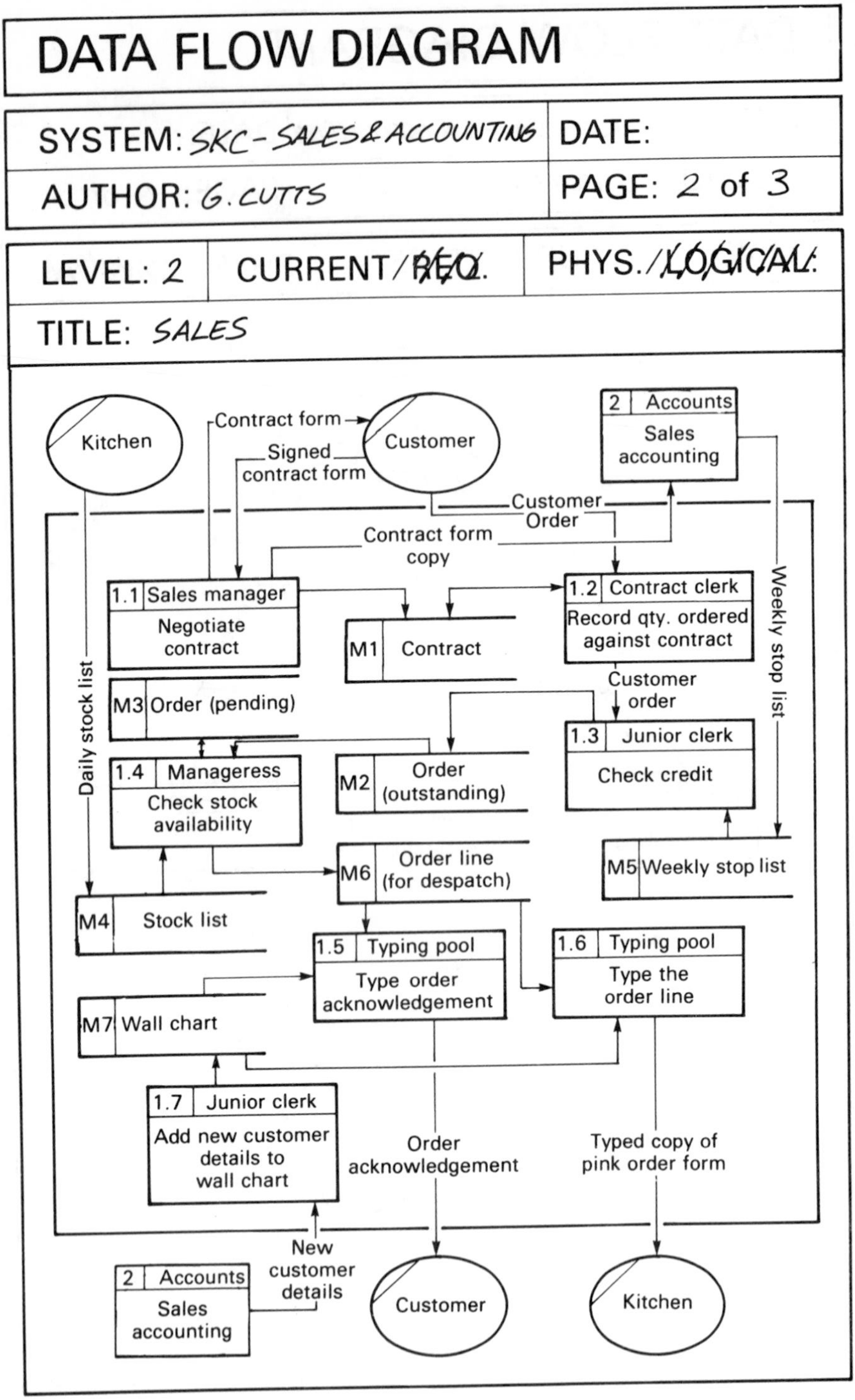

DATA FLOW DIAGRAM

SYSTEM: *SKC - SALES & ACCOUNTING* DATE:

AUTHOR: *G. CUTTS* PAGE: 2 of 3

LEVEL: 2   CURRENT/~~PROP~~.   PHYS./~~LOGICAL~~.

TITLE: *SALES*

Figure 10.3

DATA FLOW DIAGRAM

SYSTEM: *SKC-SALES & ACCOUNTING* DATE:

AUTHOR: *G. CUTTS* PAGE: *3* of *3*

LEVEL: *2* CURRENT/~~REQ~~. PHYS./~~LOGICAL~~.

TITLE: *ACCOUNTS*

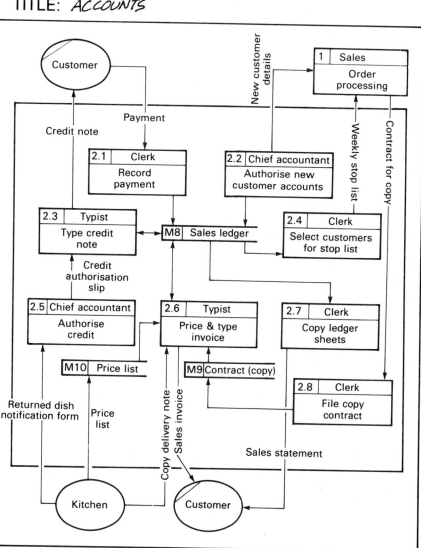

Figure 10.4

	Customer	Contract	Order head	Order line	Dish	Invoice	Payment	Credit note
Customer		*	*			*	*	*
Contract				*				
Order head				*				
Order line								
Dish		*		*				
Invoice								
Payment								
Credit note								

Figure 10.5

10.5 SKC: Current entity model, task 1.3

Figure 10.5 Entity matrix
Figure 10.6 Entity model

The order within the SKC system may exist as an outstanding order, a pending order or an order for despatch. It is necessary to be able to access the orders by this status. An operation owner, order status, is therefore shown on the entity model.

A similar argument cannot be made for customer status. There is no requirement to access all customers with a stopped status. Customer status is therefore included as an attribute of the customer entity and therefore not shown on the entity model.

10.6 SKC: Data store entity cross-references, task 1.4

Figure 10.7   Physical data store entity cross-reference
Figure 10.8   Level 2 current physical DFDs
           (Figures 10.3 and 10.4 with data flows to and from the data
           stores annotated with the entity names)
Figure 10.9   Entity model, divided into logical groups
Figure 10.10 Logical data store entity cross-reference

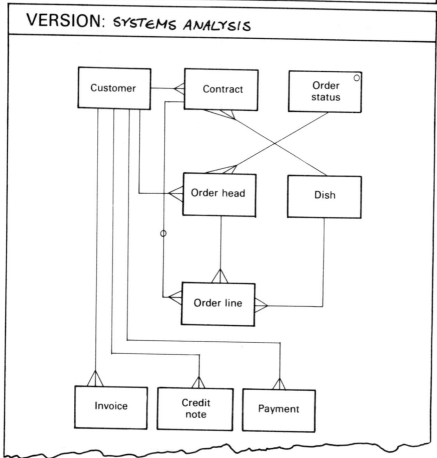

ENTITY MODEL

SYSTEM: SKC. - SALES & ACCOUNTING	DATE:
AUTHOR: G. CUTTS	PAGE: 1 of 1

VERSION: SYSTEMS ANALYSIS

Figure 10.6

The physical data store entity cross-reference indicates, for each data store, the entities within the data store. Figure 10.8 shows which entities are accessed by each function.

Four logical data stores were identified and are shown in Figure 10.9.

Data stores L3, product, and L4, sales ledger, appear very straight-forward, as also do data stores for contract and order head/order line. This

DATA STORE/ENTITY X REF.

SYSTEM: SKC - SALES & ACCOUNTING

DATE:

AUTHOR: G. CUTTS

PAGE: 1 of 1

PHYSICAL/~~LOGICAL~~:

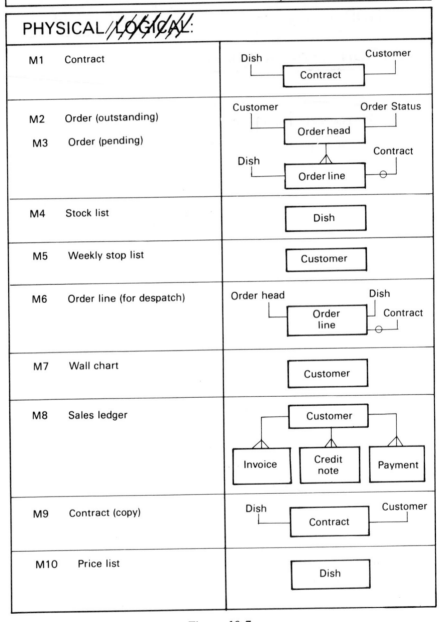

M1	Contract
M2	Order (outstanding)
M3	Order (pending)
M4	Stock list
M5	Weekly stop list
M6	Order line (for despatch)
M7	Wall chart
M8	Sales ledger
M9	Contract (copy)
M10	Price list

Figure 10.7

DATA FLOW DIAGRAM

SYSTEM: SKC- SALES & ACCOUNTING	DATE:
AUTHOR: G. CUTTS	PAGE: 2 of 3

LEVEL: 2	CURRENT/~~REQ.~~	PHYS./~~LOGICAL.~~

TITLE: SALES

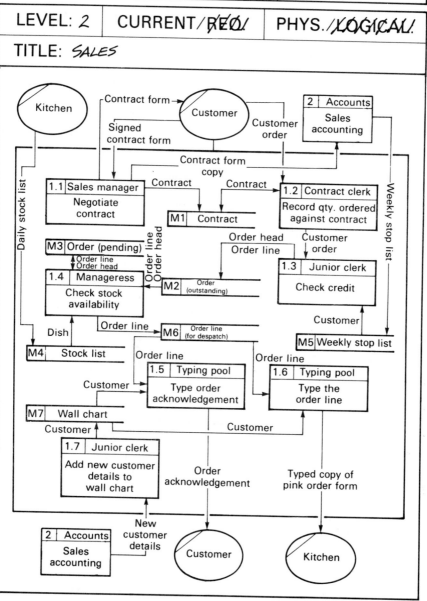

Figure 10.8

DATA FLOW DIAGRAM

SYSTEM: *SKC-SALES & ACCOUNTING*   DATE:

AUTHOR: *G.CUTTS*   PAGE: *3* of *3*

LEVEL: *2*   CURRENT/~~REQ!~~   PHYS./~~LOGICAL!~~

TITLE: *ACCOUNTS*

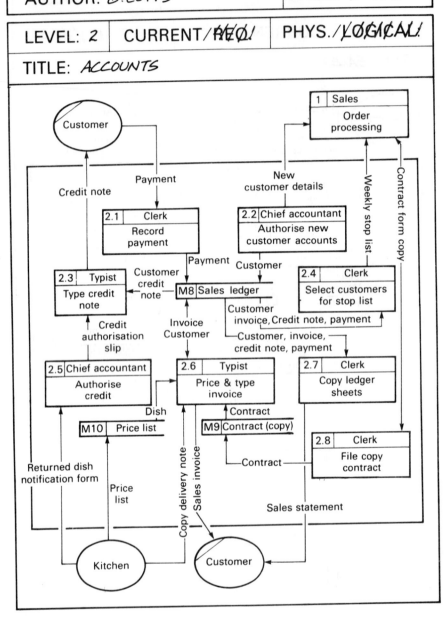

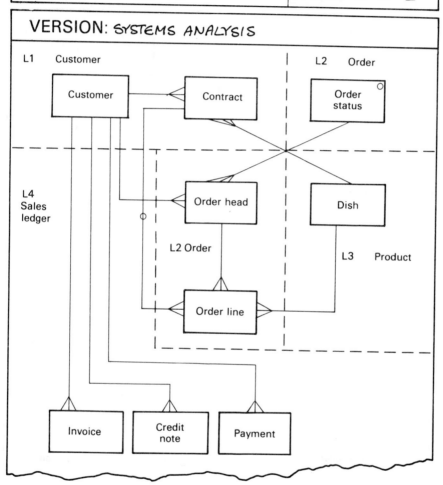

ENTITY MODEL

SYSTEM: SKC- SALES & ACCOUNTING	DATE:
AUTHOR: G. CUTTS	PAGE: 1 of 1

VERSION: SYSTEMS ANALYSIS

Figure 10.9

leaves one question: 'Where to locate the customer entity?' Possibilities are: with the contract entity, with the order head and order line entities, with the invoice, credit note and payment entities, or with none of them.

For this system, contract is chosen as the customer entity is most used,

DATA STORE/ENTITY X REF.

SYSTEM: SKC - SALES & ACCOUNTING

DATE:

AUTHOR: G. CUTTS

PAGE: 1 of 1

PHYSICAL/LOGICAL:

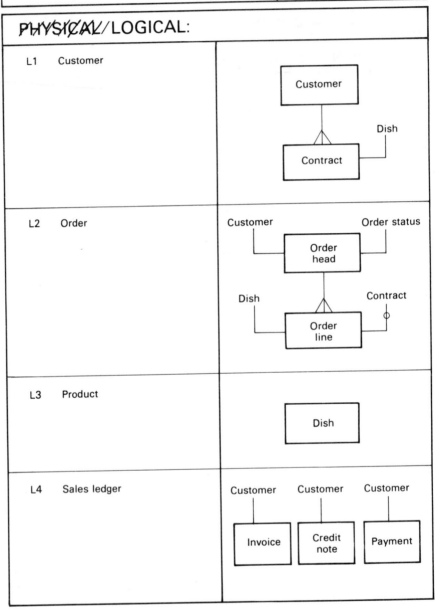

L1	Customer
L2	Order
L3	Product
L4	Sales ledger

Figure 10.10

on-line, for order processing (contract or standard order?) and invoicing (contract or standard price?).

Four logical data stores therefore seem appropriate. These are represented in Figure 10.10.

10.7 SKC: Current logical data flow diagrams, task 1.5

Figure 10.11 Level 2 current physical DFDs
            (data flows logicalised and physical functions deleted)
Figure 10.12 Level 2 current logical DFDs
Figure 10.13 Level 1 current logical DFD

Figure 10.11 shows the level 2 current physical DFDs with renamed data flows and physical functions and physical data stores deleted.

10.7.1 Step 1: Logicalise the data flows

The following data flows have been renamed in Figure 10.11:

From (physical)	To (logical)
contract form	customer contract
signed contract form	customer contract
contract form copy	customer contract
daily stock list	dish stock
weekly stop list	credit status
new customer details	customer
pink order form	despatch note
copy delivery note	delivery note
returned dish notification form	dish reference and quantity
credit authorisation slip	credit authorisation

10.7.2 Step 2: Delete time dependencies

The following functions and data stores have been marked for deletion in Figure 10.11:

Function 1.7, zero logical function
Function 2.8, zero logical function
Data stores M2 and M6, physical time dependency, logically not required

Figure 10.11 shows the level 2 current logical DFDs with renamed functions.

DATA FLOW DIAGRAM

SYSTEM: *SKC- SALES & ACCOUNTING*

DATE:

AUTHOR: *G. CUTTS*

PAGE: *2* of *3*

LEVEL: 2 | CURRENT/~~REQ~~ | PHYS./~~LOGICAL~~

TITLE: *SALES*

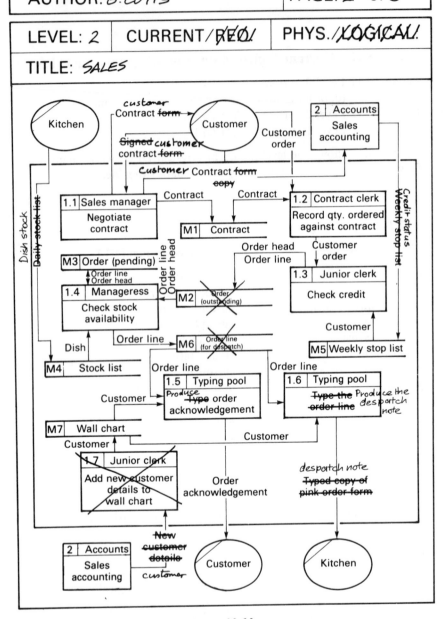

Figure 10.11

DATA FLOW DIAGRAM

SYSTEM: *SKC-SALES & ACCOUNTING* DATE:

AUTHOR: *G.CUTTS* PAGE: *3* of *3*

LEVEL: *2* CURRENT/~~REQ~~/ PHYS./~~LOGICAL~~/

TITLE: *ACCOUNTS*

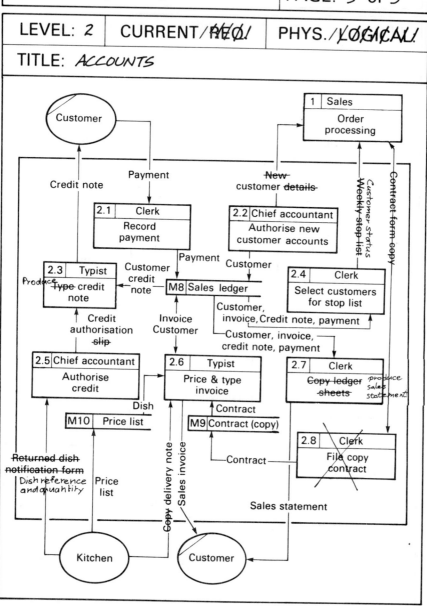

DATA FLOW DIAGRAM

SYSTEM: *SKC SALES & ACCOUNTING* DATE:

AUTHOR: *G. CUTTS* PAGE: *2* of *3*

LEVEL: *2* CURRENT/~~REQ~~. ~~PHYS~~./LOGICAL:

TITLE: *SALES*

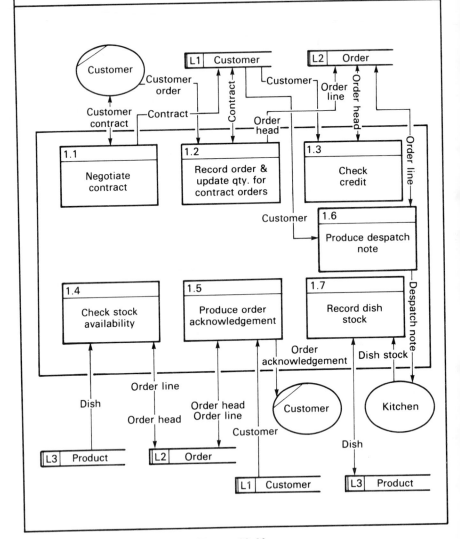

Figure 10.12

DATA FLOW DIAGRAM

SYSTEM: *SKC -SALES & ACCOUNTING*   DATE:

AUTHOR: *G.CUTTS*   PAGE: *3* of *3*

LEVEL: *2*   CURRENT/~~REQ.~~   ~~PHYS.~~/LOGICAL:

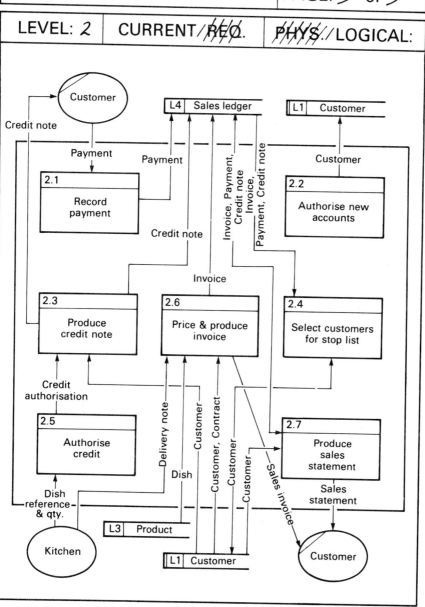

DATA FLOW DIAGRAM

SYSTEM: *SKC-SALES & ACCOUNTING*	DATE:
AUTHOR: *G. CUTTS*	PAGE: *1* of *3*

LEVEL: 1	CURRENT/~~REQ.~~	~~PHYS.~~/LOGICAL:

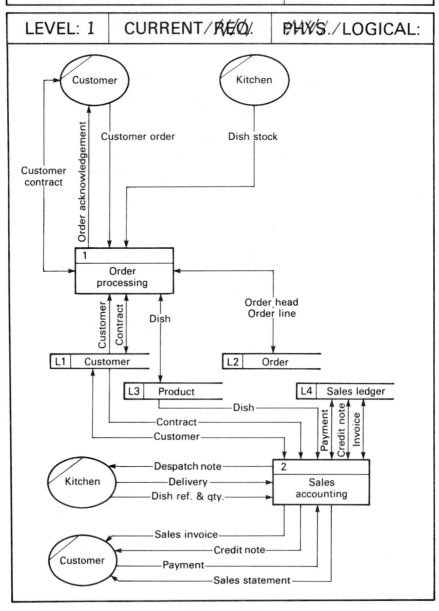

Figure 10.13

10.7.3 Step 3: Logicalise the functions

The following functions have been renamed or deleted:

1.5 type order acknowledgement	renamed produce order acknowledgement
1.6 type the order line	renamed produce despatch note
1.7 add new customer details	deleted
2.3 type credit note	renamed produce credit note
2.6 price and type invoice	renamed price and produce invoice
2.7 copy ledger sheets	renamed produce sales statement
2.8 file copy contract	deleted

10.7.4 Step 4: Create the current logical DFDs

Figures 10.12 and 10.13 show the current logical DFDs.

Logicalised data flows and functions were copied to the current logical DFDs function by function. Where a data flow accessed a data store, the physical data store was replaced by its logical equivalent.

The action taken on transfer of each function is given below:

Function

1.1 Contract is written to data store L1 for access by function 1.2 and accounts. The identical logical data flow to accounts is deleted.

1.2 The customer order represented by the entities order and order line is inserted into data store L2.

1.3 Physical data store M5 is replaced by logical data store L1. The status of the order is modified, access is not required to the order line.

1.4 M4 replaced by L3. All other transactions are performed by status manipulation.

1.5 M7 replaced by L1 and M6 by L2.

1.6 M6 replaced by L2.

1.7 A new function is required to update the quantity in stock attribute in the dish entity.

2.1 M8 replaced by L4.

2.2 The entity inserted by this function, originally on physical data store M8 with a copy of the customer entity on M7, is now inserted into logical data store L1. Sales have access to the data store.

2.3 M8 replaced by L4.

2.4 List of customer numbers replaced by status on L1. M8 replaced by L4.

2.5 No change.

2.6 M10 replaced by L3, M9 replaced by L1, and M8 replaced by L4 and L1.

2.7 M8 replaced by L4 and L1.

Figure 10.13 was then constructed from Figure 10.12 and shows the level 1 current logical DFD.

PROBLEMS/REQUIREMENTS LIST

SYSTEM: *SKC - SALES & ACCOUNTING*	DATE:
AUTHOR: *G. CUTTS*	PAGE: *1* of *1*

No.	Problem/requirement	Init.	Solution Reference
1.	Copies of contracts are not always sent to accounting. This results in incorrect pricing since orders for contract items may be priced at the standard higher price. This in turn causes customer problems.	C.A.	
2.	Three files are used for processing orders: outstanding order, pending order and order lines for despatch. This results in considerable movement of documents, loss of efficiency and lost documents. Additionally, no order can be processed until all the dishes on the order are in stock.	S.M.	
3.	There is no easy method of selecting pending orders for despatch when new stock is delivered. Many pending orders are processed each day for several weeks especially for long lead times on delivery of new stock.	S.M.	
4.	Management require a report on order throughput. Some information can be provided but other information such as average time from receipt of an order to despatch is difficult or impossible to provide.	M.D.	
5.	Invoice typing is several days behind despatch.	S.A.	
6.	A statement for customers in the current form, photocopied ledger card is not acceptable.	C.A.	
7.	The process "select slow payers" is not done. It is too complicated to summarise the ledger sheets.	C.A.	
8.	Invoices are currently raised for every delivery. It is required to invoice weekly with invoices listing all deliveries for the week.	C.A.	
9.	It is required to part deliver orders. Instead of complete orders being held pending, only order lines should be held.	S.M.	
10.	The current brought forward ledger system should be converted to an open item ledger. Credit notes and payments must be against specific invoices not on account.	C.A.	

Figure 10.14

10.8 SKC: Problems and requirements list, task 1.6

Figure 10.14 Problems and requirements list

The problems and requirements list was developed during the previous tasks and is now formally documented.

11

SKC stage 2: specification of requirements

11.1 Introduction

Chapter 11 describes the second stage of SSADM applied to SKC. A full logical specification of requirements is produced.

11.2 SKC: Required logical data flow diagrams, task 2.1

Figure 11.1 Level 1 required logical DFD
Figure 11.2 Level 2 required logical DFDs
Figure 11.3 Problems and requirements list with solution references

11.3 SKC: Required entity model, task 2.2

Figure 11.4 Required entity model

The current logical DFDs and entity model have been modified to reflect the requirements and to solve the problems listed on the problems and requirements list. This resulted in a revised set of diagrams, the required logical DFDs (Figures 11.1 and 11.2) and the required entity model (Figure 11.4).

Each problem or requirement, Figure 11.3, has a solution reference. The references are expanded below:

S1 A common contracts data store to both sales and accounting will resolve this problem.

S2 A single orders data store is proposed with order lines recorded as separate entities. Each order line entity may take the status outstanding, pending or despatched. All order lines will be processed on each stock allocation run. These measures should overcome problems 2, 3 and 9.

S3 A new function 3, produce management report, is included on the level 1 DFD.

DATA FLOW DIAGRAM

SYSTEM: SKC -SALES & ACCOUNTING	DATE:
AUTHOR: G.CUTTS	PAGE: 1 of 4

LEVEL: 1	CURRENT/REQ.	PHYS./LOGICAL:

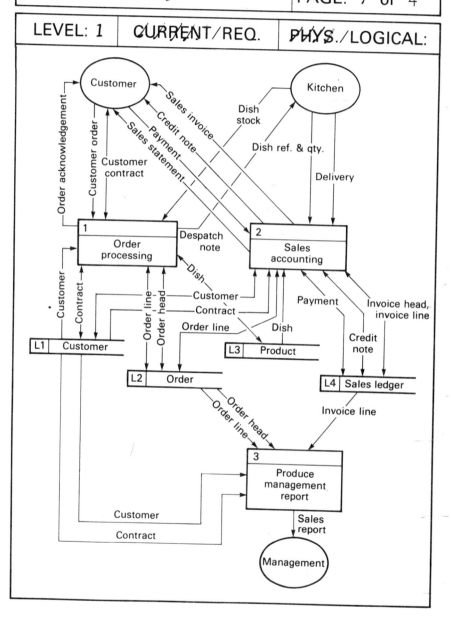

DATA FLOW DIAGRAM

| SYSTEM: *SKC – SALES & ACCOUNTING* | DATE: |
| AUTHOR: *G. CUTTS* | PAGE: *2* of *3* |

| LEVEL: *2* | ~~CURRENT~~/REQ. | ~~PHYS.~~/LOGICAL: |

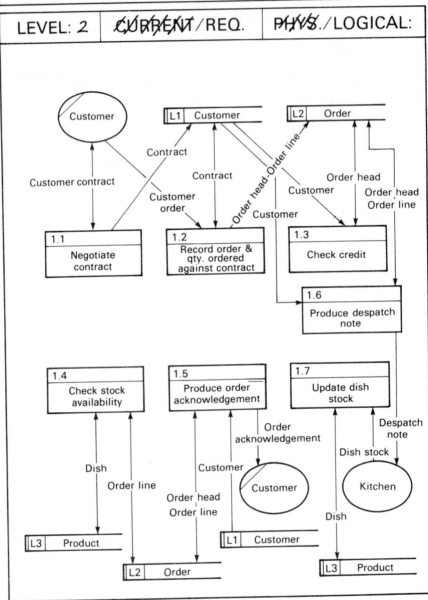

Figure 11.2

DATA FLOW DIAGRAM

SYSTEM: *SKC - SALES & ACCOUNTING* DATE:

AUTHOR: *G. CUTTS* PAGE: *3* of *3*

LEVEL: *2* | CURRENT/REQ. | PHYS./LOGICAL:

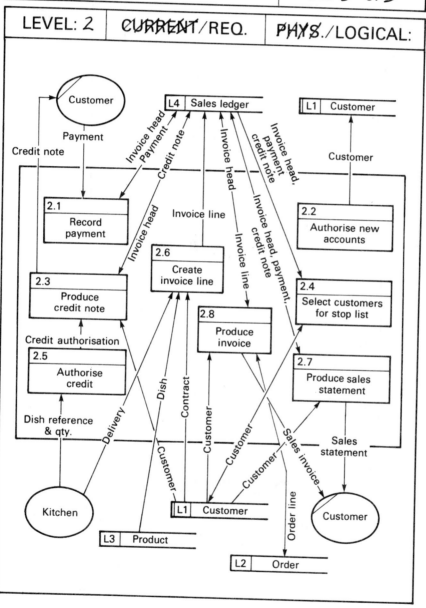

PROBLEMS/REQUIREMENTS LIST

SYSTEM: _SKC – SALES & ACCOUNTING_ DATE:

AUTHOR: _G. CUTTS_ PAGE: _1_ of _1_

No.	Problem/requirement	Init.	Solution Reference
1.	Copies of contracts are not always sent to accounting. This results in incorrect pricing since orders for contract items may be priced at the standard higher price. This in turn causes customer problems.	C.A.	S1
2.	Three files are used for processing orders: outstanding order, pending order and order lines for despatch. This results in considerable movement of documents, loss of efficiency and lost documents. Additionally, no order can be processed until all the dishes on the order are in stock.	S.M.	S2
3.	There is no easy method of selecting pending orders for despatch when new stock is delivered. Many pending orders are processed each day for several weeks especially for long lead times on delivery of new stock.	S.M.	S2
4.	Management require a report on order throughput. Some information can be provided but other information such as average time from receipt of an order to despatch is difficult or impossible to provide.	M.D.	S3
5.	Invoice typing is several days behind despatch.	S.A.	S4
6.	A statement for customers in the current form, photocopied ledger card is not acceptable.	C.A.	S4
7.	The process "select slow payers" is not done. It is too complicated to summarise the ledger sheets.	C.A.	S4
8.	Invoices are currently raised for every delivery. It is required to invoice weekly with invoices listing all deliveries for the week.	C.A.	S5
9.	It is required to part deliver orders. Instead of complete orders being held pending, only order lines should be held.	S.M.	S2
10.	The current brought forward ledger system should be converted to an open item ledger. Credit notes and payments must be against specific invoices not on account.	C.A.	S6

Figure 11.3

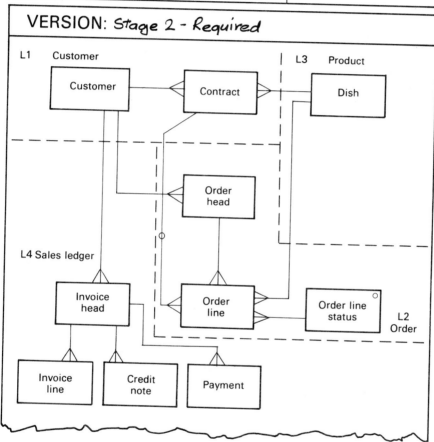

ENTITY MODEL

SYSTEM: SKC- *SALES & ACCOUNTING*

DATE:

AUTHOR: G. CUTTS

PAGE: 1 of 1

VERSION: Stage 2 - Required

Figure 11.4

S4 Problems 5, 6 and 7 are relieved by automation of the processing involved.

S5 The original function 2.6, produce an invoice for each despatch, is amended to produce an invoice line on logical data store L4 for each despatch. A new function, 2.8, will produce invoices weekly for all invoice lines inserted during the previous week.

S6   Functions 2.1 and 2.3 are amended to record payments and credit notes against invoices not against the account.

Solutions 2 and 6 require modification to be made to the entity model, as follows.

The order status has been deleted and replaced by order line status. This is to satisfy requirement 9, outstanding, pending and despatched status should be applied to order lines, thus enabling part delivery of an order.

Requirement 10 is for an open item sales ledger. A brought forward ledger simply accounts for the total debt and the total credit; it does not record individual credit notes or payment against invoices. This can cause accounting problems with bad debts or disputed invoices. An open item ledger allocates each credit note or payment to an invoice. The entity model has been revised to show customers having many invoices, with each invoice having a number of credit notes and payments.

Invoices contain many deliveries, each creating an invoice line on the invoice. Invoices, therefore, comprise an invoice head, with many invoice lines.

11.4   SKC: Entity descriptions, task 2.3

Figure 11.5 Entity descriptions

Figure 11.5 documents the entity descriptions for the nine entities shown on the required entity model.

The entity descriptions are based on reasonable assumptions.

11.5   SKC: Input/output descriptions, task 2.4

Figure 11.6 Input/output descriptions

Figure 11.6 documents the input or output descriptions for the nine data flows which are not entities.

The input and output descriptions are based again on reasonable assumptions.

11.6   SKC: Function descriptions, task 2.5

Figure 11.7 Logical function descriptions

For each DFD primitive function, a business description of the function is documented.

ENTITY DESCRIPTION

SYSTEM: SKC - SALES ACCOUNTING	DATE:
AUTHOR: G. CUTTS	PAGE: 01. of 9

NAME: CONTRACT - STAGE 2

NARRATIVE: A contract for one dish requiring orders up to a fixed minimum quantity at a special. Contract numbers unique.

Key	Data item	Format	Len.	Comment
✓	Contract number			
	Customer number			
	Dish reference			
	Contract date			
	Expiry date			
	Contract quantity			
	Quantity ordered to date			
	Contract price			

VOLUMETRICS	
ENTITY SIZE	
No. OF OCCURRENCES	
TOTAL	

Figure 11.5

ENTITY DESCRIPTION

SYSTEM: SKC-SALES ACCOUNTING	DATE:
AUTHOR: G. CUTTS	PAGE: 2 of 9

NAME: CREDIT NOTE - STAGE 2

NARRATIVE: A negative or inverse invoice for a returned dish. A credit note is issued against a specific invoice.

Key	Data item	Format	Len.	Comment
✓ ✓ ✓	Credit note number Invoice number Customer number			Credit note numbers consecutively allocated within invoice & customer
	Credit note date Credit value			

VOLUMETRICS	
ENTITY SIZE	
No. OF OCCURRENCES	
TOTAL	

ENTITY DESCRIPTION

SYSTEM: SKC-SALES & ACCOUNTING	DATE:
AUTHOR: G.CUTTS	PAGE: 3 of 9

NAME: CUSTOMER

NARRATIVE: Customer data not related to a specific order or contract.

Key	Data item	Format	Len.	Comment
✓	Customer number			
	Customer name			
	Customer address			5 lines
	Stop listed			yes/no
	Credit limit			£ value
	Credit time			Number of months
	Management clearance			Yes/no
	Activity			

VOLUMETRICS	
ENTITY SIZE	
No. OF OCCURRENCES	
TOTAL	

ENTITY DESCRIPTION

SYSTEM: SKC - SALES ACCOUNTING	DATE:
AUTHOR: G. CUTTS	PAGE: 4 of 9

NAME: DISH

NARRATIVE: All data relevant to a specific dish. (not recipe).

Key	Data item	Format	Len.	Comment
✓	Dish reference			
	Dish description			
	Number of portions in pack			
	Quantity in stock			
	Standard price			

	VOLUMETRICS	
	ENTITY SIZE	
	No. OF OCCURRENCES	
	TOTAL	

ENTITY DESCRIPTION

NAME: *INVOICE HEAD - STAGE 2*

NARRATIVE: *The heading of an invoice which collects together all the invoice lines for one week.*

Key	Data item	Format	Len.	Comment
✓	{ Customer number			
✓	{ Invoice number			Invoice numbers are unique within customer
	Invoice date			

VOLUMETRICS	
ENTITY SIZE	
No. OF OCCURRENCES	
TOTAL	

ENTITY DESCRIPTION

NAME: INVOICE LINE – STAGE 2

NARRATIVE: A line on an invoice for one delivery of one dish.

Key	Data item	Format	Len.	Comment
✓	Invoice number			Invoice number added after initial insertion of the entity
✓	Customer number			
✓	Order sequence			
✓	Dish reference			
	Standard price			
	Contract price			
	Quantity delivered			
	Invoice line value			

VOLUMETRICS

ENTITY SIZE	
No. OF OCCURRENCES	
TOTAL	

ENTITY DESCRIPTION

SYSTEM: *SKC-SALES ACCOUNTING*	DATE:
AUTHOR: *G. CUTTS*	PAGE: *7* of *9*

NAME: *ORDER HEAD – STAGE 2*

NARRATIVE: *Order data not related to a specific dish on an order.*

Key	Data item	Format	Len.	Comment
✓ ✓	{ Customer number { SKC order number } (Order number) Date of order (Delivery address) Order stopped			SKC order numbers are allocated within each customer Yes/No

	VOLUMETRICS	
	ENTITY SIZE	
	No. OF OCCURRENCES	
	TOTAL	

ENTITY DESCRIPTION

SYSTEM: *SKC-SALES ACCOUNTING*	DATE:	
AUTHOR: *G. CUTTS*	PAGE: *8* of *9*	

NAME: *ORDER LINE*

NARRATIVE: *The detail of an order for one dish as part of a total order.*

Key	Data item	Format	Len.	Comment
√ √ √	Customer number SKC order number Dish reference Quantity ordered (Contract price) Order line status			 Pending/despatched

	VOLUMETRICS	
	ENTITY SIZE	
	No. OF OCCURRENCES	
	TOTAL	

ENTITY DESCRIPTION

SYSTEM: SKC-SALES ACCOUNTING	DATE:
AUTHOR: G. CUTTS	PAGE: 9 of 9

NAME: PAYMENT - STAGE 2

NARRATIVE: A payment of cash or cheque reducing the overall outstanding debt. Payments are recorded against a specific invoice.

Key	Data item	Format	Len.	Comment
√ √ √	Payment number Customer number Invoice no. Payment type Payment date Payment value			Payment numbers are unique within customer & invoice.

	VOLUMETRICS	
	ENTITY SIZE	
	No. OF OCCURRENCES	
	TOTAL	

INPUT OUTPUT DESCRIPTION

SYSTEM: *SKC-SALES ACCOUNTING*	DATE:
AUTHOR: *G. CUTTS*	PAGE: *1* of *9*

NAME: *CREDIT NOTE*	

NARRATIVE: *A credit note is allocated against a specific invoice for a given customer.*

Key	Data item	Format	Len.	Comment
	Customer number			
	Name			
	Address			
	Credit note number			Credit note number unique within invoice & customer
	Credit note date			
	Credit value			
	Invoice number			Credit can only be given against a specific invoice

VOLUMETRICS

Figure 11.6

INPUT OUTPUT DESCRIPTION

SYSTEM: *SKC-SALES ACCOUNTING*	DATE:
AUTHOR: *G. CUTTS*	PAGE: *2* of *9*

NAME: *CUSTOMER CONTRACT*

NARRATIVE: *The content of the negotiation between a customer and SKC.*

Key	Data item	Format	Len.	Comment
	Contract number			A unique number within SKC
	Customer number			
	Name			
	Address			
	Dish reference			
	Dish description			
	Contract date			
	Expiry date			
	Quantity contracted			
	Contract price			

VOLUMETRICS

INPUT OUTPUT DESCRIPTION

SYSTEM: SKC- SALES ACCOUNTING	DATE:
AUTHOR: G. CUTTS	PAGE: 3 of 9

NAME: CUSTOMER ORDER/ORDER ACKNOWLEDGEMENT

NARRATIVE: *The order document received from a customer and the context of the order acknowledgement.*

Key	Data item	Format	Len.	Comment
	Customer number			Order sequence
	Order sequence			Allocated
	Name			consecutively within
	Address			customer to
	(Order number)			make the order
	Date of order			unique
	(Delivery address)			
	Dish reference			
	Dish description			
	Quantity ordered			
	(Contract price)			

VOLUMETRICS

INPUT OUTPUT DESCRIPTION

SYSTEM: *SKC-SALES ACCOUNTING*	DATE:
AUTHOR: *G. CUTTS*	PAGE: *4* of *9*

NAME: *DELIVERY & DESPATCH NOTE*

NARRATIVE: *A deliverey of one dish to a customer*

Key	Data item	Format	Len.	Comment
	Customer number			
	Name			
	Address			
	(Delivery address)			
	Dish reference			
	Dish description			
	Quantity ⎡ to be delivered ⎤ ⎣ delivered ⎦			
	Order sequence			
	Contract delivery			Yes/No

VOLUMETRICS

INPUT OUTPUT DESCRIPTION

SYSTEM: SKC - SALES & ACCOUNTING	DATE:
AUTHOR: G. CUTTS	PAGE: 5 of 9

NAME: DISH STOCK	

NARRATIVE: A list of the quantities of all dishes put into stock.

Key	Data item	Format	Len.	Comment
	Dish reference			
	Quantity produced			

	VOLUMETRICS		

INPUT OUTPUT DESCRIPTION

SYSTEM: SKC - SALES & ACCOUNTING	DATE:
AUTHOR: G. CUTTS	PAGE: 6 of 9

NAME: PAYMENT

NARRATIVE: A payment received from a customer. Payments are recorded against a specific invoice consecutively.

Key	Data item	Format	Len.	Comment
	Customer number			
	Customer name			
	Invoice number			
	Payment number			Payment number allocated by SKC within the invoice number
	Payment date			
	Payment value			

	VOLUMETRICS		

INPUT OUTPUT DESCRIPTION

NAME: SALES INVOICE

NARRATIVE: *An invoice comprising many invoice lines where each invoice line represents a delivery of a dish.*

Key	Data item	Format	Len.	Comment
	Customer number			
	Customer name			
	Customer address			
	Invoice number			
	Invoice date			
	Order sequence			
	Dish reference			
	Dish description			
	Standard price			
	Contract price			
	Quantity delivered			
	Invoice line value			
	Total invoice value			

VOLUMETRICS

INPUT OUTPUT DESCRIPTION

SYSTEM: SKC - SALES & ACCOUNTING	DATE:
AUTHOR: G. CUTTS	PAGE: 8 of 9

NAME: SALES REPORT/MANAGEMENT REPORT

NARRATIVE: For each customer produce the following report.

Key	Data item	Format	Len.	Comment
	Customer number			
	Name			
	Dish reference			From the order-line entity
	Dish description			
	Order sequence			
	Qty. ordered			
	Order stopped			Yes/No
	(Qty. delivered)			
	(Invoice line value)			
	(Contract number)			
	(Contract price)			

VOLUMETRICS

INPUT OUTPUT DESCRIPTION

SYSTEM: SKC · SALES ACCOUNTING	DATE:
AUTHOR: G. CUTTS	PAGE: 9 of 9

NAME: SALES STATEMENT	

NARRATIVE: A statement of the current invoices, payments and credit notes.

Key	Data item	Format	Len.	Comment
	Customer number			
	Name			
	Address			
	Invoice number			
	Date			
	Total invoice value			
	(Credit note number			
	Credit note date			
	(Credit value			
	(Payment number			
	Payment date			
	(Payment value			

VOLUMETRICS

LOGICAL FUNCTION DESCRIPTIONS

| SYSTEM: *SKC-SALES ACCOUNTING* | DATE: |
| AUTHOR: *G. CUTTS* | PAGE: *1* of *5* |

DFD Ref.	Name	Description
1.1	Negotiate contract	Insert contract details into the system.
1.2	Record order & qty. ordered against contract	Insert sales order details into the system. If any dish ordered contains a contract price, record the quantity ordered for that dish on the appropriate contract.
1.3	Check credit	For all orders inserted by function 1.2, check that the customer is not stop listed. Modify the order to reflect the stop list status.
1.4	Check stock availability	For each dish on the order which has a pending status or outstanding status, check if there is sufficient stock for the order. If stock is sufficient, then mark the order for despatch (i.e. change its status) else mark the status as pending. All pending orders must be processed before outstanding orders. Decrement the stock for dishes despatches.

Figure 11.7

LOGICAL FUNCTION DESCRIPTIONS

SYSTEM: *SKC - SALES ACCOUNTING*   DATE:

AUTHOR: *G. CUTTS*   PAGE: *2* of *5*

DFD Ref.	Name	Description
1.5	Produce order acknowledgement	For all orders not previously acknowledged, generate an order acknowledgement.
1.6	Produce despatch note	For all order lines with status ready to despatch, produce a despatch note. Change the status to indicate that a despatch note has been produced.
1.7	Update dish stock	Increment the dish quantity in stock for all dishes recorded on the dish production list.

LOGICAL FUNCTION DESCRIPTIONS

SYSTEM: SKC - SALES ACCOUNTING	DATE:
AUTHOR: G. CUTTS	PAGE: 3 of 5

DFD Ref.	Name	Description
2.1	Record payment	For each payment received, examine the latest sales statement, allocate the payment to an invoice and insert the payment into the system.
2.2	Authorise new accounts	Insert newly authorised customer details into the system.
2.3	Produce credit notes	For each credit authorisation insert the credit into the system and generate a credit note for the customer. Credits must be allocated to invoices.
2.4	Select customers for stop list	Examine all customer accounts. Where a customer has exceeded the credit limit or credit time and has not obtained management clearance, then the customer status must be changed to stop listed.

Credit limit exceeded	Y	—	—	N
Credit time exceeded	—	Y	—	N
Management exception	N	N	Y	N

Stop list	X	X		
OK			X	X

LOGICAL FUNCTION DESCRIPTIONS

SYSTEM: SKC - SALES ACCOUNTING	DATE:
AUTHOR: G. CUTTS	PAGE: 4 of 5

DFD Ref.	Name	Description
2.5	Authorise credit	For all returned dishes, authorise credit according to management guidelines.
2.6	Create invoice line	For all deliveries, insert an invoice line into the system. For deliveries against a contract, use the contract price, for all other deliveries use the standard price to generate the invoice line value.
2.7	Produce sales statement	Generate a sales statement for each customer showing all outstanding invoices, credit notes and payments.
2.8	Produce invoice	For all invoice lines inserted into the system, with a status of not printed, generate sales invoice showing all the invoice lines. Insert the invoice head into the system.

LOGICAL FUNCTION DESCRIPTIONS

SYSTEM: SKC - SALES ACCOUNTING	DATE:
AUTHOR: G. CUTTS	PAGE: 5 of 5

DFD Ref.	Name	Description
3	Produce management report	For all customers, generate a report showing for each dish ordered by the customer the quantity ordered, and the quantity invoiced. Also show if the dish was a standard or contract order and the contract price. Indicate all orders stopped because of credit violations.

11.7 SKC: Entity function matrix, task 2.6

Figure 11.8 Entity function matrix
Figure 11.9 New and revised function descriptions
Figure 11.10 Revised entity function matrix
Figure 11.11 Revised required logical DFDs

The entity function matrix shown in Figure 11.8 was constructed directly from the required logical DFDs and the required entity model.

By reading across the rows, it can be easily seen that the following functions are required:

1 A function to insert and modify the entity dish.
2 No entities are deleted or archived from the database. Additional functions and modifications to existing functions are required as follows.

Allow the dish maintenance function to delete obsolete entity occurrences.

Allow function 2.7, produce sales statements, to delete all invoice heads, invoice lines, credit notes and payments when the total credit note value plus payment value equals the invoice value and when all entities have been printed on a sales statement.

Create a new function to delete order head and order line entities when all order lines for the order have been invoiced. This requires a modification to function 2.8, produce invoice.

A monthly review of customers and contracts should provide for the archiving of inactive customer entities and completed contracts.

New functions
  Function 4.1   Maintain dish
  Function 4.2   Archive order head and order line
  Function 4.3   Archive customer and contract

Revised functions
  Function 2.7   Allow deletion of invoice head, invoice line, credit note and payment
  Function 2.8   Modify order lines to show that they have been invoiced.

The new and revised functions are documented and shown in Figure 11.9. A revised entity function matrix is shown in Figure 11.10.

It is also necessary to update the required logical DFDs with the new and revised functions. Figure 11.11 shows the revised required logical DFDs.

ENTITY/FUNCTION MATRIX

| SYSTEM: SKC – SALES ACCOUNTING | DATE: |
| AUTHOR: G. CUTTS | PAGE: 1 of 1 |

Entity name \ Function name	1.1 Negotiate contract	1.2 Record order & qty. against contract	1.3 Check credit	1.4 Check stock availability	1.5 Produce order acknowledgement	1.6 Produce despatch note	1.7 Update dish stock	2.1 Record payment	2.2 Authorise new accounts	2.3 Produce credit note	2.4 Select customers for stop list	2.5 Authorise credit	2.6 Create invoice line	2.7 Produce sales statement	2.8 Produce invoice	3 Produce management report
Contract	I	M											R			R
Credit note										I	R			R		
Customer			R		R	R			I	R	M			R	R	R
Dish				M			M						R			
Invoice head								R		R	R			M	I	
Invoice line													I		M	R
Order head			I	M		M	R									R
Order line			I		M	R	M									R
Payment								I				R		R		

Figure 11.8

LOGICAL FUNCTION DESCRIPTIONS

SYSTEM: *SKC-SALES ACCOUNTING*	DATE:
AUTHOR: *G. CUTTS*	PAGE: / of /

DFD Ref.	Name	Description
2.7	Produce sales statement (additional)	Printing must continue until invoice value $\leqslant$ credit value + payment value then delete invoice head, invoice line, credit & payment & print the final values.
2.8	Produce invoice (additional)	Modify the order line to indicate an invoice has been produced.
4.1	Maintain dish	This function inserts, modifies or deletes all attributes associated with the entity dish.
4.2	Archive order head & order line	Archive (delete from the system) all order & order line entities when all order lines have been invoiced.
4.3	Achieve customer & contract	Archive (delete from the system) all customer and contract entities indicated via the input.

Figure 11.9

ENTITY/FUNCTION MATRIX

SYSTEM: SKC - SALES ACCOUNTING	DATE:
AUTHOR: G. CUTTS	PAGE: 1 of 2

Entity name \ Function name	1.1 Negotiate contract	1.2 Record order & qty. against contract	1.3 Check credit	1.4 Check stock availability	1.5 Produce order acknowledgement	1.6 Produce despatch note	1.7 Update dish stock	2.1 Record payment	2.2 Authorise new accounts	2.3 Produce credit note	2.4 Select customer for stop list	2.5 Authorise credit	2.6 Create invoice line	2.7 Produce sales statement	2.8 Produce invoice	3 Produce management report
Contract	I	M											R			R
Credit note									I	R				R/D		
Customer			R		R	R			I	R	M			R	R	R
Dish				M			M						R			
Invoice head								R		R	R			M/D	I	
Invoice line													I	D	M	R
Order head	I	M			M	R										R
Order line	I			M	R	M									M	R
Payment								I				R		R/D		

Figure 11.10

ENTITY/FUNCTION MATRIX

SYSTEM: SKC - SALES ACCOUNTING	DATE:
AUTHOR: G. CUTTS	PAGE: 2 of 2

Function name / Entity name	4.1 Maintain dish	4.2 Archive order & order line	4.3 Archive customer & contract													
Contract			D													
Credit note																
Customer			D													
Dish	I/M/D															
Invoice head																
Invoice line																
Order head		D														
Order line		D														
Payment																

DATA FLOW DIAGRAM

SYSTEM: SKC - SALES & ACCOUNTING	DATE:
AUTHOR: G. CUTTS	PAGE: 1 of 4

LEVEL: 1	CURRENT/REQ.	PHYS./LOGICAL:

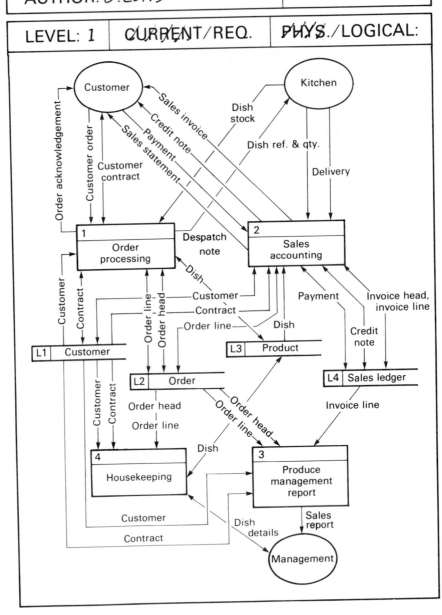

DATA FLOW DIAGRAM

SYSTEM: *SKC SALES & ACCOUNTING*   DATE:

AUTHOR: *G. CUTTS*   PAGE: 4 of 4

LEVEL: 2 | ~~CURRENT~~/REQ. | ~~PHYS.~~/LOGICAL:

TITLE: HOUSEKEEPING

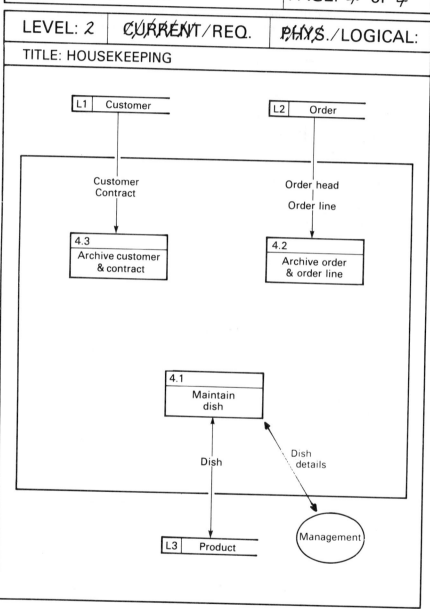

11.8 SKC: Entity life histories, task 2.7

Figure 11.12 Entity life histories

Figure 11.12 documents the entity life histories for the nine entities.

Three entity life histories have been enhanced to show possible abnormal lives. The order head life can deadlock at the function, check credit, by continual failure. Two new functions are required. Function 1.9 rejects and deletes the order and function 1.10 accepts the order without passing the credit check. An order may also be cancelled by the customer. Cancellation may be processed from any status.

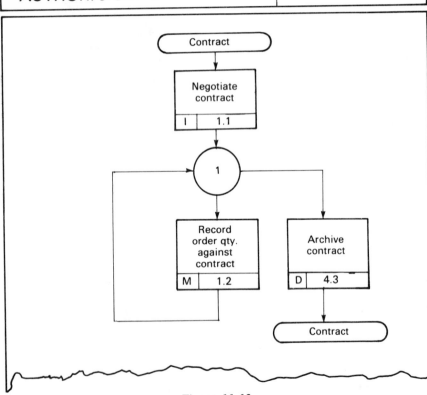

Figure 11.12

ENTITY LIFE HISTORY

SYSTEM: *SKC- SALES & ACCOUNTING*	DATE:
AUTHOR: *G. CUTTS*	PAGE: 2 of 9

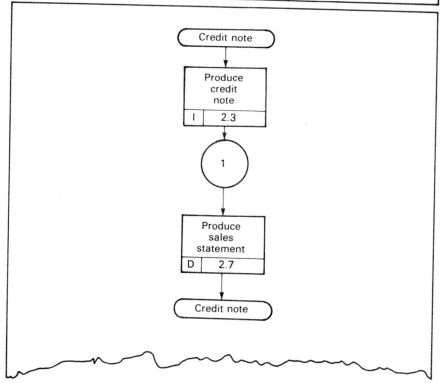

If an order is rejected, function 1.9, then the order line entity must be deleted. Similarly, if an order is cancelled, then the order line entity must be deleted. Cancel order is only acceptable before a despatch note is produced. Order line statuses 1 and 2 are therefore connected to function 1.8, cancel order.

If an order is cancelled after the allocation of stock, function 1.4, then this must be notionally returned to stock. Function 1.8, cancel order, must therefore modify the dish entity.

An entity function matrix is shown in Figure 11.13 for functions 1.8, cancel order, 1.9, reject order, and 1.10, accept order.

ENTITY LIFE HISTORY

SYSTEM: SKC - SALES AND ACCOUNTING | DATE:

AUTHOR: G. CUTTS | PAGE: 3 of 9

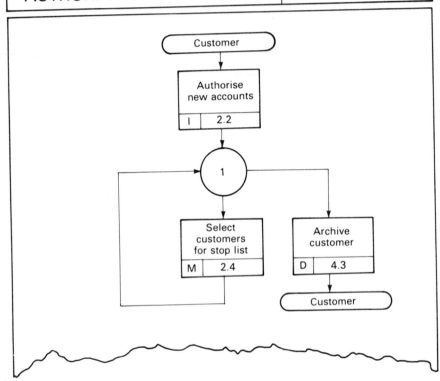

ENTITY LIFE HISTORY

SYSTEM: SKC-SALES AND ACCOUNTING	DATE:
AUTHOR: G. CUTTS	PAGE: 4 of 9

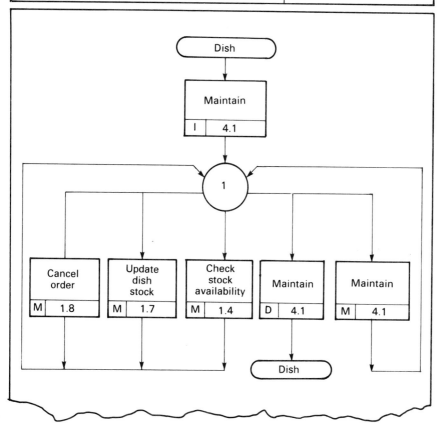

ENTITY LIFE HISTORY

SYSTEM: SKC - SALES AND ACCOUNTING	DATE:
AUTHOR: G. CUTTS	PAGE: 5 of 9

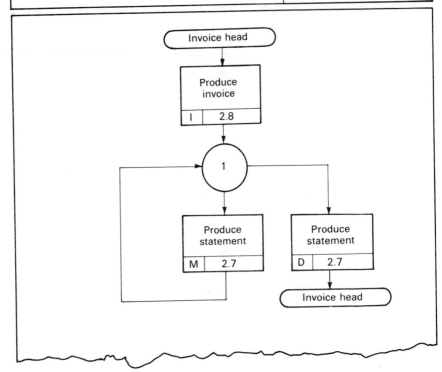

ENTITY LIFE HISTORY

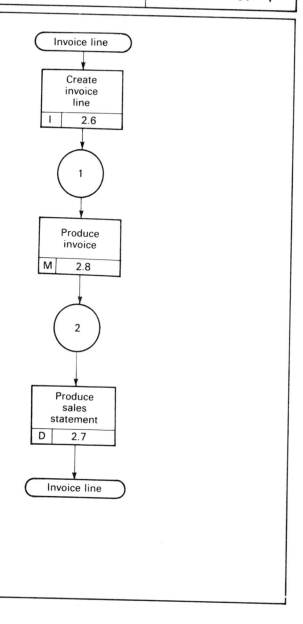

ENTITY LIFE HISTORY

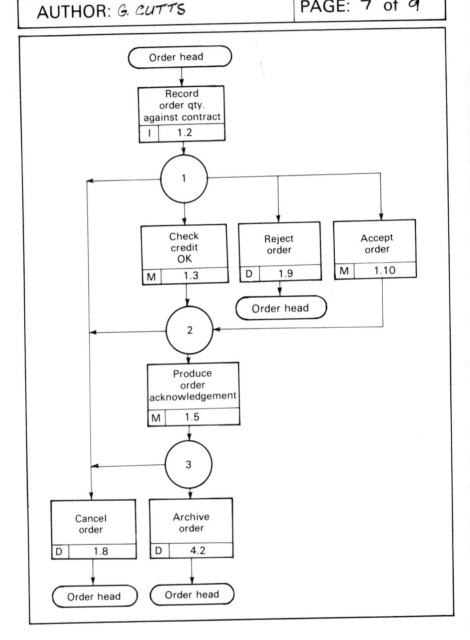

ENTITY LIFE HISTORY

SYSTEM: SKC-SALES & ACCOUNTING

DATE:

AUTHOR: G. CUTTS

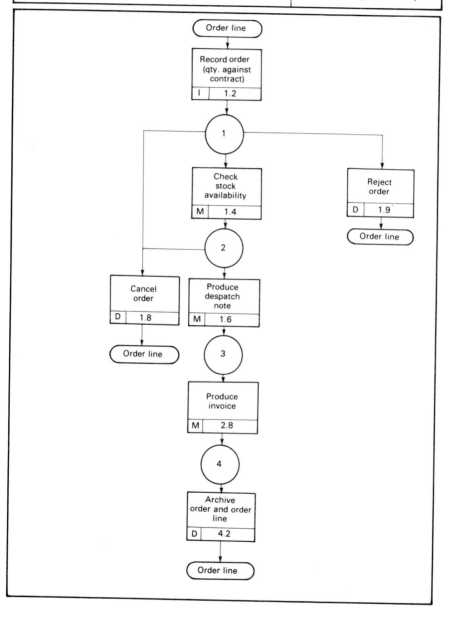

ENTITY LIFE HISTORY

| SYSTEM: SKC - SALES & ACCOUNTING | DATE: |
| AUTHOR: G. CUTTS | PAGE: 9 of 9 |

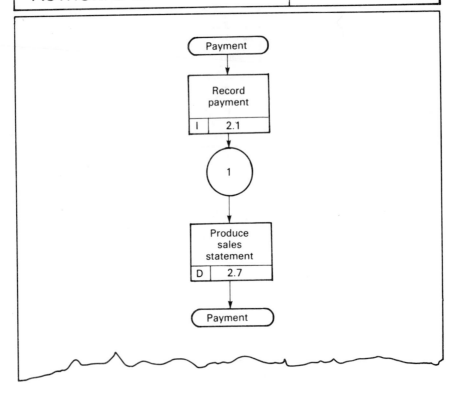

ENTITY/FUNCTION MATRIX

SYSTEM: SKC - SALES AND ACCOUNTING				DATE:							
AUTHOR: G. CUTTS				PAGE: I of I							

Event name ⟍ Entity name	1.8 Cancel order	1.9 Reject Order	1.10 Accept order								
Contract											
Credit note											
Customer											
Dish	M										
Invoice head											
Invoice line											
Order head	D	D	M								
Order line	D	D									
Payment											

Figure 11.13

LOGICAL FUNCTION DESCRIPTIONS

SYSTEM: SKC-SALES AND ACCOUNTING		DATE:	
AUTHOR: G. CUTTS		PAGE: 1 of 1	

DFD Ref.	Name	Description
1.8	Cancel order	Delete the order head and order lines from the system. If stock has been allocated to the order line, increment the dish stock with the quanity allocated.
1.9	Reject order	Delete the order head and order lines.
1.10	Accept order	Modify the order head to indicate that processing may continue.

Figure 11.14

The logical function descriptions for functions 1.8, 1.9 and 1.10 are shown in Figure 11.14.

The revised level 2 required logical DFD for sales incorporating functions 1.8, 1.9 and 1.10 is shown in Figure 11.15.

DATA FLOW DIAGRAM

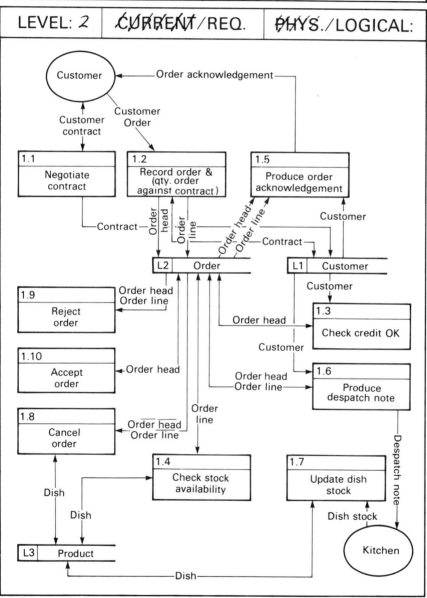

Figure 11.15

12

SKC stage 3: selection of system option

For the purpose of this case study, only one option is postulated. The level 1 and level 2 required physical DFDs are shown in Figure 12.1.

DATA FLOW DIAGRAM

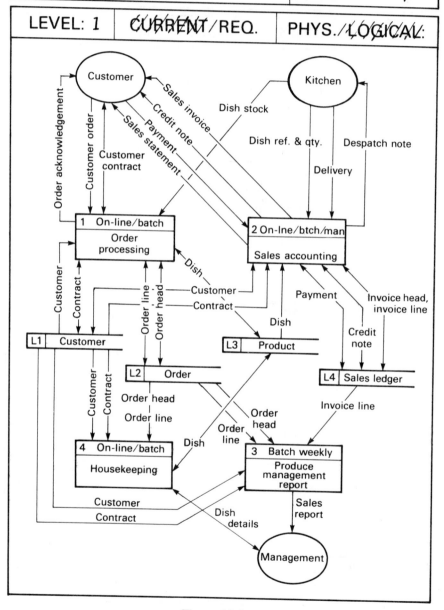

Figure 12.1

DATA FLOW DIAGRAM

SYSTEM: *SKC SALES & ACCOUNTING*   DATE:

AUTHOR: *G. CUTTS*   PAGE: 2 of 4

LEVEL: 1   ~~CURRENT~~/REQ.   PHYS./~~LOGICAL~~:

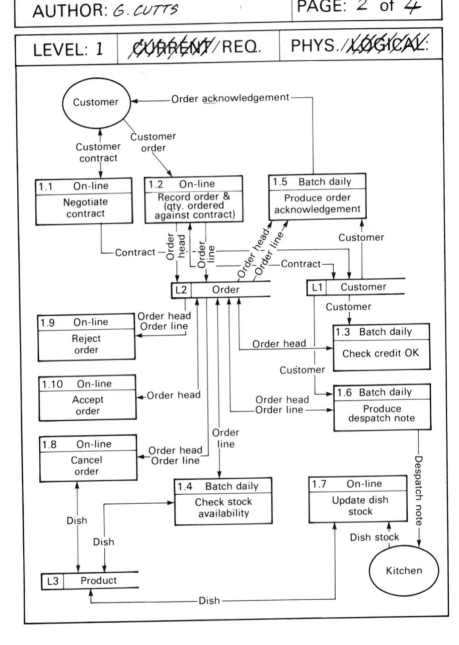

DATA FLOW DIAGRAM

SYSTEM: *SKC - SALES & ACCOUNTING*	DATE:
AUTHOR: *G. CUTTS*	PAGE: 3 of 4

LEVEL: 2	CURRENT / REQ.	PHYS. / LOGICAL:

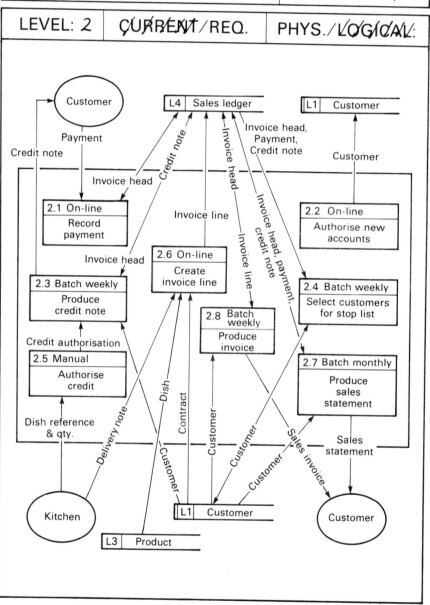

DATA FLOW DIAGRAM

SYSTEM: *SKC SALES & ACCOUNTING*   DATE:

AUTHOR: *G. CUTTS*   PAGE: *4* of *4*

LEVEL: *2*   ~~CURRENT~~/REQ.   PHYS./~~LOGICAL~~:

TITLE:

13

SKC stage 4: logical data design

13.1 SKC: Selected data structures, task 4.1

All of the input and output to the required computer functions were selected for normalisation.

13.2 SKC: Data structures in 3NF, task 4.2

Figure 13.1 Data structures

The data structures in third normal form are documented in Figure 13.1.

13.3 SKC: Entity descriptions, task 4.3

Figure 13.2 Entity descriptions

The third normal form data structures have been merged to produce nine entity descriptions, shown in Figure 13.2.

13.4 SKC: Entity model, task 4.4

Figure 13.3 Entities
Figure 13.4 Entities—compound key relationships
Figure 13.5 Entity model

Figure 13.3 shows the entities reproduced from the stage 4 entity descriptions. Each entity rectangle is annotated with its key. Foreign keys within the entity's attributes are listed below the lower horizontal line.

The invoice line and order line entities have compound keys. Invoice line may become a member of the invoice head–invoice line relationship via the composite key customer number–invoice number. It may also becomes a member of the order line–invoice line relationship via the compound key comprising the composite key customer number–order sequence and the

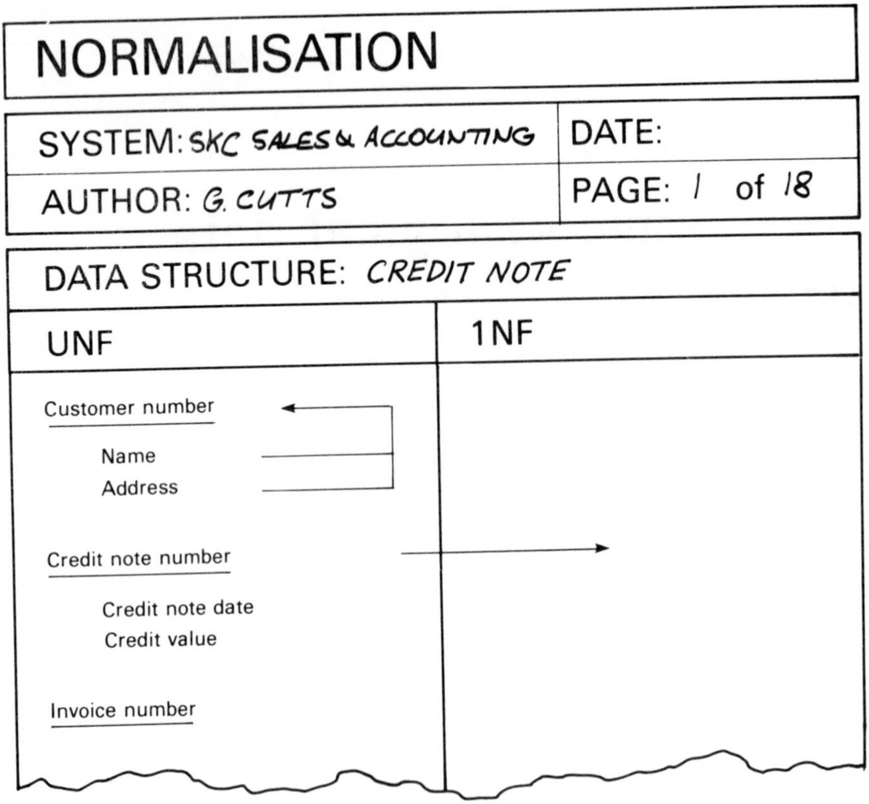

NORMALISATION

SYSTEM: SKC SALES & ACCOUNTING	DATE:
AUTHOR: G. CUTTS	PAGE: 1 of 18

DATA STRUCTURE: *CREDIT NOTE*

UNF	1NF
Customer number ⟵	
Name	
Address	
Credit note number ⟶	
Credit note date	
Credit value	
Invoice number	

Figure 13.1

NORMALISATION

SYSTEM: SKC SALES & ACCOUNTING	DATE:
AUTHOR: G. CUTTS	PAGE: 2 of 18

DATA STRUCTURE: CREDIT NOTE

2NF	3NF
Customer number Customer name ⟶ Customer address	
⎧ Customer number ⎫ ⎨ Credit note number ⎬ ⎩ Invoice number ⎭ Credit note date ⟶ Credit value	

NORMALISATION

SYSTEM: *SALES ACCOUNTING*	DATE:
AUTHOR: *G. CUTTS*	PAGE: *3* of *16*

DATA STRUCTURE: *CUSTOMER CONTRACT*

UNF	1NF
Contract number	
Customer number	
Name	
Address	
Dish reference	
Dish description	
Contract date	
Expiry date	
Quantity contracted	
Contract price	

NORMALISATION

SYSTEM: *SALES ACCOUNTING*	DATE:
AUTHOR: *G. CUTTS*	PAGE: *4* of *18*

DATA STRUCTURE: *CUSTOMER CONTRACT*

2NF	3NF
2NF is identical to 1NF since there is only a simple key	<u>Customer number</u> Name Address
<u>Contract number</u>	
Customer number Name Address Dish reference Dish description Contract date Expiry date Quantity contracted Contract price	<u>Dish reference</u> Dish description
	<u>Contract number</u> Customer number* Dish reference* Contract date Expiry date Quantity contracted Contract price

NORMALISATION

SYSTEM: *SKC SALES & ACCOUNTING*	DATE:
AUTHOR: *G. CUTTS*	PAGE: *5* of *18*

DATA STRUCTURE: *CUSTOMER ORDER/ ORDER ACKNOWLEDGEMENT*

UNF	1NF
{ Customer number } { Order sequence } Name Address (Order number) Date of order (Delivery address) Dish reference Dish description Quantity ordered (Contract price) Order sequence added to provide a unique generated composite key for each order. Order sequence numbers are unique only with a customer number.	{ Customer number } { Order sequence } Name Address (Order number) Date of order (Delivery address) { Customer number } { Order sequence } Dish reference Dish Description Quantity ordered (Contract price)

NORMALISATION

SYSTEM: *SALES ACCOUNTING*	DATE:
AUTHOR: *G. CUTTS*	PAGE: 6 of *18*

DATA STRUCTURE: *CUSTOMER ORDER* / *ORDER ACKNOWLEDGMENT*

2NF	3NF
<u>Customer number</u> Name Address (Delivery address) →	
{ <u>Customer number</u> (<u>Order sequence</u> (Order number) Date of order →	
<u>Dish reference</u> Dish description →	
{ <u>Customer number</u> (<u>Order sequence</u> <u>Dish reference</u> Quantity ordered (Contract price)	{ <u>Customer number</u> (<u>Order sequence</u> <u>Dish reference</u> Quantity ordered (Contract number)*
	The contract price is replaced by its implied key contract number, which becomes a foreign key.

NORMALISATION

SYSTEM: SKC SALES & ACCOUNTING	DATE:
AUTHOR: G. CUTTS	PAGE: 7 of 18

DATA STRUCTURE: DELIVERY/DESPATCH NOTE

UNF	1NF
{ Customer number { Order sequence Name Address (Delivery address) Dish reference Dish description Quantity [to be delivered delivered] Contract delivery	

NORMALISATION

SYSTEM: *SKC SALES & ACCOUNTING*	DATE:
AUTHOR: *G. CUTTS*	PAGE: *8* of *18*

DATA STRUCTURE: *DELIVERY/DESPATCH*

2NF	3NF
<u>Customer number</u> Name Address (Delivery address	⟶
<u>Dish reference</u> Dish description	⟶
{ <u>Customer number</u> } { <u>Order sequence</u> } <u>Dish reference</u> ⎡ Quantity to be delivered ⎤ ⎣ Quantity delivered ⎦	⟶

NORMALISATION

SYSTEM: SKC SALES & ACCOUNTING	DATE:
AUTHOR: G. CUTTS	PAGE: 9 of 18

DATA STRUCTURE: DISH STOCK	
UNF	1NF
Dish reference ⟶ Quantity produced	⟶

NORMALISATION

SYSTEM: SKC SALES & ACCOUNTING	DATE:
AUTHOR: G. CUTTS	PAGE: 10 of 18

DATA STRUCTURE: DISH STOCK	
2NF	3NF
⟶	⟶

NORMALISATION

SYSTEM: SKC SALES & ACCOUNTING	DATE:
AUTHOR: G. CUTTS	PAGE: 11 of 18

DATA STRUCTURE: PAYMENT

UNF	1NF
Customer number ◄──────┐ Customer name ──────────┘ Invoice number Payment number ─────────────► Payment date Payment value	

NORMALISATION

SYSTEM: SKC SALES & ACCOUNTING	DATE:
AUTHOR: G. CUTTS	PAGE: 12 of 18

DATA STRUCTURE: PAYMENT

2NF	3NF
Customer number Name ─────────────► Customer number } Invoice number Payment number } ─────────────► Payment date Payment value	

NORMALISATION

SYSTEM: *SALES ACCOUNTING*	DATE:
AUTHOR: *G.CUTTS*	PAGE: *13* of *18*

DATA STRUCTURE: *SALES INVOICE*

UNF	1NF
Customer number Name Address Invoice number Invoice date Order sequence Dish reference Dish description Quantity delivered ⌈ Standard price ⌉ ⌊ Contract price ⌋ Invoice line value Total invoice value	{ Customer number } { Invoice number } ←———— Name ———————— Address ———————— Invoice date Total invoice value
Invoice numbers are only unique within a customer number.	{ Customer number } { Invoice number } { Customer number } { Order sequence } Dish reference ←———— Dish description ———— Quantity delivered ⌈ Standard price ⌉———— ⌊ Contract price ⌋ Invoice line value

NORMALISATION

SYSTEM: *SALES ACCOUNTING*

DATE:

AUTHOR: *G. CUTTS*

DATA STRUCTURE: *SALES INVOICE*

2NF	3NF
Customer number Name Address ⟶	
{ Customer number { Invoice number Invoice date Total invoice value ⟶	
Dish reference Dish description Standard price ⟶	
{ Customer number } { Invoice number } { Customer number } { Order sequence } Dish reference Quantity delivered Invoice line value Contract price	{ Customer number } { Invoice number } Dish reference { Customer number } { Order sequence } Quantity delivered Invoice line value (Contract number)* Contract price replaced by Contract number.

NORMALISATION

SYSTEM: SKC SALES & ACCOUNTING	DATE:
AUTHOR: G. CUTTS	PAGE: 15 of 18

DATA STRUCTURE: SALES REPORT

UNF	1NF
Customer Number Customer name	Customer number Name
Dish reference Dish description Order sequence Quantity ordered Order stopped (Qty. delivered) (Invoice line value) (Contract number) (Contract price)	Customer number Order sequence Dish reference Dish description Qty. ordered Order stopped (Qty. delivered) (Invoice line value) (Contract number) (Contract price)

NORMALISATION

SYSTEM: SKC SALES & ACCOUNTING	DATE:
AUTHOR: G. CUTTS	PAGE: 16 of 18

DATA STRUCTURE: SALES REPORT

2NF	3NF
⟶	⟶
<u>Dish reference</u> Dish description ⟶	
{ <u>Customer number</u> Order sequence } ⟶ Order stopped	
{ <u>Customer number</u> Order sequence } <u>Dish reference</u> Qty. ordered (Qty. delivered) (Invoice line value) (Contract number) ⟵ (Contract price)	{ <u>Customer number</u> Order sequence } <u>Dish reference</u> Qty. ordered (Qty. delivered) (Invoice number)* (Contract number)*
	<u>Contract number</u> Contract price

NORMALISATION

SYSTEM: *SALES ACCOUNTING*	DATE:
AUTHOR: *G. CUTTS*	PAGE: *17* of *18*

DATA STRUCTURE: *SALES STATEMENT*

UNF	1NF

Customer number
  Name
  Address
	Customer number
	  Name
	  Address

Invoice number Invoice date Total invoice value	{ Customer number } { Invoice number } Invoice date Total invoice number
(Credit note number) Credit note date Credit value (Payment number) Payment date Payment value	{ Customer number } { Invoice number } (Credit note number) Credit note date Credit value
	(Customer number) (Invoice number) (Payment number) Payment Date Payment Value

NORMALISATION

SYSTEM: *SALES ACCOUNTING*	DATE:
AUTHOR: *G. CUTTS*	PAGE: *18* of *18*

DATA STRUCTURE: *SALES STATEMENT*

2NF	3NF
→ →	→
→ →	→
→	→
→	→

ENTITY DESCRIPTION

SYSTEM: SKC SALES & ACCOUNTING	DATE:
AUTHOR: G. CUTTS	PAGE: 1 of 9

NAME: CONTRACT - STAGE 4

NARRATIVE:

Key	Data item	Format	Len.	Comment
✓	Contract number			
	Customer number*			
	Dish reference*			
	Contract date			
	Expiry date			
	Quantity contracted			
	Contract price			

	VOLUMETRICS	
	ENTITY SIZE	
	No. OF OCCURRENCES	
	TOTAL	

Figure 13.2

ENTITY DESCRIPTION

SYSTEM: SKC SALES & ACCOUNTING	DATE:
AUTHOR: G. CUTTS	PAGE: 2 of 9

NAME: CREDIT-STAGE 4

NARRATIVE:

Key	Data item	Format	Len.	Comment
✓	Customer number			
✓	Credit note number			
✓	Invoice number			
	Credit note date			
	Credit value			

	VOLUMETRICS	
	ENTITY SIZE	
	No. OF OCCURRENCES	
	TOTAL	

ENTITY DESCRIPTION

SYSTEM: SKC SALES & ACCOUNTING	DATE:
AUTHOR: G. CUTTS	PAGE: 3 of 9

NAME: CUSTOMER —STAGE 4

NARRATIVE:

Key	Data item	Format	Len.	Comment
✓	Customer number			
	Name			
	Address			
	(Delivery address)			

	VOLUMETRICS	
	ENTITY SIZE	
	No. OF OCCURRENCES	
	TOTAL	

ENTITY DESCRIPTION

NAME: DISH - STAGE 4

NARRATIVE:

Key	Data item	Format	Len.	Comment
✓	Dish reference			
	Dish description			
	Standard price			
	Quantity produced			

VOLUMETRICS

ENTITY SIZE	
No. OF OCCURRENCES	
TOTAL	

ENTITY DESCRIPTION

| SYSTEM: SKC SALES & ACCOUNTING | DATE: |
| AUTHOR: G. CUTTS | PAGE: 5 of 9 |

NAME: INVOICE HEAD – STAGE 4

NARRATIVE:

Key	Data item	Format	Len.	Comment
✓ ✓	{ Customer number } { Invoice number } Invoice date Total invoice value			

VOLUMETRICS	
ENTITY SIZE	
No. OF OCCURRENCES	
TOTAL	

ENTITY DESCRIPTION

NAME: *INVOICE LINE – STAGE 4*

NARRATIVE:

Key	Data item	Format	Len.	Comment
✓	{ Customer number }			
✓	{ Invoice number }			
✓	Dish reference			
✓	{ Customer number }			
✓	{ Order sequence }			
	Quantity delivered			
	Invoice line value			
	(Contract number)*			

	VOLUMETRICS	
	ENTITY SIZE	
	No. OF OCCURRENCES	
	TOTAL	

ENTITY DESCRIPTION

SYSTEM: SKC - SALES & ACCOUNTING	DATE:
AUTHOR: G. CUTTS	PAGE: 7 of 9

NAME: ORDER HEAD - STAGE 4

NARRATIVE:

Key	Data item	Format	Len.	Comment
	{ Customer number { Order sequence (Order number) Date of order Order stopped			Yes/No

VOLUMETRICS	
ENTITY SIZE	
No. OF OCCURRENCES	
TOTAL	

ENTITY DESCRIPTION

SYSTEM: SKC SALES & ACCOUNTING	DATE:
AUTHOR: G. CUTTS	PAGE: 8 of 9

NAME: ORDER LINE - STAGE 4

NARRATIVE: Not merged with invoice line since it is created first.

Key	Data item	Format	Len.	Comment
✓ ✓ ✓	{ Customer number { Order sequence Dish reference Quantity ordered (Contract number)* Quantity to be delivered Quantity delivered			
✓ ✓	{ Customer number { Invoice number			

VOLUMETRICS	
ENTITY SIZE	
No. OF OCCURRENCES	
TOTAL	

ENTITY DESCRIPTION

SYSTEM: SKC SALES & ACCOUNTING	DATE:
AUTHOR: G. CUTTS	PAGE: 9 of 9

NAME: PAYMENT - STAGE 4

NARRATIVE:

Key	Data item	Format	Len.	Comment
✓ ✓ ✓	Customer number Invoice number Payment number Payment date Payment value			

VOLUMETRICS	
ENTITY SIZE	
No. OF OCCURRENCES	
TOTAL	

ENTITY MODEL

SYSTEM: *SKC SALES & ACCOUNTING* **DATE:**

AUTHOR: *G. CUTTS* **PAGE:** / of /

VERSION: *STAGE 4*

Customer

Customer
number

Dish

Dish
reference

Invoice head

{Customer number}
{ Invoice number }

Contract

Contract number
Customer number*
Dish reference*

Order head

{Customer number}
{ Order sequence }

Invoice line

{ Customer number }
{ Invoice number }
{ Customer number }
{ Order sequence }
Dish reference

(Contract number)*

Order line

{Customer number}
{ Order sequence }
Dish reference

{ Invoice number }
{Customer number}

(Contract number)*

Payment

{Customer number }
{ Payment number }
{ Invoice number }

Credit

{Customer number }
{Credit note number}
{ Invoice number }

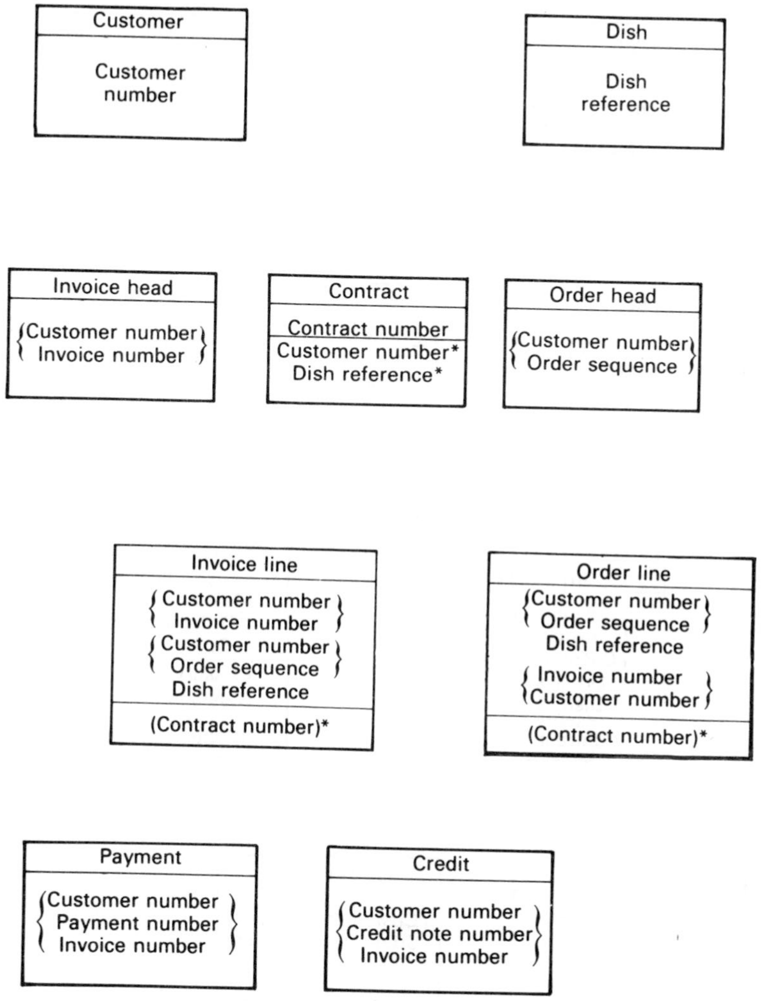

Figure 13.3

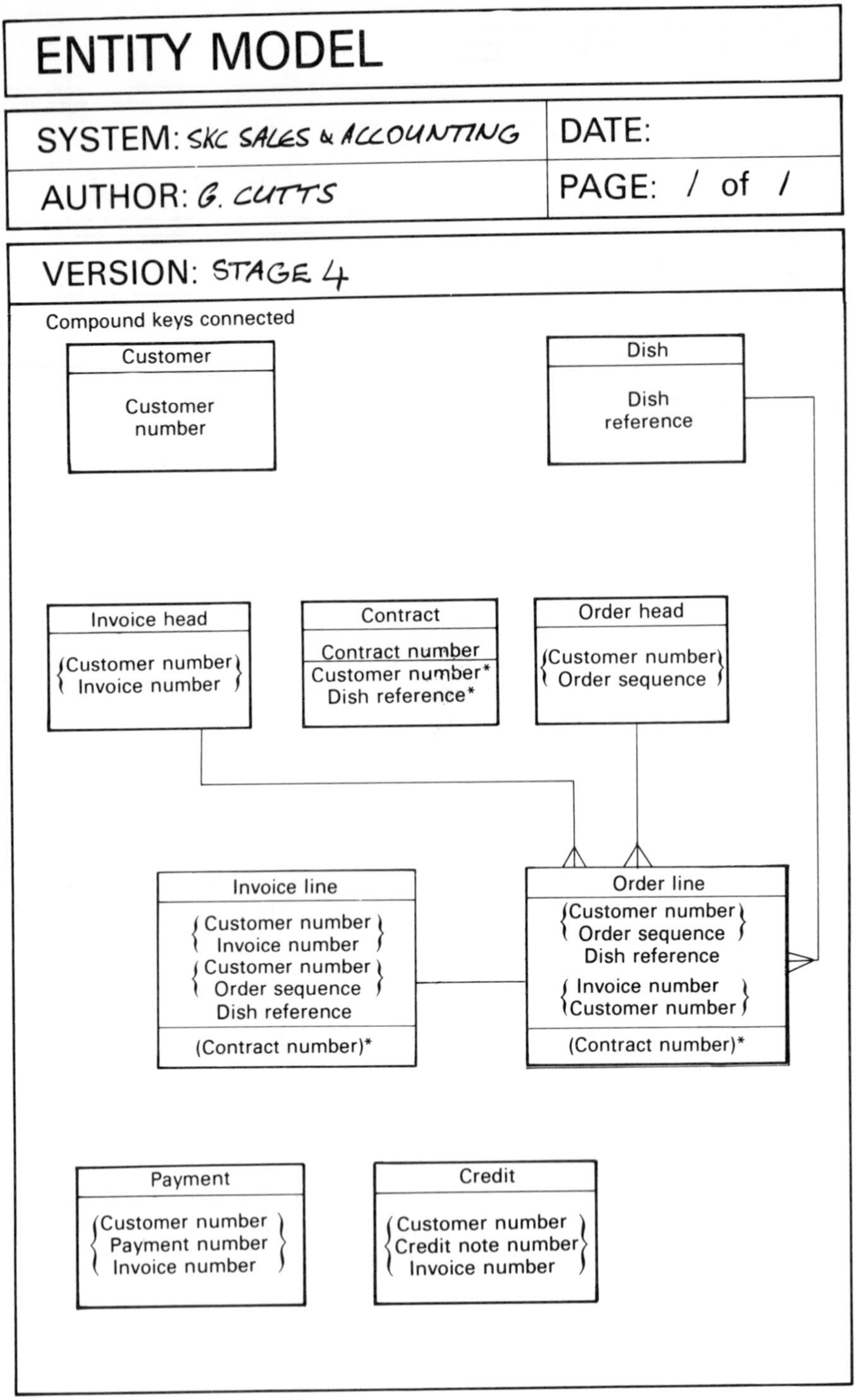

ENTITY MODEL

VERSION: STAGE 4

Compound keys connected

Customer
Customer number

Dish
Dish reference

Invoice head
{Customer number} {Invoice number}

Contract
Contract number
Customer number* Dish reference*

Order head
{Customer number} {Order sequence}

Invoice line
{Customer number} {Invoice number} {Customer number} {Order sequence} Dish reference
(Contract number)*

Order line
{Customer number} {Order sequence} Dish reference {Invoice number} {Customer number}
(Contract number)*

Payment
{Customer number} {Payment number} {Invoice number}

Credit
{Customer number} {Credit note number} {Invoice number}

Figure 13.4

ENTITY MODEL

SYSTEM: SKC SALES & ACCOUNTING   DATE:

AUTHOR: G. CUTTS   PAGE: 1 of 1

VERSION: STAGE 4

Compound, composite and foreign keys connected

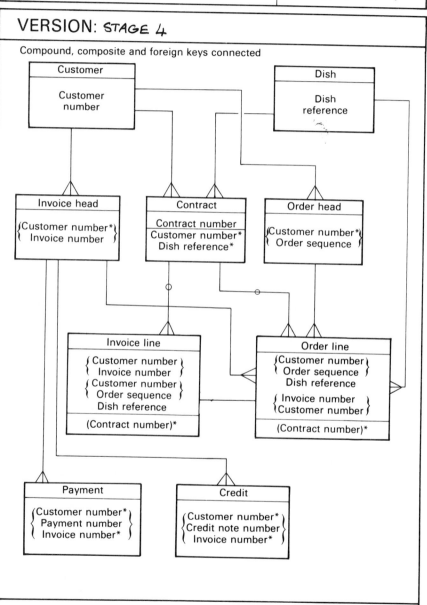

Figure 13.5

simple key dish reference. In fact the order line–invoice line relationship is sufficient.

Similarly, order line is a member of the order head–order line and the dish order–line relationship.

The relationships are shown in Figure 13.4.

The final step is to mark the dominant part of the composite keys as foreign keys and to connect these and the genuine foreign keys. Figure 13.5 shows the entity model derived from the third normal form data structures.

13.5   SKC: Logical entity model, task 4.5

Figure 13.6 Logical entity model

The logical entity model derived from the entity model, stage 2, Figure 11.4, and the entity model, stage 4, Figure 13.5, is shown in Figure 13.6.

The nine common entities and the order line status are retained. The order line status represents a specific user requirement. All of the relationships from the stage 2 model are retained. There are three additional relationships on the stage 4 model. They are:

Invoice head to order line. This relationship is not carried across to the logical entity model since the relationship is correctly from invoice line to order line.

Invoice line to order line. This relationship is retained. Each order line results in one delivery which results in one invoice line. The relationship is one to one.

Invoice line to contract. This relationship is not carried across to the logical entity model as a relationship exists via the order line entity.

13.6   SKC: Logical entity descriptions, task 4.6

Figure 13.7 Logical entity descriptions

The logical entity descriptions are derived from the entity descriptions, stage 2, Figure 11.5, and the entity descriptions, stage 4, Figure 13.2. They are shown in Figure 13.7.

The logical entity descriptions were formed by simple merging of the attribute lists with the exception of the following entity descriptions.

Dish   The quantity produced is used to update the quantity in stock. Quantity produced is deleted, quantity in stock is retained. There is no requirement to store the number of portions in a pack. The attribute is therefore deleted from the logical entity description.

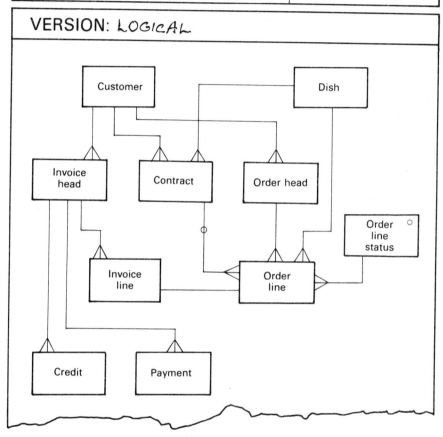

ENTITY MODEL

SYSTEM: SKC SALES & ACCOUNTING	DATE:
AUTHOR: G. CUTTS	PAGE: / of /

VERSION: LOGICAL

Figure 13.6

Order head The SKC order number is equivalent to the order sequence.
The delivery address is not retained with the order as
customers are only allowed one current delivery address.

Order line The SKC order number is equivalent to the order sequence.

ENTITY DESCRIPTION

SYSTEM: SKC SALES & ACCOUNTING	DATE:
AUTHOR: G. CUTTS	PAGE: 1 of 9

NAME: CONTRACT   LOGICAL

NARRATIVE:

Key	Data item	Format	Len.	Comment
✓	Contract number			
	Customer number*			
	Dish reference*			
	Contract date			
	Expiry date			
	Quantity contracted			
	Contract price			
	Quantity ordered to date			

VOLUMETRICS	
ENTITY SIZE	
No. OF OCCURRENCES	
TOTAL	

Figure 13.7

ENTITY DESCRIPTION

NAME: CREDIT   LOGICAL

NARRATIVE:

Key	Data item	Format	Len.	Comment
✓ ✓ ✓	Customer number Credit note number Invoice number Credit note date Credit value			

	VOLUMETRICS	
	ENTITY SIZE	
	No. OF OCCURRENCES	
	TOTAL	

ENTITY DESCRIPTION

SYSTEM: SKC SALES & ACCOUNTING	DATE:
AUTHOR: G. CUTTS	PAGE: 3 of 9

NAME: CUSTOMER	LOGICAL

NARRATIVE:

Key	Data item	Format	Len.	Comment
✓	Customer number			
	Name			
	Address			5 lines
	(Delivery address)			5 lines
	Stop listed			Yes/No
	Credit limit			£ value
	Credit time			Number of months
	Management clearance			Yes/No
	Activity			

	VOLUMETRICS	
	ENTITY SIZE	
	No. OF OCCURRENCES	
	TOTAL	

ENTITY DESCRIPTION

SYSTEM: *SKC SALES & ACCOUNTING*	DATE:
AUTHOR: *G. CUTTS*	PAGE: *4* of *9*

NAME: *DISH*	*LOGICAL*

NARRATIVE:

Key	Data item	Format	Len.	Comment
✓	Dish reference			
	Dish description			
	Standard price			
	Quantity in stock			

	VOLUMETRICS	
	ENTITY SIZE	
	No. OF OCCURRENCES	
	TOTAL	

ENTITY DESCRIPTION

NAME: *INVOICE HEAD*   *LOGICAL*

NARRATIVE:

Key	Data item	Format	Len.	Comment
	{ Customer number { Invoice number			
	Invoice date Total invoice value			

VOLUMETRICS

ENTITY SIZE		
No. OF OCCURRENCES		
TOTAL		

ENTITY DESCRIPTION

NAME: *INVOICE LINE*   *LOGICAL*

NARRATIVE:

Key	Data item	Format	Len.	Comment
✓	Customer number			
✓	Invoice number			
✓	Order sequence			
✓	Dish reference			
	Quantity delivered			
	(Standard price)			
	Invoice line value			
	(Contract number)*			

VOLUMETRICS		
ENTITY SIZE		
No. OF OCCURRENCES		
TOTAL		

ENTITY DESCRIPTION

NAME: *ORDER HEAD* *LOGICAL*

NARRATIVE:

Key	Data item	Format	Len.	Comment
✓ ✓	{ Customer number } { Order sequence }			
	(Order number)			
	Date of order			
	Order stopped			Yes/No
	SKC order number = Order sequence			

VOLUMETRICS	
ENTITY SIZE	
No. OF OCCURRENCES	
TOTAL	

ENTITY DESCRIPTION

SYSTEM: *SKC SALES & ACCOUNTING*	DATE:
AUTHOR: *G. CUTTS*	PAGE: *7* of *9*

NAME: *ORDER LINE*   *LOGICAL*

NARRATIVE:

Key	Data item	Format	Len.	Comment
✓	(Customer number)			
✓	(Order sequence			
✓	Dish reference			
	Quantity ordered			
	(Contract number)*			
	Quantity to be delivered			
	Quantity delivered			

	VOLUMETRICS	
	ENTITY SIZE	
	No. OF OCCURRENCES	
	TOTAL	

ENTITY DESCRIPTION

NAME: PAYMENT LOGICAL

NARRATIVE:

Key	Data item	Format	Len.	Comment
✓ ✓ ✓	Customer number Invoice number Payment number			
	Payment date Payment value Payment type			

	VOLUMETRICS		
	ENTITY SIZE		
	No. OF OCCURRENCES		
	TOTAL		

14

SKC stage 5: logical process design

14.1 Introduction

Stage 4 did not introduce any new entities. The entity function matrix, entity life histories and function descriptions produced during stage 2 are therefore up to date. Task 5.1, review the stage 2 documentation, is therefore trivial.

14.2 SKC: Logical process catalogue, task 5.2

Figure 14.1 Logical process catalogue

The primitive functions from the required physical DFDs, Figure 12.1, have been posted to the logical process catalogue. The catalogue is shown in Figure 14.1.

14.3 SKC: Logical process outlines, task 5.3

Figure 14.2 Logical process outlines

Seventeen logical process outlines have been produced to correspond with the ten on-line entries and the seven batch mode entries in the logical process catalogue. The logical process outlines are shown in Figure 14.2.

LOGICAL PROCESS CATALOGUE

SYSTEM: *SKC SALES & ACCOUNTING*   DATE:

AUTHOR: *G. CUTTS*   PAGE: *1* of *1*

Mode/ Process no.	DFD function nos.	Name	Brief description
On-line			
1	1.1	Insert contract details	
2	1.2	Insert sales order details	
3	1.7	Update dish stock	
4	1.8	Sales order cancellation	
5	1.9	Sales order rejection	
6	1.10	Sales order special acceptance	(See the logical process outlines)
7	2.1	Record a customer's payment	
8	2.2	Insert account details	
9	2.6	Insert invoice line detils	
10	4.1	Maintain dish details	
Batch daily			
11	1.3	Produce order acknowledgment	
	1.5		
12	1.4	Produce despatch note	
	1.6		
Batch weekly			
13	2.3	Produce invoices and credit notes	
	2.4		
	2.8		
14	3	Produce management report	
Batch monthly			
15	2.7	Produce sales statement	
16	4.3	Archive customers and contracts	
17	4.2	Archive sales orders	

Figure 14.1 Process catalogue

LOGICAL PROCESS OUTLINE

SYSTEM: SKC SALES & ACCOUNTING	DATE:
AUTHOR: G. CUTTS	PAGE: 1 of 19

PROCESS No: 1 NAME: Insert contract details

MODE: On-line FREQUENCY: VOLUME:

BRIEF DESCRIPTION: Contract details are inserted into the database on completion of successful negotiation.

DFD Functions. 1·1

ENTITY NAME	Contract								
EFFECT	I								
VALID PREV.	—								
SET TO	1								

Op. no.	Entity Name	Entity Effect	Status Ind. Valid prev.	Status Ind. Set to	Description Narrative	Ref.	I/O ref.	Error ref.
1					Display screen format		F1	
2					Accept & validate the entries.	V1		E1
3	Contract	I	—	1	Insert the contract details.			

Figure 14.2

LOGICAL PROCESS OUTLINE

SYSTEM: SKC SALES & ACCOUNTING	DATE:
AUTHOR: G. CUTTS	PAGE: 2 of 19

PROCESS No: 2	NAME: INSERT SALES ORDER DETAILS
MODE: On-line	FREQUENCY: VOLUME:

BRIEF DESCRIPTION: Sales orders and inserted into the system.

DFD Functions. 1·2

ENTITY NAME	Contract	Order head	Order line					
EFFECT	M	I	I					
VALID PREV.	1	—	—					
SET TO	1	1	1					

Op. no.	Entity Name	Effect	Status Ind. Valid prev.	Set to	Description Narrative	Ref.	I/O ref.	Error ref.
1					Display screen format.		F2	
2					Accept & validate the entries.	V2		E2
3	Order head	I	—	1	Insert the order head details.			
4					Repeat 4 for all dish references on the order.			
4.1	Order line	I	—	1	Insert the order line details.			
4.2	Contract	M	1	1	If the order line contains a contract price obtain the relevant contract and add order line. quantity ordered to contract. quantity contracted.			

LOGICAL PROCESS OUTLINE

SYSTEM: *SKC SALES & ACCOUNTING*	DATE:
AUTHOR: *G. CUTTS*	PAGE: *3* of *19*

PROCESS No: *3*   NAME: *UPDATE DISH STOCK*

MODE: *On-line*   FREQUENCY: VOLUME:

BRIEF DESCRIPTION: *Quantities of dishes produced are used to update the stock quantity available for sale.*

DFD Functions. *1·7*

ENTITY NAME	Dish									
EFFECT	M									
VALID PREV.	1									
SET TO	1									

Op. no.	Entity Name	Effect	Status Ind. Valid prev.	Set to	Description Narrative	Ref.	I/O ref.	Error ref.
1					Display screen format.		F3	
2					Accept & validate the entries.	V3		E3
3	Dish	M	1	1	Add the dish stock. quantity produced to dish. quantity in stock.			

LOGICAL PROCESS OUTLINE

SYSTEM: SKC-SALES & ACCOUNTING	DATE:
AUTHOR: G. CUTTS	PAGE: 4 of 19

PROCESS No: 4   NAME: SALES ORDER CANCELLATION

MODE: On-Line   FREQUENCY: VOLUME:

BRIEF DESCRIPTION: The processing required following
DFD Functions. 1·8   an order cancellation.

ENTITY NAME	Dish	Order head	Order line					
EFFECT	M	D	D					
VALID PREV.	1	1,2,3,	1,2,					
SET TO	1	—	—					

Op. no.	Entity Name	Effect	Status Ind. Valid prev.	Set to	Description Narrative	Ref.	I/O ref.	Error ref.
1					Display screen format.		F4	
2					Accept and validate the entries.	V4		E2
3					Repeat 3 for all order lines on the order.			
3.1	Order line	R	—	—	If the order line status = 2 then operation 3.2.			
3.2	Dish	M	1	1	Add order line. quantity to be delivered to dish. quantity in stock.			
3.3	Order line	D	1,2	—	Delete the order line.			
4	Order head	D	1,2,3	—	Delete the order head.			

LOGICAL PROCESS OUTLINE

SYSTEM: *SKC SALES & ACCOUNTING*	DATE:
AUTHOR: *G. CUTTS*	PAGE: *5* of *19*

PROCESS No: *5*   NAME: *SALES ORDER REJECTION*

MODE: *On-line*   FREQUENCY: VOLUME:

BRIEF DESCRIPTION: *The processing required following the*
DFD Functions. *1-9*   *rejection by SKC of a sales order.*

ENTITY NAME	Order head	Order line							
EFFECT	D	D							
VALID PREV.	1	1							
SET TO	—	—							

Op. no.	Entity Name	Effect	Valid prev.	Set to	Description Narrative	Ref.	I/O ref.	Error ref.
1					Display screen format.		F5	
2					Accept & validate the entries.	V5		E5
3					Repeat 3 for all order lines on the order.			
3.1	Order line	D	1	—	Delete the order line.			
4	Order head	D	1	—	Deleter the order head.			

LOGICAL PROCESS OUTLINE

SYSTEM: *SKC SALES & ACCOUNTING*	DATE:
AUTHOR: *G. CUTTS*	PAGE: *6* of *19*

PROCESS No: *6*	NAME: *SALES ORDER SPECIAL ACCEPTANCE*
MODE: *On-line*	FREQUENCY: VOLUME:

BRIEF DESCRIPTION: *The processing of a sales order after*
DFD Functions. *1-10   Special acceptance by SKC management.*

ENTITY NAME	Order head									
EFFECT	M									
VALID PREV.	1									
SET TO	2									

Op. no.	Entity Name	Effect	Status Ind. Valid prev.	Set to	Description Narrative	Ref.	I/O ref.	Error ref.
1					Display screen format.		F6	
2					Accept & validate the entires.	V6		E6
3	Order head	M	1	2	Set order head. Order stopped = no.			

LOGICAL PROCESS OUTLINE

SYSTEM: SKC SALES & ACCOUNTING	DATE:
AUTHOR: G. CUTTS	PAGE: 7 of 19

PROCESS No: 7   NAME: RECORD A CUSTOMERS PAYMENT

MODE: On-line   FREQUENCY: VOLUME:

BRIEF DESCRIPTION: Payments from customers are
recorded against invoices.

DFD Functions: 2.1

ENTITY NAME	Invoice head	Payment							
EFFECT	R	I							
VALID PREV.	—	—							
SET TO	—	1							

Op. no.	Entity Name	Effect	Status Ind. Valid prev.	Set to	Description / Narrative	Ref.	I/O ref.	Error ref.
1					Display screen format.		F7	
2					Accept & validate the input.	V7		E7
3					Repeat 3 until the input (3.2) = A (allocate).			
3.1	Invoice head	R	—	—	Read & display the details of the first/next invoice head.		F8	
3.2					Accept & validate the input.	V8		E8
4	Payment	I	—	1	Insert the payment details.			

LOGICAL PROCESS OUTLINE

SYSTEM: *SKC SALES & ACCOUNTING*	DATE:
AUTHOR: *G. CUTTS*	PAGE: *8* of *19*

PROCESS No: *8*	NAME: *INSERT ACCOUNT DETAILS*	
MODE: *On-line*	FREQUENCY:	VOLUME:

BRIEF DESCRIPTION: *Account details are inserted into the database following authorsating of the customer's details.*

DFD Functions. *2·2*

ENTITY NAME	Customer										
EFFECT	I										
VALID PREV.	—										
SET TO	1										

Op. no.	Entity Name	Effect	Status Ind. Valid prev.	Set to	Description Narrative	Ref.	I/O ref.	Error ref.
1					Display the screen format.		F9	
2					Accept & validate the input.	V9		E9
3	Customer	I	—	1	Insert the customer details.			

LOGICAL PROCESS OUTLINE

SYSTEM: *SKC SALES & ACCOUNTING*	DATE:
AUTHOR: *G. CUTTS*	PAGE: *9* of *19*

PROCESS No: *9*	NAME: *INSERT INVOICE LINE DETAILS*

MODE: *On-line* **FREQUENCY:** **VOLUME:**

BRIEF DESCRIPTION: *For cash delivery an invoice line is inserted into the database.*

DFD Functions. 2·6

ENTITY NAME	Contract	Dish	Invoice line				
EFFECT	R	R	I				
VALID PREV.	—	—	—				
SET TO	—	—	1				

Op. no.	Entity Name	Effect	Status Ind. Valid prev.	Set to	Description Narrative	Ref.	I/O ref.	Error ref.
1					Display screen format		F10	
2					Accept and validate the input	V10		E10
					If delivery. contract delivery = yes then operation 3 else operation 4.			
3	Contract	R			Set invoice line. price each = contract. contract price.			
4	Dish	R			Set invoice line. price each = dish. standard price.			
5	Invoice line	I	—	1	Insert the invoice line details.			

LOGICAL PROCESS OUTLINE

SYSTEM: SKC SALES & ACCOUNTING	DATE:
AUTHOR: G. CUTTS	PAGE: 10 of 19

PROCESS No: 10   NAME: MAINTAIN DISH DETAILS

MODE: On-line   FREQUENCY: VOLUME:

BRIEF DESCRIPTION:
All processing of dish static detail.
DFD Functions. 4.1

ENTITY NAME	Dish	Dish	Dish					
EFFECT	I	M	D					
VALID PREV.	—	1	1					
SET TO	1	1						

Op. no.	Entity Name	Effect	Status Ind. Valid prev.	Set to	Description / Narrative	Ref.	I/O ref.	Error ref.
1					Display screen format.		F11	
2					Accept & validate the input.	V11		E11
					If input = I then 3			
					input = M then 4			
					input = D then 5			
3.1					Display screen format.		F12	
3.2					Accept & validate the input.	V12		E12
3.3	Dish	I	—	1	Insert the dish details.			
4.1	Dish	R			Read the dish entity referenced by the input & display screen format.		F13	
4.2					Accept & validate the input.	V13		E13
4.3	Dish	M	1	1	Insert the dish details to replace the current occurrence.			
5	Dish	D	1	—	Delete the dish details referenced by the input.			

LOGICAL PROCESS OUTLINE

SYSTEM: SKC SALES & ACCOUNTING	DATE:
AUTHOR: B. CUTTS	PAGE: 11 of 19

PROCESS No: 11 **NAME:** PRODUCE ORDER ACKNOWLEDGEMENT

MODE: BATCH **FREQUENCY:** DAILY **VOLUME:**

BRIEF DESCRIPTION: All newly inserted sales orders are checked for credit violation. If OK an order acknowledgement is produced.

DFD Functions. 1·3 & 1·5

ENTITY NAME	Customer	Order head	Order line				
EFFECT	R	M	R				
VALID PREV.	—	1	—				
SET TO	—	3	—				

Op. no.	Entity Name	Effect	Status Ind. Valid prev.	Set to	Description Narrative	Ref.	I/O ref.	Error ref.
1	Order head	R			Repeat for all order head where order head. status = 1. Read the first/next order head.			
2	Customer	R			Read the customer given by order head. customer number.			
3	Order head	M	1	1	If the customer. stop listed = yes then set order head. order stopped = yes : END.			
4					If the customer. stop listed = no then set order head. order stopped = no and operations 5 & 6			
5	Order line	R			Produce an order acknowledgement containing all of the order lines.		O19	
6	Order head	M	1	3	Modify the order head. status.			

LOGICAL PROCESS OUTLINE

SYSTEM: SKC SALES & ACCOUNTING	DATE:
AUTHOR: G. CUTTS	PAGE: 12 of 19

PROCESS No: 12   NAME: PRODUCE DESPATCH NOTE

MODE: BATCH   FREQUENCY: DAILY   VOLUME:

BRIEF DESCRIPTION: All accepted sales orders are checked with regard to stock availability. For all order lines with sufficient stock available then a despatch note is produced.

DFD Functions. 1·4, 1·6

ENTITY NAME	Dish	Order line	Order head	Customer		
EFFECT	M	M	R	R		
VALID PREV.	1	1	—	—		
SET TO	1	3	—	—		

Op. no.	Entity Name	Effect	Status Ind. Valid prev.	Set to	Description Narrative	Ref.	I/O ref.	Error ref.
					Repeat all operations for all order head entity occurrences.			
1	Order head	R			Read the first/next order head entity occurrence.			
2					If the order head. order stopped = yes then ignore.			
					Repeat 3 for every order with status 1 on the order head.			
3.1	Order line	R			Read the first/next order line,			
3.2	Dish	R			Read the dish referenced by order line.dish reference.			
3.3	Dish	M	1	1	If dish. quantity in stock ⩾ order line. quantity ordered then decrement dish. quantity in stock.			
3.4	Customer	R			Produce a despatch note.			
3.5	Order line	M	1	3	Modify the order line status.		011	

LOGICAL PROCESS OUTLINE

SYSTEM: *SKC SALES & ACCOUNTING*	DATE:
AUTHOR: *G. CUTTS*	PAGE: *13* of *19*

PROCESS No: *13*   NAME: *PRODUCE INVOICES & CREDIT NOTES*

MODE: *BATCH*   FREQUENCY: *WEEKLY* VOLUME:

BRIEF DESCRIPTION: *All invoices & credit notes not previously produced should be printed. Customer credit limits are checked.*

DFD Functions. *2·3, 2·4, 2·8*

ENTITY NAME	Credit note	Customer	Invoice head	Invoice line	Order line	
EFFECT	I	M	I	M	M	
VALID PREV.	—	1	—	1	3	
SET TO	1	1	1	2	4	

Op. no.	Entity Name	Effect	Status Ind. Valid prev.	Set to	Description / Narrative	Ref.	I/O ref.	Error ref.
					Repeat all operations for all customers.			
1	Customer	R	—	—	Read the first/next customer.			
2	Credit note	I	—	1	If a credit authorisation exists for this customer insert the credit note into the system & produce a credit note.		I10 O12	
					For all invoice lines. status = 1			
3.1	Invoice head	I	—	1	Insert an invoice head with invoice head. invoice number incremented by 1.			
3.2					Print a sales invoice.		O13	
3.3	Invoice line	M	1	2	Modify all invoice lines.			
					Where invoice lines. invoice number = invoice head. invoice number.			
3.4	Order line	M	3	4	Modify all order lines.			

LOGICAL PROCESS OUTLINE

SYSTEM: SKC SALES & ACCOUNTING	DATE:
AUTHOR: G. CUTTS	PAGE: 14 of 19

PROCESS No: 13   NAME: PRODUCE INVOICES & CREDIT NOTES

MODE: BATCH   FREQUENCY: WEEKLY   VOLUME:

BRIEF DESCRIPTION: All invoices & credit notes not previously produced should be printed. Customer credit limits are checked.
DFD Functions. 2·3, 2·4, 2·8

ENTITY NAME	Credit note	Customer	Invoice head	Invoice line	Order line	
EFFECT	I	M	I	M	M	
VALID PREV.	—	1	—	1	3	
SET TO	1	1	1	2	4	

Op. no.	Entity Name	Effect	Status Ind. Valid prev.	Set to	Description Narrative	Ref.	I/O ref.	Error ref.
4.1	Invoice head	R	—	—	Read all the invoice heads, payment & credit notes.			
4.2	Payment	R	—	—				
4.3	Credit note	R	—	—				
4.4	Customer	R	—	—	Check if management clearance exists for the customer. (i.e. customer. management clearance = yes.)			
4.5	Customer	M	1	1	Modify the customer. status. If there are no invoice head inserts, add 1 to customer. activity else set customer. activity = 0	DT1		

LOGICAL PROCESS OUTLINE

SYSTEM: SKC SALES & ACCOUNTING	DATE:
AUTHOR: G. CUTTS	PAGE: 15 of 19

PROCESS No: 14   NAME: PRODUCE MANAGEMENT REPORT
MODE: BATCH   FREQUENCY: WEEKLY   VOLUME:
BRIEF DESCRIPTION: By reference to orders, invoices and
DFD Functions: 3   contracts produce the weekly management report.

ENTITY NAME						
EFFECT						
VALID PREV.						
SET TO						

Op. no.	Entity Name	Effect	Status Ind. Valid prev.	Set to	Description Narrative	Ref.	I/O ref.	Error ref.
1	Customer	R			Repeat all operations for all customers. Read the first/next customer.			
2.1	Order head	R	—	—	Repeat 2 for all order heads. Read the order head.			
2.2					If order head. order stopped = yes then produce a line on the report else repeat 3 for all order lines.		O20	
3.1	Order line	R	—	—	Read the order line.			
3.2	Invoice line	R	—	—	Read the invoice line & contract for the order line.			
3.3	Contract	R	—	—				
3.4					Produce a line on the report.		O21	

LOGICAL PROCESS OUTLINE

SYSTEM: SKC SALES & ACCOUNTING	DATE:
AUTHOR: G. CUTTS	PAGE: 16 of 19

PROCESS No: 15   NAME: PRODUCE SALES STATEMENT

MODE: BATCH   FREQUENCY: MONTHLY   VOLUME:

BRIEF DESCRIPTION: For each active customer produce a sales statement.

DFD Functions. 2.7

ENTITY NAME	Credit note	Credit note	Customer	Invoice head	Invoice head	Invoice line	Payment	Payment
EFFECT	R	D	R	M	D	D	R	D
VALID PREV.	—	1	—	1	1	2	—	1
SET TO	—	—	—	1	—	—	—	—

Op. no.	Entity Name	Effect	Status Ind. Valid prev.	Set to	Description Narrative	Ref.	I/O ref.	Error ref.
					Repeat all operations for each customer.			
1	Customer	R	—	—	Read the customer & produce a statement head.		O30	
					Repeat 2 for each invoice head.			
2.1	Invoice head	R			Read the first/next invoice head.			
2.2	Payment	R			Read all the payments for the invoice head.			
2.3	Credit note	R			Read all the credit notes for the invoice head.			
2.4					If invoice head. total invoice value ≤ total (payment. payment value + credit note. credit value) then operation 4, continue.			
2.5					Produce a statement line for invoice head payment credit note		O31 O32 O33	
3					Produce a statement trailer.		O34	
					continued			

LOGICAL PROCESS OUTLINE

SYSTEM: SKC SALES & ACCOUNTING	DATE:
AUTHOR: G. CUTTS	PAGE: 17 of 19

PROCESS No: 15   NAME: PRODUCE SALES STATEMENT

MODE: BATCH   FREQUENCY: MONTHLY VOLUME:

BRIEF DESCRIPTION: For each active customer
DFD Functions. 2.7   produce a sales statements.

ENTITY NAME	Credit note	Credit note	Customer	Invoice head	Invoice head	Invoice line	Payment	Payment
EFFECT	R	D	R	M	D	D	R	D
VALID PREV.	—	1	—	1	1	2	—	1
SET TO	—	—	—	1	—	—	—	—

Op. no.	Entity Name	Effect	Status Ind. Valid prev.	Set to	Description Narrative	Ref.	I/O ref.	Error ref.
4.1	Invoice line	D	2	—	Delete all invoice line for the invoice head.			
4.2	Payment	D	1	—	Delete all payment for the invoice head.			
4.3	Credit note	D	1	—	Delete all credit note for the invoice head.			
4.4	Invoice head	D	1	—	Delete the invoice head. Return.			

LOGICAL PROCESS OUTLINE

SYSTEM: Skc SALES & ACCOUNTING	DATE:
AUTHOR: G. CUTTS	PAGE: 18 of 19

PROCESS No: 16	NAME: ARCHIVE CUSTOMERS & CONTRACTS
MODE: BATCH	FREQUENCY: MONTHLY VOLUME:

BRIEF DESCRIPTION: For all non-active customers and completed contracts copy the details from the database to the archive files.

DFD Functions: 4.3

ENTITY NAME	Contract	Customer							
EFFECT	D	D							
VALID PREV.	1	1							
SET TO	—	—							

Op. no.	Entity Name	Effect	Status Ind. Valid prev.	Set to	Description Narrative	Ref.	I/O ref.	Error ref.
					Repeat all processing for each customer.			
					Repeat 1 for all contracts for the customer.			
1	Customer	D	1	—	If there are no contracts and customer. activity ≥ 26 then delete the customer.			
2	Contract	D	1	—	If contract. quantity ordered to date ≥ contract. quantity contracted then delete the contract.			

LOGICAL PROCESS OUTLINE

SYSTEM: SKC SALES & ACCOUNTING	DATE:
AUTHOR: G. CUTTS	PAGE: 19 of 19

PROCESS No: 17   NAME: ARCHIVE SALES ORDERS

MODE: BATCH   FREQUENCY: MONTHLY VOLUME:

BRIEF DESCRIPTION: For all orders where all odd lines have

DFD Functions: 4.2   been invoiced, copy the details to the archive files.

ENTITY NAME	Order head	Order line							
EFFECT	D	D							
VALID PREV.	3	4							
SET TO	—	—							

Op. no.	Entity Name	Effect	Status Ind. Valid prev.	Set to	Description Narrative	Ref.	I/O ref.	Error ref.
1					Repeat for all order head. Read first/next order head.			
					Repeat 2 for all order lines invoiced: = 0; order lines: = 0			
2.1	Order line	R			Read first/next order line.			
2.2					If order line. status = 4 then invoiced = invoiced + 1			
2.3					Order lines = order lines + 1			
					If order lines = invoiced then 3			
3.1	Order line	D	4	—	Delete all order lines.			
3.2	Order head	D	3	—	Delete the order head.			

Appendix A

SSADM standard forms

Figure

DOCUMENT FLOW

SYSTEM:	DATE:
AUTHOR:	PAGE: of

Figure A.1

DATA FLOW DIAGRAM

SYSTEM:	DATE:
AUTHOR:	PAGE: of

LEVEL: 1	CURRENT/REQ.	PHYS./LOGICAL

Figure A.2

DATA FLOW DIAGRAM

SYSTEM:	DATE:
AUTHOR:	PAGE: of

LEVEL:	CURRENT/REQ.	PHYS./LOGICAL
TITLE:		

Figure A.3

ENTITY MODEL

SYSTEM:	DATE:
AUTHOR:	PAGE: of

VERSION:

Figure A.4

DATA STORE/ENTITY X REF.

SYSTEM:	DATE:
AUTHOR:	PAGE: of

PHYSICAL/LOGICAL

Figure A.5

PROBLEMS/REQUIREMENTS LIST

SYSTEM:	DATE:
AUTHOR:	PAGE: of

No.	Problem/requirement	Init.	Solution Reference

Figure A.6

ENTITY DESCRIPTION

SYSTEM:	DATE:
AUTHOR:	PAGE: of

NAME:	VERSION:

NARRATIVE:

Key	Data item	Format	Len.	Comment

	VOLUMETRICS	
	ENTITY SIZE	
	No. OF OCCURRENCES	
	TOTAL	

Figure A.7

INPUT OUTPUT DESCRIPTION

SYSTEM:	DATE:
AUTHOR:	PAGE: of

NAME:

NARRATIVE:

Key	Data item	Format	Len.	Comment

VOLUMETRICS

Figure A.8

LOGICAL FUNCTION DESCRIPTIONS

SYSTEM:	DATE:
AUTHOR:	PAGE: of

DFD Ref.	Name	Description

Figure A.9

ENTITY/FUNCTION MATRIX

| SYSTEM: | DATE: |
| AUTHOR: | PAGE: of |

Function name / Entity name											

Figure A.10

ENTITY LIFE HISTORY

SYSTEM:	DATE:
AUTHOR:	PAGE: of

Figure A.11

NORMALISATION

SYSTEM:	DATE:
AUTHOR:	PAGE: of

DATA STRUCTURE:

UNF	1NF

Figure A.12

NORMALISATION

SYSTEM:	DATE:
AUTHOR:	PAGE: of

DATA STRUCTURE:

2NF	3NF

LOGICAL PROCESS CATALOGUE

SYSTEM:	DATE:
AUTHOR:	PAGE: of

Mode/ Process no.	DFD function nos.	Name	Brief description

Figure A.13

LOGICAL PROCESS OUTLINE

SYSTEM:	DATE:
AUTHOR:	PAGE: of

PROCESS No: NAME:
MODE: FREQUENCY: VOLUME:

BRIEF DESCRIPTION:

DFD Functions.

ENTITY NAME										
EFFECT										
VALID PREV.										
SET TO										

Op. no.	Entity Name	Effect	Status Ind. Valid prev.	Set to	Description Narrative	Ref.	I/O ref.	Error ref.

Figure A.14

PHYSICAL ACCESS PATHS

SYSTEM:	DATE:
AUTHOR:	PAGE: of

PROCESS No:	PROCESS NAME:

Operation no.	Entity name	Effect	Access path

Figure A.15

Appendix B

The differences between SSADM (as described) and LSDM version 3.2

The relationship between the methodology described in this book and LSDM version 3.2 is described in this appendix.

LSDM comprises six stages:

Systems analysis
1   Analysis of the current system and identification of problems
2   Specification of requirements
3   Selection of technical options
Systems design
4   Logical data design
5   Logical process design
6   Physical design

The stages and tasks within LSDM are shown diagrammatically. Alongside each diagram the tasks, described in the text, which correspond with the LSDM tasks, are listed.

LSDM includes tasks for project initiation and stage review. These tasks are considered to be implicit throughout the book.

As well as the differences in the stages and tasks, LSDM places a different emphasis on the use of some of the techniques within the method.

LSDM draws a clear distinction between functions, processes and events. A function is a logical grouping of one or more processes, usually from the level 2 data flow diagrams. An event is a smaller unit which gives rise to a change of state of the system. There will be usually several events associated with each update function.

LSDM uses an additional technique in stage 2 for the design of logical dialogues for on-line systems. The events, which form the basis of ELHs, become logical transactions which are the basic unit of design for dialogues. Subsequently, even smaller units, known as exchanges, are identified and used in the development of process outlines.

STAGE 1: ANALYSIS OF CURRENT SYSTEM AND IDENTIFICATION OF PROBLEMS

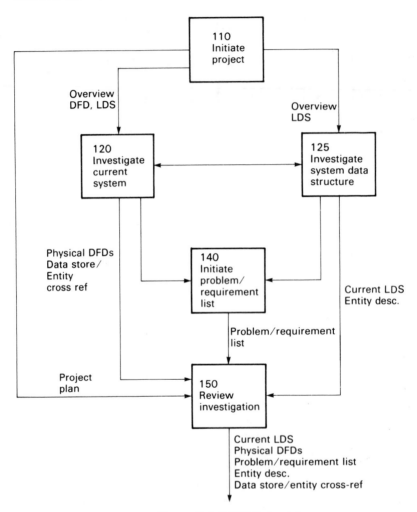

Figure B.1 LSDM stage 1

LSDM task	Structured Systems Analysis & Design Task
110 Initiate project	
120 Investigate current system	1.1 Investigation 1.2 Create the current physical DFDs 1.4 Create the physical data store/entity cross ref.
125 Investigate system data structures	1.1 Investigate 1.3 Create the current entity model LDS — logical data structure ≡ entity model 2.3 Document the entity descriptions
140 Initiate the problem/ requirements list	1.6 Create the problems & requirements list
150 Review investigation	

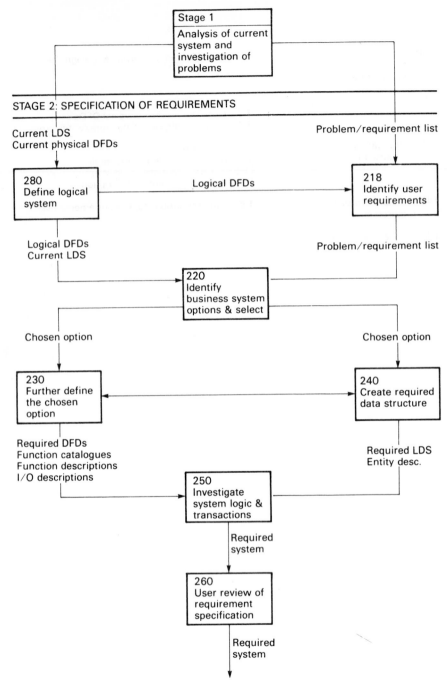

Figure B.2 LSDM stage 2

LSDM task	Structured Systems Analysis Design Task
200 Define logical system	1.5 Create the current logical DFDs
	1.3 Create the current entity model
210 Identify user requirements	1.6 Create the problems & requirements list
220 Identify business system options & select	2.1 Create the required logical DFDs
	2.4 Document the input & output descriptions
230 Further define the chosen option	2.5 Document the function descriptions
240 Create required data structure	2.2 Create the required entity model
250 Investigate system logic & transactions	2.6 Create the entity function matrix
	2.7 Create the entity life histories
260 User review of requirement specification	

STAGE 2

Specification of
requirements

STAGE 3: SELECTION OF TECHNICAL OPTION

Requires data flows and data descriptions
Problems/requirement list, function catalogues,
Entity life histories and error handling narratives

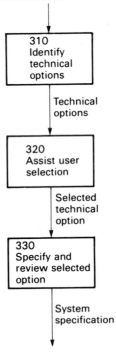

310
Identify
technical
options

Technical
options

320
Assist user
selection

Selected
technical
option

330
Specify and
review selected
option

System
specification

Figure B.3 LSDM stage 3

LSDM task	Structured Systems Analysis & Design task
310 Identify technical options	3.1 Postulate system options
320 Assist user selection	3.2 Review & select option
330 Specify & review selected option	3.3 Set the design constraints

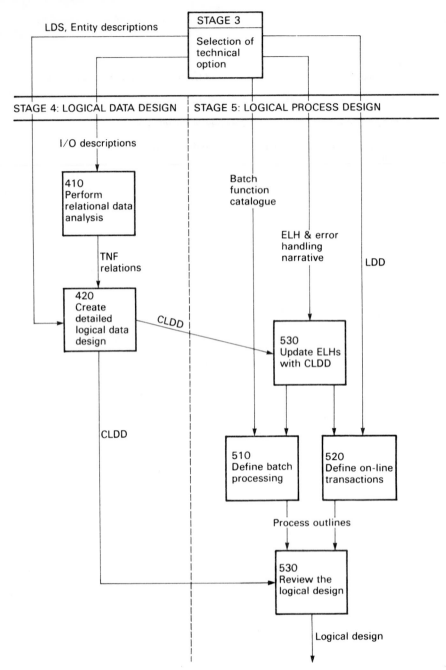

Figure B.4 LSDM stages 4 and 5

LSDM task	Structured Systems Analysis & Design task
410 Perform relational data analysis	4.1 Select data structures
	4.2 Normalisation
420 Create detailed logical data design	4.3 Create the entity descriptions
	4.4 Create the entity model
	4.5 Compare & rationalise the entity model (Logical entity model ≡ composite logical data design)
	4.6 Compare & rationalise the entity descriptions
500 Update ELHs with CLDD	5.1 Review the Stage 2 documentation
510 Define batch processing } 520 Define on-line transactions }	5.2 Create the process catalogue
530 Review the logical design	

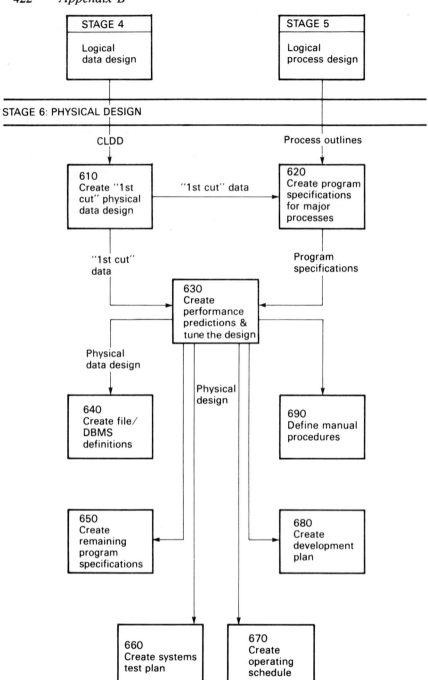

Figure B.5 LSDM stage 6

LSDM task	Structured Systems Analysis & Design Task
610 Create "1st cut" physical data design	6.1 Create the physical files or database specification
640 Create file DBMS definitions	
620 Create program specifications for major processes	6.2 Specify the access paths
650 Create remaining program specifications	6.3 Create the program specifications
630 Create performance predictions & tune the design	6.4 Design tuning
660 Create the systems test plan 680 Create the development plan	6.5 Create the implementation plan
670 Create operating schedule	6.6 Create the operations manual
690 Define manual procedures	6.7 Create the user manual

Index